Dear Bob and Sue

Matt and Karen Smith

Disclaimer: This book reflects the opinions of the authors related to their experiences while traveling to the national parks. Some names and details of people mentioned were changed to protect their privacy.

How to Contact Us

Email: mattandkarensmith@gmail.com

Dedication

To our three children Rachel, Emily and Matthew, and our son-in-law Justin. If they thought we were crazy for quitting our jobs, they never showed it. Instead, they offered us encouragement, advice, unique insights and their constant love and support. Our journey through the parks was all the richer for it.

Photos from our trips and a map of all the parks can be found on www.dearbobandsue.com.

Preface

We don't remember the moment or even the day we decided to visit all 58 national parks, but it called us just the same. We had spent the previous 28 years working and raising kids. Once they were grown and out of the house, we no longer needed to be home for them; it was time to take a break. The deciding factor may have been that we'd seen friends and family members, our age and younger, die before they did all the things they wanted to do.

So, in the spring of 2010, during the worst economy in our lifetime – with no guarantee we would find employment when we finished – we quit our jobs and began the journey.

Our interest in the national parks came from our dear friends, Bob and Sue. Their passion for the parks began before we met them. From the time their kids were babies, they spent most of their vacations visiting the parks. Their stories inspired us. We wish they had joined us on this adventure, but since they didn't, we sent them updates on our progress with occasional emails, texts, phone calls, and a couple of in-person visits.

In the fall of 2010, we began writing about our trip, but struggled with the tone and format for the book. It was then that I sent the letter from the Ahwahnee Hotel (dated September 14, 2010) to Bob and Sue along with gifts from our hotel room. I said to Karen, "I wish that writing the book were as easy as writing to Bob and Sue." That's when the idea came to us. We would write about our trip as a series of letters to Bob and Sue; later we changed the format to emails. (If we were 20 or 30 years younger, we would have written this book as a series of text messages.) In the interest of full disclosure, we didn't send all these emails to Bob and Sue on the dates indicated. But, they are real people; their names really are Bob and Sue, and the events we've written about actually happened.

This is not a guide to the national parks. It's a series of snapshots and impressions based on our experience. We didn't have time to see everything we wanted to see in every park, and we know we missed a lot of great stuff. We didn't camp, rock climb, scuba dive, or snorkel, but we did what we love: we hiked, drank beer, and had the time of our lives.

We hope you enjoy reading it and are inspired to create your own memories in the national parks.

Matt and Karen Smith, 2012

From: **Matt Smith**
Subject: **Mouse-on-head**
Date: **April 16, 2010**

Dear Bob and Sue,

Planning our parks trip is harder than I thought it would be. Karen refuses to stay any place where there's a possibility she'll wake up in the middle of the night with a mouse on her head. She read a review for a motel in Utah where a woman described waking up to see a mouse on her husband's head. Now, before I book any room, Karen wants to check the online reviews. On top of the other logistical challenges with planning a 58-park trip, I also have to wait for her to give me the all clear before I can book a room.

It's surprising how many mouse complaints there are online. A lodge in one of the national parks had several mouse mentions in their reviews. The manager posted a response in the lodge's defense. He made the point that the lodge is in a national park where there's a greater chance that animals would be in or around the property. And, all the animals in the park are protected, including mice, so the lodge is limited in what they can do to prevent them from being in the rooms. The parks service doesn't allow them to kill the mice.

I said to Karen, "Why are you making such a big deal about this? I'm sure there have been times when mice were in our hotel room at night, maybe even running across our bodies, and you didn't know it." This, I'll admit, was a poor choice of words. She pulled her shoulders close to her ears and shivered as if she'd stuck her tongue in a light socket.

I tried a different approach. "Karen, Sweetie, you'll have to get used to roughing it a little. There might be rodents in our future."

I can't wait to see what she does when we see our first tarantula.

Your friend,
Matt

Note to reader: There's something you should know about Karen: she's not a fan of rodents. She didn't like them before, but after her close encounter with a squirrel a few years ago, she wants nothing to do with them.

One spring day, I was away on a business trip; Karen was home with the kids. It was a warm afternoon, and she was sitting with our son Matthew at the computer in my office. The kitchen door that leads to the backyard was open. They were reviewing a homework project when they heard what sounded like fingernails scratching on the hardwood floors in the kitchen followed by a thumping gallop from our cat Sox. An instant later, a squirrel raced into the office with the cat at its heels. In a panic, Karen grabbed Matthew and the cat, and ran out of the office slamming the door behind her.

Her plan was to leave the squirrel in my office and let me deal with it when I got home in a few days; the homework could wait. However, 30 minutes and two glasses of Merlot later, Karen saw the flaw in her plan. She wasn't worried so much about sticking me with the task of removing a hungry, pissed-off squirrel from my office as she was the possibility of the squirrel shredding everything in there before I got home. Or worse, she feared the house would permanently smell of dead squirrel. There was a decent chance her scream gave it a heart attack.

Luckily, the window in my office was open that afternoon. The only problem, there was a screen in the window. Karen figured if she could remove the screen, the squirrel, if it were still alive, would find its way back to the great outdoors.

My office was on the first floor, so she was able to remove the screen easily from the outside. Standing in the backyard at a safe distance, she watched the open window, but no squirrel appeared. Venetian blinds were down covering the window opening. Karen thought, "If I just reach in and pull the cord on the blinds I can raise them enough for the little rodent to see his escape route."

Taking deep breaths while standing on the third rung of our stepladder, Karen thought through exactly what she had to do: raise the blinds with one hand, pull the cord with the other, lock it in place and get the hell out of there. No problem, the squirrel was no doubt cowering in the corner.

Not quite.

As soon as she raised the blinds, the squirrel – according to Karen who was the only witness – saw daylight and flew through the air, landing on her head. Its toes were caught in Karen's hair as it made a desperate attempt to free itself. Karen said, "It was running in place on top of my head." She fell off the ladder and ran screaming through the backyard with the squirrel stuck to her head. (I'm sure it was only a few seconds, but time stands still when there's a squirrel on your head.) It eventually freed its claws, jumped off her head and ran away.

Sue was the first person Karen called after she calmed down enough to speak. They discussed the situation thoroughly and agreed that shampooing several times with Head and Shoulders, rubbing the tiny scratch marks on her scalp with alcohol and drinking the rest of the bottle of Merlot were the proper steps to prevent rabies. I was her second call.

Karen gave me a second-by-second recounting of the event, complete with sound effects and a graphic description of how the squirrel's toes felt as they dug into her scalp. Then she told me the whole thing was my fault because I wasn't home to protect the family when it happened. Apparently being away earning a living was not an acceptable excuse.

She also said she learned a valuable lesson that day. "Not to leave the back door open?" I guessed. No, the lesson was that all squirrels are evil and out to get her. (She also decided that she doesn't like "any animal related to squirrels," whatever that means.)

~.~.~.~.~.~.~

From: **Matt Smith**
Subject: **OC without the D**
Date: **April 30, 2010**

Dear Bob and Sue,

We're getting ready for our parks trip, so I made a list of things I need to carry in my backpack. I like being prepared. Karen thinks I over-prepare; she calls this my OCD. I correct her every time, telling her, "I'm OC, without the D." (I do *not* have a disorder.)

Karen shouldn't complain; she benefits from my OC. When we're traveling and need a flashlight, I have one. When we need a bottle opener, I have two. (I carry two in case I lose one. I hid a third in Karen's backpack just in case I lose both of mine.) There's no "D," and I wish she would stop saying it.

Today Karen saw my list on our dresser. I was trying to keep her from seeing it because she makes fun of my lists. With a straight face, she started to ask me a question about it, but before the question came out, she looked like she was going to cry and covered her face with her hands. She laughed so hard she couldn't speak and walked out of the room. Ten minutes later she came back. As soon as she saw me: crying face, hands up, walked out of the room.

Why is this funny? We're going into the wilderness and need to be prepared. If I don't have a list, I'll forget something, and then what? What if we need duct tape and don't have any? What would we do? Probably not survive, that's what.

If she thinks I'm going to share my stuff with her when we're out in the wild, she's mistaken. Maybe if I need her body warmth, I'll barter.

I want to travel light, so I'm keeping my list to the bare minimum: snacks, emergency space blanket, zip lock bags, analog compass, sunglasses, binoculars, postcard stamps, sunscreen, chap stick with SPF 15 or higher, bug spray, Purell, bottle opener, Advil, liquid bandage, dental floss, finger and/or toenail clippers, reading glasses, peppermint patties, extra house keys, 30' section of nylon cord (I don't know why I need this, but it's on all the lists of things to have in case of an emergency), medical tape, wet wipes, extra flashlight batteries, napkins, water, snacks, GPS, extra batteries for the GPS, scissors, tweezers, tick remover, small roll of duct tape, Imodium A-D, small tripod, camera, backup bottle opener, knife, fire starter, bear spray, Spork (combination spoon/knife/fork), blister patch, snacks, gauze, earplugs, Dramamine and micro puff vest.

All that's in Karen's backpack is three wadded up Kleenex, four and a half candy corn, the bottle opener I hid in there, two Corona Light bottle caps, and a tampon. It's all a big joke until she needs something and doesn't have it. Then my OC isn't that funny. She better hope she doesn't need my Imodium A-D on our flight to American Samoa. I'm not sure I'll have any to spare.

Your friend,
Matt

~.~.~.~.~.~.~

From: **Matt Smith**
Subject: **Our national parks passport**
Date: **May 10, 2010**

Dear Bob and Sue,

It's a memorable moment when your spouse says, "You were right and I was wrong." I'm only guessing of course because Karen has never said this.

I found her today admiring her national parks passport, the little blue book you introduced to us years ago. At first Karen laughed at the idea of a national parks passport, but now she's proud of hers. She can't wait to get a stamp from every national park.

I bought my passport in April 2006 at Grand Canyon National Park. When I was in the checkout line at the Grand Canyon bookstore, I asked Karen if she wanted me to buy her one. I suggested to her that she start collecting park stamps with me on that trip. She gave me her best annoyed-to-have-to-answer-such-a-stupid-question look and said, "No thanks, I'm a grown up." For the last four years, I've endured her rolling of eyes whenever I would hunt for the stamp at a national park. All the while I was accumulating an impressive collection.

Then it happened – as I knew it would someday. It was earlier this year, and we were packing for a trip to Tucson. Karen said to me, "Don't forget our national parks passport." I paused for effect then replied, "*Our* passport? (pause again) Sweetie, *we* don't have a passport. *I* have a passport."

She tried to get me to acknowledge that it was now *our* passport, even using her "everything we have belongs to both of us because we're companions-for-life and so much in love, yada, yada, yada" line. Shameless. I didn't give in.

On that trip, she bought her very own passport at Saguaro National Park. She carries it with her everywhere, and if anyone asks, will show it with pride. Now she wishes she had it all those times we visited national parks before. I guess I was right. At least she has one now – with fewer stamps than me.

Your friend,
Matt

~.~.~.~.~.~.~

From: **Matt Smith**
Subject: **#1 – North Cascades National Park**
Date: **June 6, 2010**

Dear Bob and Sue,

I'm writing you from the ferryboat on our way out of Stehekin. Why were we in Stehekin instead of visiting our first national park? Good question.

It is impossible to drive to North Cascades National Park. I don't mean difficult, I mean impossible. Rather, I should say nearly impossible. Looking at a map there is no reasonably accessible road into the park. You can hike into the park, but even then it is confusing to tell when you are within the park boundaries.

There's a north and a south unit of North Cascades NP, and Ross Lake National Recreation Area divides the two units. Highway 20, the only road that runs east-west over the mountains is in Ross Lake National Recreation Area, not the national park. The visitor centers, the park signs, none of these are in the national park. No lodging, no restaurants. In fact, of the top 12 things to do in North Cascades NP listed on Tripadvisor, 11 are not in the park.

To make things even more confusing, there's a third national park unit, Lake Chelan National Recreation Area, which is adjacent and to the south of the other two units. The National Park Service manages all three units as a single park complex.

We had no idea how we were going to visit the park, so we talked with several rangers at the visitor center in Newhalem (not in the park) about this dilemma. They seemed defensive; they must get this question a lot. Their consistent response was, "You are in the park, it's a park complex and North Cascades National Park is part of the complex." Sorry, maybe it's my OC with a lowercase "d" talking, but you are either in the park or you're not, and the map says, "not".

It's a shame that it's so inaccessible, because North Cascades National Park is remarkable: remote mountains, deep valleys and more than 300 glaciers. But since we'd always wanted to stay at the lodge in Stehekin (in Lake Chelan NRA), we decided to see if we could hike or bike into the park from there. That's why we were in Stehekin this weekend.

Three of the kids went with us – Rachel, Justin, and Matthew. Emily is home studying for finals (so she says). We're glad the kids joined us on our first park trip, but just Karen and I will be going to the other 57.

Thursday night we drove from Issaquah (Issaquah, Washington is 15 miles east of Seattle) to Chelan where we spent the night. At 8:30am on Friday we took the two and a half hour Lady of the Lake ferry from Chelan to Stehekin. The only way to get to Stehekin is by boat, floatplane, horse or by hiking in. There's a 23-mile road in the Stehekin valley that is mostly gravel. Locals can arrange to have their vehicles put on a barge that runs every few weeks if they need them brought from or taken to Chelan. This is what I meant when I said there is no reasonably accessible road into the park.

As we traveled up the lake, the surrounding hills gradually increased in elevation. Near Chelan, the hills are low and gently rolling; in the summer, they're the color of straw except for the neatly spaced lines of green made by the irrigated orchards and vineyards. At Stehekin, the peaks are more than 7,000 feet and rise nearly vertically out of the 1,486-foot deep lake. By the time the boat docked, we felt we were in a different world than the one we came from only a few hours before. We had reservations at Stehekin Landing Resort, which sits right on the water by the ferry dock.

There was time to kill before we could check into our cabin, so we walked the mile and a half to the valley bakery for lunch. Stehekin has fewer than 100 year-round residents. It's not a crowded place, but while we were walking, four different people in pickup trucks stopped and asked if we wanted a ride. Normally, we wouldn't consider taking a ride from a stranger, but here it's what people do; the residents all know one another and treat visitors like neighbors. It's an exceptionally safe place. We declined the offers, not out of concern, but because we needed to stretch our legs after the long boat ride.

Lunch at the bakery was fantastic: chili, huge deli sandwiches and fresh baked cookies. Afterward, we walked back and checked into our cabin. It didn't have air-conditioning, TV, Internet, or cell phone service, but it had electricity, hot water, a coffee maker, and a magnificent view of the lake.

Later that afternoon, Karen and I hiked a few miles of the Lakeshore Trail. It was beautiful, but Karen walked with her head down the whole way, scanning for snakes and listening for rattles. Every time my foot hit a rock she jumped three feet in the air. Before the hike we spoke with a ranger at the Golden West Visitor Center. We asked for hiking suggestions and she recommended this hike. Her only warning, "Watch out for rattlesnakes sleeping in the sun on the trail."

She went on to tell us, "If they bite you, they probably won't use their venom. They can sense you're too big to eat by the vibrations you make when you walk, so they won't waste their venom on you." This didn't comfort me. It was like someone telling me that they're going to shoot me in the calf with a nail gun, but don't worry, the nails are clean. Karen wasn't comforted either. She wanted to see the ranger's diploma from snake school.

Whenever we hike in an area with rattlesnakes, Karen has a scenario running through her head where a rattlesnake strikes from out of nowhere and sinks its fangs into her leg. I make an incision with my pocketknife just above the bite, suck out the venom before it reaches her heart and save her life. What she fails to realize is by the time I found my pocketknife, sharpened it with my honing stone and sterilized both it and the bite area with my travel-size alcohol wipes, the venom would have done its damage. Fortunately, we had the trail to ourselves – no snakes and few people.

Yesterday (Saturday), Karen and I got out of bed about 7am; we knew we had several hours to ourselves before there would be any sign of life from the other three. It was a beautiful morning, so we walked along the valley road. We could smell the bakery before we could see it. We enjoyed a relaxed breakfast of coffee and a shared cinnamon roll the size of a football.

At mid-morning, the five of us were at the bike rental stand across the road from the resort. Our plan was to ride along the valley road toward the park boundary. I asked the woman renting us the bikes if she had locks for us to use. She laughed and said, "We don't need locks here. No one's going to take your bike. And if they do, they'll bring it back."

Our first stop along the valley road was the old Stehekin one-room schoolhouse. It was built in 1921 and used until the community built the new school in 1988. A short distance from the schoolhouse is Rainbow Falls where we ate lunch at a Paul Bunyan-sized picnic table within mist range of the 312-foot falls.

After lunch, we left our bikes in the grass alongside the valley road across from the falls, and walked to the 50-acre historic Buckner Orchard. The ranger at the visitor center made a point of telling us that *we* own Buckner Orchard since it's part of the park system, so we thought the least we could do is check it out and see how *our* orchard was doing. From the valley road a half-mile away, a hand-dug irrigation ditch diverted water into the orchard from Boulder Creek just below Rainbow Falls. Water ran swiftly through the 100-year old ditch as if the Buckners dug it only a few years ago.

Our day of biking in the valley was perfect – sunny and temperatures in the 70's – it was like riding a bike through a postcard. Just one problem, we didn't make it to the North Cascades National Park border. After all our side trips, we didn't have the energy to bike the remaining miles to the boundary. (We also weren't sure exactly where the boundary was.) I don't think we can count this as an official park visit, despite the rangers' assurances that it's all one big happy park complex.

This morning (Sunday) we woke up to the sound of rain on the metal roof of our cabin. Fortunately, we hadn't planned on doing much today except taking the ferry back to Chelan and driving home. Our butts were sore from yesterday's bike ride, and the rain was making it hard to get out of bed to pack for home.

Sitting inside the Lady of the Lake ferry on our trip back to Chelan, there hasn't been much conversation. I've been doing my best to try and stay awake, but the rain and the sound of the boat's engine are making me sleepy. After a long silence, Karen said, "Justin, I've been meaning to tell you about an article I read this week about the dangers of using a laptop. Researchers think that men who use a laptop while it's resting on their lap can damage their sperm. The laptop can cook their testicles. You don't use your laptop while it's on your lap do you?"

Justin looked terrified, so I jumped in to rescue him. "Karen, first, please don't use the phrase 'cook your testicles' *ever* again. Second, Justin doesn't want to talk about his testicles or his sperm with his mother-in-law."

"I'm serious," she continued. "It can cook his testicles. We want to have grandchildren someday." I put an end to the testicle discussion, but Justin seems to have disappeared.

So our very first park trip was a false start. It was a great visit to a beautiful national recreation area, but we still have 58 national parks to go. I'm happy the kids came with us, but I think they've had enough of us for a while.

Your friend,
Matt

~.~.~.~.~.~.~

From: **Matt Smith**
Subject: **It's blinking!**
Date: **June 10, 2010**

Dear Bob and Sue,

Today we hiked into North Cascades National Park, so we could claim that we've officially visited the park. After studying the park map, we found a trail off Highway 20 where we could hike a few miles to the park boundary. We never saw a sign indicating that we had entered the national park, but we're trusting the map and crossing this one off the list.

On our way to the trailhead, we stopped to take our picture in front of the park sign in Sedro-Woolley, the park headquarters. We've added "taking our picture in front of the park sign" to the list of things we plan on doing in every park.

We parked close to the sign, so I could balance my digital camera on the hood of the car. I set the timer for ten seconds, giving me enough time to get in position for the picture. There's a light on the front of the camera that starts blinking once the timer is set. When I pressed the button to start the timer, Karen yelled, "It's blinking!" She scared the shit out of me. I thought someone threw a hand grenade at us. She says this every time we take a picture with the timer. Even after I've explained that I know when it is blinking because I'm the one pushing the button that's making it blink, she still yells, "It's blinking!"

The picture came out slanted because of the slope of the car's hood; I tried setting the camera on the ground. The perspective from down there made us look like giants in the picture. I found a box of saltines in the car and put the camera on the box. This was a slight improvement.

At first we were embarrassed about posing for our picture in front of the park sign. We waited until no one was around, but after a few takes, we stopped caring. People in passing cars would honk and shout at us, usually compliments such as, "Nice cracker box!"

It took many tries to get the picture just right. Karen didn't know what to do with her hands. At first she put them in front of her about waist high, limp at the wrist. I called this her squirrel pose. She insisted she was not holding her hands like a squirrel until I showed her the picture. We tried again. I ran back from the camera after setting the timer and said in a soft voice, "No squirrel" just before the flash went off.

Drawing attention to her squirrel pose made it harder for her not to hold her hands that way. On the second picture, she had one hand in squirrel position. Half-squirrel. On the third picture, she put her hands straight down at her sides as if she was jumping off a diving board. I called this the high-dive. Naming the poses made matters worse.

After each take, I would go back to the camera, and Karen would stay in position next to the sign. While I checked the picture Karen would yell, "Is it okay?" and I would yell back, "Full squirrel again," or "High dive," reset the camera and run back. Eventually we were laughing so hard that the picture came out perfect.

Your friend,
Matt

~.~.~.~.~.~.~

From: **Karen Smith**
Subject: **#2 – Olympic National Park**
Date: **June 23, 2010**

Dear Bob and Sue,

I realized as we left the visitor center in Port Angeles that I had forgotten to bring my raincoat on our visit to the rainforest. There was no way I'd make it through the trip without needing one, but I didn't want to tell Matt. I knew he would ask me if a raincoat was on my list of things to bring. I don't ever make a list of things to bring, but maybe I should. I can't let Matt see my lists though, after laughing at his. We'll keep this just between us.

We drove the 17-mile Hurricane Ridge Rd., climbing steeply in elevation, to the Hurricane Ridge Visitor Center. There we stamped our passports, and took pictures of the amazing views of Olympic National Park and beyond. The road to the Hurricane Hill trailhead was free of snow, so we headed over there and hiked the easy three-mile round-trip trail. About a mile into the hike, we came across a scraggly old marmot. By the look of his fur, he'd seen one too many winters in the Olympic Mountains. Matt was very excited about this rare wildlife sighting until, farther up the trail, we came across many more. The trail was thick with marmots. At first Matt kept his distance; he wasn't sure if they were biters, but after seeing other hikers casually walk past them, he became more comfortable. Soon he was right in their faces taking pictures. They didn't move. These marmots were accustomed to hikers and cameras. Seeing so many of them close to the trail creeped me out; they're like giant squirrels. I never made eye contact with them, but I could still feel their beady little eyes following me.

When we were finished hiking and Matt was done taking pictures of people pushing strollers up Hurricane Hill, we drove to Lake Crescent Lodge where several weeks ago we reserved one of the Singer Tavern Cottages along the lake.

We're staying there for two nights. On our way to check in at the main lodge, we were walking past the cottages when Matt pointed out that one of them was in an odd spot. It didn't face the lake; it was sitting at a 45-degree angle, facing the other cottages. Matt made comments about the poor suckers who end up with that cottage. Guess who the poor suckers were today?

An hour after checking in, it was still eating at him that we got the dud cabin. When he couldn't stand it any longer, we went to the lodge, and Matt asked the manager if we could move to another cottage. I went over to sit by the fireplace, acting like we weren't together, but I could still hear their conversation. The manager told Matt that all the other cottages were taken. He tried to smooth it over by saying we were *lucky* because our cottage was "one of the most requested cottages at the lodge." When I heard that I thought, "Uh oh." Matt has a low tolerance for bullshit (as if you didn't already know). He couldn't let that slide, "So, let me get this straight. What you're telling me is that when people call to reserve a cottage, they say, 'I want the cottage that *doesn't* face the lake. I don't want any of the other cottages – the ones with a lake view. I want the cottage *without* the lake view.' Is this what you're telling me?" I let Matt go on for a couple of minutes, then went to the front desk and said, "I'm sorry to interrupt, but is it okay if we take our beers outside to the lawn by the lake?" Matt knew my interruption was code for, "stop being an asshole, you're only going to piss off the manager."

We relaxed in Adirondack chairs at the edge of the lake with a beer. Several beers. It was lovely and tranquil. We may have napped. Eventually, we dragged our cooler into the lobby/bar area and found comfortable chairs close to the fireplace. We discovered on a trip to Crater Lake Lodge last year that you're allowed to bring your own food and beverages into the lobbies of national park lodges, even if you're not staying there.

When it was time for dinner, we decided to stay put and eat in the bar area instead of the dining room. We ordered hamburgers, and after waiting for about half an hour, we saw a kitchen worker bring out our hamburgers and leave them at the end of the bar. From across the room, we watched our hamburgers sit at the end of the bar. About five minutes later, we saw the bartender look at our hamburgers, say something to our waitress and shrug his shoulders. We then watched the bartender and waitress eat our hamburgers. I gave Matt a look with a raised eyebrow as if to say, "This is what happens when you piss them off." It took another half an hour, and several confused conversations with our waitress, to get new hamburgers. We keep reminding ourselves that staying in the national park lodges is about the park experience and not the food or the service.

The lodge was crowded with people returning from their day of activities in the park. They milled about while waiting for tables to open in the dining room. We could see them eyeing us, wondering how we got the comfortable chairs next to the fire, and if we were leaving any time soon. There was no way we were giving up our prime real estate. We sat there and read for a couple of hours. The front doors of the lodge were open and a small red squirrel kept running into the great room; his little toenails made a skidding/scratching sound as he raced from place to place. I couldn't stand it, so I read with my feet on top of the cooler.

Close by, two couples sat on couches while they waited for their table. They were talking about all the parks they had been to, national parks and others. Their list was impressive. It made me realize we're novices, this being the second park of our trip. There are so many incredible parks that we haven't seen yet. One of the men said, "I don't know what it is, but when I see those brown park signs my heart beats a little faster." Matt and I looked at each other. That's exactly how we feel.

This morning we drank our coffee while gazing out the window of our cottage at the reflection of the lake in the windows of the other cottages. We were up and out early.

Olympic National Park has three completely different ecosystems: mountains, rainforest, and ocean beach, and our plan was to see parts of each on this trip. The drive from Lake Crescent to the Hoh Rain Forest Visitor Center took nearly two hours. We hiked the Hall of Mosses Loop, and then several miles of the Hoh River Trail. Years ago we hiked in the Quinault Rain Forest at the southern end of the park. I love rainforests. The draping, dripping moss on the giant western hemlocks and Douglas firs makes them look like an enchanted forest straight out of a storybook.

We didn't bring lunch with us, so we backtracked to the town of Forks and ate at Sully's Drive-In. Sully's is an old dairy freeze style hamburger place. The area in front of the walk-up order window was enclosed; it looked like it had originally been open to the outside. There was a weird mix of customers having lunch; everyone in their own way looked out of place: loggers in their canvas overalls, three college students with laptops and University of Washington t-shirts – their car overflowing with camping equipment – several pairs of Goth-looking tourists, and Matt and I in our hiking clothes.

In Forks, we saw several tour buses. These buses were not taking people into Olympic National Park; they were touring the town. Since you have a teenager, you probably know that the *Twilight* vampire books and movies are set in Forks. It seems odd that people would pay money to tour places where fictional characters hang out. It's all made up. They didn't even film the movies in Forks.

After lunch, we headed to the Pacific Coast; much of the Pacific coastline on the Olympic Peninsula is part of the park. We drove to a parking lot adjacent to Rialto Beach and walked a mile or two along the beach to the Hole-in-the-Wall, a sea-carved arch. The coastline is gorgeous, wild, and rugged. It was windy and the spray off the high waves made us damp. There were interesting pieces of driftwood everywhere; even wood that might have been construction debris – small lengths of two by four – had been rounded smooth as if they'd spent a month in a giant rock tumbler. I picked up a piece of driftwood that looked like a dinosaur with a long neck, and was planning to take it home with me until Matt said it looked like a giant penis. Before I could disagree with him, he held out his camera and showed me the picture of me holding it tightly by the "neck" with a stupid grin on my face. I immediately dropped it on the beach. It's just as well; you're not supposed to remove anything from a national park anyway.

Right now we're back in the Lake Crescent Lodge bar again, having a beer and wishing you were here. We just ordered hamburgers. It looks like a different bartender tonight. Hopefully, he's already eaten dinner.

Your friend,
Karen

~.~.~.~.~.~.~

From: **Matt Smith**
Subject: **#3 – Mount Rainier National Park**
Date: **June 30, 2010**

Dear Bob and Sue,

I learned during our visit to Mount Rainier National Park that it's against the law to impersonate a national park ranger. Last night we stayed at Paradise Inn, inside the park on the south side of the mountain. Before leaving the lodge this morning, I asked a park ranger how one would go about getting an official park ranger uniform. We thought it would be a nice birthday gift for you, Bob. I can see you now in those dark green wool trousers, a straw hat with its pinecone-embossed leather band and a bear spray holster loaded and ready. You could wear the uniform in your back yard, and practice for when you retire and become a park ranger. When friends come over, you could rope off rooms in your house and give make-believe tours as if it was Harry Truman's house. Or, you could wear it on the weekends when you go to the Home Depot to get a bag of nails, or whatever it is you get there.

The ranger seemed concerned that I was trying to get an official uniform. She said something about it being a federal offense to impersonate a park ranger. I can't imagine this is a big problem for the National Park Service, fake rangers leading unauthorized interpretive hikes. Regardless, keep this in mind if you're planning on going out in public in the ranger uniform I'm going to find for you.

I hadn't gotten off to a good start with this ranger. I told her about our plan to visit all 58 national parks. She said, "You know there are more than 58 national parks, don't you?" I acknowledged that there were 300+ park units, but told her that we decided to go to only the 58 that were named *national park*. She didn't seem too happy that we were placing a higher priority on some of the park units than others; she was a bit— severe. She then asked, "How many parks have you been to so far?" When I told her that Mount Rainier was our third, she smiled and said "Good luck."

Mount Rainier National Park is a two-hour drive southeast of Seattle, Washington. It was made the 5th national park in 1899 to preserve the wilderness around the volcano: the old growth forests and the sub-alpine wildflower meadows. The centerpiece of the park is the massive 14,410-foot volcanic peak of Mount Rainier; its year-round glacier covered peak is nature's lighthouse for the entire Pacific Northwest. It has the highest topographic prominence of any mountain in the lower 48 states. This means it looks taller than mountains its same size because the land that surrounds it is so much lower in elevation. Sea level is only 50 miles away.

On a clear day, we can see Mount Rainier from Issaquah. For years, I've thought about climbing it, but Karen discouraged me. She thinks it's dangerous. She also didn't want to raise three kids by herself; I can't blame her.

Over the last 30 years, there have been an average of two deaths per year of people climbing Mount Rainier, an unfortunate number, but a small percentage of those who try. In 1966, the number of climbers attempting the summit was 2,000. By 1994, the number had grown to 10,000. It's stayed close to that level ever since. During the 2009 climbing season (October 2008 – September 2009), 10,616 climbers took a shot at it; about half succeeded in reaching the summit.

By far the most popular routes to the summit start at the Henry M. Jackson Memorial Visitor Center parking lot (adjacent to Paradise Inn). Most climbers hike from the visitor center to Camp Muir – about a 5,000-foot vertical climb – spend the night, and start an early morning push to the summit, which is another 4,000 vertical feet. Most climbers, whether they are successful at summiting or not, make it down without injury or need for rescue or assistance because almost half use one of the three professional guide companies licensed by the park service.

Last year there were 18 climbing related search-and-rescue incidents in the park: climbers breaking bones (ankles, legs, ribs, pelvis), one climber was hit in the face with a rock and lost consciousness, several suffered acute mountain sickness (headache, nausea, dizziness), and one incident involved a ranger who fell 30 feet into a crevasse after accidentally skiing into it. He was lucky to have survived.

Karen and I didn't attempt to climb Mount Rainier on this trip; we settled for hiking in the forests in the lower regions of the park. With all the attention on the summit, the trails through the old growth forests are nearly deserted. The park service issues more permits for climbing the summit than for overnight backpacking in the entire rest of the park. That's quite amazing since the park is 368 square miles.

Yesterday, when we got here, we entered through the Stevens Canyon Entrance in the southeast corner of the park. The trailhead for the Grove of the Patriarchs Trail is just inside the park. The grove consists of Western Hemlock, Douglas fir, and Western red cedar trees. Some are more than one thousand years old. We hiked the short loop to the patriarchs, and then continued hiking several miles north along the Ohanapecosh River.

A couple of miles into the hike, we met park workers who were building bridges using blown down trees. They were improving the trail enough to get tools and stock to a river crossing farther north where they needed to prepare footings for a steel span bridge being delivered by helicopter later this summer. It looked like a fun job: chain saws, hard hats, large trees attached to steel cables being winched into place. I could easily imagine them being a CCC (Civilian Conservation Corps) crew from the 1930's. The lead ranger said the CCC built some of the bridges they were replacing. He told us of a bridge farther up the trail that the CCC built in the 1930's that's still in excellent shape. The original square head nails they used on the planks, now smooth from the better part of a century of hiking boots passing over them, are still visible.

After leaving the bridge builders, we hiked to the river crossing where they told us the steel span bridge was to go. The existing bridge was a single log stretching 30 feet across the Ohanapecosh River at a point where the river drops about 100 feet. The falls were beautiful, but I was nervous walking across the log. One misplaced step would have ended our parks trip.

I videotaped Karen as she walked slowly across the log, looking down and carefully putting one foot in front of the other. She accused me of doing this so, if she fell, I'd have proof I didn't push her. I was deeply offended.

After our hike, we drove to Paradise Inn. The inn, at 5,400 feet elevation, opened in 1917. There have been several attempts over the years to make Paradise a recreation destination; they built a golf course and towrope for skiing, but those are gone now – they weren't economically sustainable. Today the main activity is hiking and climbing.

Paradise Inn has been remodeled several times; the most recent project was a two-year renovation from mid-2006 to mid-2008 when the inn was reinforced to withstand a major earthquake. Mount Rainier is an active volcano, and, in an average month, there are several small earthquakes on the mountain. There are seismic sensors on the mountain, and scientists believe that if (or when) it erupts, there will be enough warning to evacuate visitors from the park safely. But you never know. Even though the last major eruption was in the mid-nineteenth century, Mount Rainier is one of the most dangerous volcanoes in the world because of its proximity to the Seattle-Tacoma metropolitan area. If Mount Rainier blows in the direction of our house, well, let's just say the park would be visiting us – in a hurry.

We'd wanted to stay at Paradise Inn since it re-opened in 2008; our parks trip was a good excuse to do it. Last night, we sat in the great room for hours reading and writing postcards. Karen is sending a postcard to each of our kids from every national park we visit. After 58 parks, they will each have a complete set of postcards. Wow! What 20-something year-old wouldn't want a postcard from all 58 national parks?

This morning, there was still five feet of snow next to the road leading away from the inn; the snowpack is 200 percent of normal for this time of the year. Driving down the mountain, there was a mile-long section of the road where we saw several marmots. They were odd looking, as if they were made from marmot spare parts. Their heads were black, their nose and mid-section blonde, and the back third of their bodies light brown. They were Hoary Marmots, which are different from the Olympic Marmots we saw in Olympic National Park. Marmots prefer a very narrow band of elevation; that's why we saw so many in one place on our hike in Olympic, and why we saw so many in one place along the road this morning.

Before heading home, we hiked several miles of the Wonderland Trail, a 93-mile path that circles Mount Rainier. About 250 people each year hike the entire trail, which takes an average of 14 days to complete. The park service requires a permit to hike the entire trail. They want to keep track of backcountry hikers and to ensure the backcountry campsites aren't overcrowded. In November 2006, a storm caused flooding that destroyed most of the trail's log bridge creek crossings; it was August 2007 before the trail re-opened. Ironically, people who have hiked the Wonderland Trail say that even though the trail circles the mountain, the mountain is rarely visible from the trail. The section we hiked was relatively easy. The elevation gains were small, and for most of the way, the trail followed Stevens Creek through a valley south of the main park road.

We're lucky that three of the national parks are a short drive from our house; we've made a good start without leaving Washington. But the trips close to home are over now. Next week we start traveling farther. We'll be visiting Cuyahoga Valley National Park in Ohio.

Your friend,
Matt

~.~.~.~.~.~.~.~

From: **Karen Smith**
Subject: **#4 – Cuyahoga Valley National Park**
Date: **July 6, 2010**

Dear Bob and Sue,

Before planning our parks trip, we'd never heard of Cuyahoga Valley National Park. Just south of Cleveland, it includes 33,000 acres along 22 miles of the Cuyahoga River. The river is the most famous part of the park – for being polluted. So polluted, it caught fire *at least 13 times* between 1868 and 1969. But the health of the river is improving, and while the National Park Service hasn't prohibited recreational activities in the river, they seriously discourage them. The park newsletter warns that the river is contaminated with pathogens such as E. coli. Signs are posted that say "No Swimming, No Wading, No Boating." We didn't need signs to keep us away – they had us at E. coli.

We arrived at the park yesterday just after noon. It was warm and humid, even for July. Our first stop was the Canal Visitor Center, in the north end of the park, where we stamped our passports and looked around the museum. Anxious to see the park, we drove south to Hunt Farm Visitor Center, stopping at the two other visitor centers along the way. Immediately, we noticed the park didn't have the "you've entered a sacred, pristine place" feeling that we get in the other national parks. It was a hodgepodge of forest, houses, small businesses, and highways crisscrossing overhead. The road we drove through the park, Canal Road, unexpectedly changed names, took us out of the park and changed names again. There were so many roads in and out of the park that we were never sure when we were in the park and when we weren't. It felt like a typical rural area in the Midwest rather than a national park.

We knew, before we got here, that Cuyahoga Valley National Park was different from the other national parks. It didn't become a national park to protect a rare or unusual landscape or other natural resource. It became a national park because the local citizens wanted it to be a national park. By the 1960's, the valley was in danger of becoming an unbroken chain of urban development from Cleveland to Akron. Local leaders decided it needed the protection that a National Park Service site is assured.

The park service and Department of the Interior resisted, not wanting to divert funds from the western *crown jewel* parks like Yellowstone and Yosemite. In 1973, the National Park Service director declared, "I will tell you one thing. (The Cuyahoga Valley) will be a park over my dead body!" The following year, President Ford, under pressure from environmental groups, reluctantly signed the bill that established Cuyahoga Valley National Recreation Area.

Over the following 34 years, more than $200 million was spent to purchase land for the park, restore nearly 100 historic structures and establish activities for visitors. Eventually, supporters called for full national *park* status, and they got it. In 2000, the name was changed to Cuyahoga Valley National Park. In a nutshell, locals got the federal government to purchase and restore their polluted landscape, manage these outdoor spaces, and provide recreation and cultural activities for the millions of people living just outside its borders.

One activity we'd been looking forward to was riding the Cuyahoga Valley Scenic Railroad. It's "one of the oldest, longest, and most scenic tourist excursion railways in the country, running 51 miles from Independence, Ohio through the park and continuing to Akron and Canton." You can board the train at the north end of the park at Rockside Station, get off at stops throughout the park, and re-board later for the return trip. But, when we asked a ranger about the train, he told us that it doesn't run on Mondays or Tuesdays (the only days we're here).

Since we planned a whole day around riding the train, we found ourselves with time to fill. We asked the rangers for recommendations of things to do. One of them suggested we go to the beaver marsh at dawn or dusk to see beaver activity. They are understandably proud of their beaver activity, because, by 1900, there were almost no beavers left in the Cuyahoga Valley due to unrestricted hunting. The ranger told us beavers created a marsh on top of what was previously an automobile junkyard. We were expecting to hear a feel-good story about how the park service removed the trash and restored the area to its natural state, but the beavers moved too quickly. They took matters into their own paws, dammed the stream and created a marsh on top of the junked cars.

Today instead of riding the train, we hiked to Brandywine Falls and then the Ledges and Pine Grove trails. It was hot and humid again, temps in the 90's. The Ledges Trail is an easy 2.2-mile loop through a hemlock forest that passes by several 30- to 60-foot tall sandstone cliffs (the ledges). It also goes by Ice Box Cave, which isn't a real cave but a 50-foot deep, narrow slit in the rock hillside. At the entrance, we felt cold air coming out of the cave. It would have been the perfect day to sit inside. I peered into the darkness.

"Let's go in and look around," I said to Matt. "Do you have a flashlight?" Matt shrugged his shoulders. He hates caves. "I know you have a flashlight. For God's sake, you have everything from batteries to a tick remover. Surely you have a flashlight."

He replied, "Do you have a tick that needs removing?"

"Come on. You could supply a medical clinic with what you have in your backpack. Do you really expect me to believe you don't have a flashlight?"

He said, "Look, it would be easy to hand you my flashlight, but then you wouldn't have learned anything. We're in a national park; you need to work on your survival skills. Take those two Corona Light bottle caps out of your backpack and try rubbing them together to get a spark. Use your dirty Kleenex as kindling." Matt never wastes an opportunity to point out my lack of preparation.

Just then, 20 kids – who looked to be about fourth grade age – arrived and swarmed the area in and around the cave. One of them ran right into Matt, got behind him and grabbed Matt's legs. He was hiding from his friends behind Matt like Matt was a tree. The kid peeked around Matt's backpack then ran away with a squeal. Matt was momentarily trapped in the scrum of children. I continued down the trail, "See ya back at the car, honey."

We thought about renting bikes and then riding along the Towpath trail, but it was too hot. The Towpath Trail is the same path that mules once walked while towing canal boats along the Ohio and Erie Canal. The canal was a 308-mile waterway built in the 1820's to carry freight, but the arrival of railroads made it obsolete, which explains why the part of the canal we saw looked like a ditch choked with weeds. It's hard to imagine boats filled with cargo ever using this as a means of transportation, but they did. Twenty miles of the trail run though the park, and it's usually crowded with walkers, runners, strollers and bicyclists – more than 2.5 million people annually – but very few of them were out today.

After looking through the newsletter and map for the tenth time, we realized we were running out of things to do. I talked Matt into visiting Hale Farm and Village (an outdoor living history museum depicting life in the mid-1800's) by telling him they have farm animals he can pet. I neglected to mention that they have crafts like broom making, basket weaving, candle making, butter churning and spinning. And, you can tour historical houses with interpreters dressed in period costume. Matt isn't a fan of crafts or places where people dress in costume and reenact history. He tries to trick them into coming out of character by asking questions like, "Do you have a website that tells more about your village?" It didn't matter anyway: when we got there we learned that Hale Farm is also closed on Mondays and Tuesdays. We chose the worst two days of the week to visit the park.

We ended up at the Winking Lizard Tavern in Peninsula, Ohio, a small historic town in the middle of the park. Between yesterday and today, we've been there three times. They're currently hosting their 24th annual World Tour of Beers. A Tour Card electronically keeps track of the beers you've consumed, and when you've had 100 beers from their World Tour of Beers list, you receive the coveted World Tour jacket. If we were spending a few more days in the park, we'd wear our World Tour jackets back to Seattle, but tomorrow we're heading home.

Your friend,
Karen

~.~.~.~.~.~.~

From: **Matt Smith**
Subject: **#5 – Rocky Mountain National Park**
Date: **July 21, 2010**

Dear Bob and Sue,

Visiting Rocky Mountain National Park today brought back memories from when our kids were young and we spent summer vacations in Estes Park. They always enjoyed the town of Estes Park more than the national park. It's hard for rocks, trees, and tundra to compete for a child's attention when there are go-carts and a giant slide close by.

I came here as a kid myself. It was my introduction to the national parks. Then, in the 1970's, tourists swarmed Colorado. Developers, it seemed, built as many condominiums as they could get away with – something John Denver could not comprehend – to accommodate the crowds. Against this backdrop, the park became a safe base for people who valued wilderness. Build your golf courses, ski slopes, and Olympic Villages along the I-70 corridor, but leave Rocky Mountain National Park unspoiled.

We drove through the park on Trail Ridge Road, entering from the east. The road climbs to the Continental Divide before it bends south to the town of Grand Lake. Workers were re-paving the road, so alternating directions of traffic had to take turns going around them. The drive was slow as we climbed to nearly 12,000 feet. Being so high, the road is above the tree line for a long stretch. One of my favorite family photos is of the kids and me, above the tree line along Trail Ridge Road, with the mountain peaks in the background and clouds below. It looks like we just climbed to a remote summit, instead of driving there in a minivan with a *Fievel Goes West* videotape playing in the back.

Halfway through the park, at the Alpine Visitor Center, we stopped and stamped our passports. At the stamp station, a man wearing a Kansas State t-shirt stood uncomfortably close to me and stared at what I was doing. He watched me stamp my passport, as if I was one of the park's interpretive exhibits. I looked up at him, thinking he wanted to use the stamp or maybe say hello. Why else would he be invading my personal space? Then, he just walked away without grunting a word.

From the visitor center, we drove toward Grand Lake. Along the drive, we saw elk, sometimes in the distance, and sometimes near the road. In a couple of places, they were so close that people stopped their cars to take pictures. One man turned off his car in the middle of the road, got out and left his driver's side door open. Oncoming traffic had to drive onto the shoulder of the road to avoid hitting the door. He walked about 30 feet into the grass and stood with his hands on his hips, looking at the elk while traffic piled up behind him. Bob, by any chance were you in Rocky Mountain National Park today?

We exited the park at the southern end and entered the town of Grand Lake where we're staying for two nights. There we could see the widespread damage from the ongoing pine beetle epidemic. It's shocking. Huge areas of pine forest are dying, and it's happening from Mexico to Canada. The park service newsletter says, "There is no effective means of controlling a large beetle outbreak in such a vast area as the park's backcountry, which comprises about 95 percent of the park." The National Park Service's efforts are limited to trying to keep the trees alive near facilities such as visitor centers and campgrounds.

Enough with the beetles; tomorrow we hike.

Your friend,
Matt

~.~.~.~.~.~.~

From: **Matt Smith**
Subject: **Rocky Mountain day two**
Date: **July 22, 2010**

Dear Bob and Sue,

Today's main activity was an 11-mile round-trip hike to Lone Pine Lake starting from the East Inlet Trailhead on the west side of Rocky Mountain National Park. A park ranger stood at the entrance of the trail checking hikers on their way in. He was making sure no one was bringing a dog with them on the trail and that everyone was wearing appropriate footwear and clothing. We've seen people wear crazy stuff on hiking trails. I once saw a woman on Tiger Mountain, a half-mile from the summit, hiking in flip-flops. There was six inches of snow on the ground at the time. I'm sure the ranger turned a few hikers away today. But not us; he deemed our clothing appropriate and wished us a pleasant day.

About a mile into the hike, we saw two foxes standing on the trail about 30 yards ahead of us. Their coats were thick and fluffy like they just had a bath. We haven't seen many foxes in the wild to compare them with, but these two looked very healthy. They didn't seem concerned that we were there, they looked at us and calmly continued on their way.

Another mile or so down the trail, a yellow-bellied marmot ran across our path and hid among the rocks. I tried to get a good look at him, but he was better at hiding than I was at finding him. I'm 49 years old and as of a month ago, I'd never seen a marmot. Since then I've seen four different species: Olympic (Olympic National Park), hoary (Mount Rainier National Park), groundhog (Michigan, visiting you) and yellow-bellied (Rocky Mountain National Park). Four different kinds of marmots in a month! I enthusiastically shared this with Karen, and she said, "No one cares. They're rodents."

No one cares? I care.

As soon as we reached Lone Pine Lake, we stood there looking at it for as long as it took to eat a granola bar, and then turned around to hike back. Karen and I enjoy the hiking part of the hike much more than the sitting and looking part. Karen says she wants us to stop more often and enjoy the scenery on our hikes, but I've tested her on this. Any pause longer than 30 seconds brings a response of, "What are we doing? Are you ready to go?"

The main reason Karen wants to keep moving is she doesn't like to pee on the trail. Many of our hikes are three to four hours long, and often the deciding factor in choosing our hike for the day is which one has a restroom at the end. I don't care where I pee; I'm fine peeing next to the trail. We've made a pact that whenever I stop to pee on a hike Karen's job is to be the lookout. She's supposed to warn me of approaching hikers by calling out, "Whip-poor-will, whip-poor-will." So far, the only thing I've heard from her is heavy exhales. She's jealous that I can pee anywhere. She would prefer that I hold it, in a show of solidarity, until she can go also.

We were lucky we didn't stay long at Lone Pine Lake. A few minutes after we headed for the car, we heard thunder, even though the sky was nearly cloud free. We knew from growing up in the Midwest that afternoon thunderstorms can develop quickly, especially in the Rockies.

We quickened our pace. Each time we heard thunder we sped up more. A mile from the car, we were surprised to see hikers passing us going in the other direction with no raincoats, backpacks, or umbrellas – no rain gear of any kind. Some even had expensive cameras, out of their cases and hanging around their necks. I could hear Karen behind me say softy, as if talking to the passing hikers, "It's cloudy; it's windy; there's thunder and lightning; you're gonna be drowned rats in about ten minutes."

About a half-mile from the car, we felt small drops and strong wind gusts. We knew we only had a few minutes before the heavy rain would reach us. The last 200 yards was a dash for the car through a downpour and small hail. We sat in the car, dripping wet, watching it rain and feeling the car rock back and forth from the wind. As strange as it sounds, we miss the Midwest thunderstorms. It was a perfect end to a perfect hike.

Tomorrow we're driving to Black Canyon of the Gunnison National Park. I have to confess; I don't know what a Gunnison is.

Your friend,
Matt

~.~.~.~.~.~.~

From: **Matt Smith**
Subject: **#6 – Black Canyon of the Gunnison National Park**
Date: **July 24, 2010**

Dear Bob and Sue,

We must look soft. Ranger Betty at the BCoftheG Visitor Center seemed to think so. We told her that we wanted to do the Gunnison Route hike from the rim of the canyon down to the river, but she strongly discouraged us. She listed many reasons why we shouldn't do that hike, emphasizing that even though it's one mile down to the river, it's an 1,800-foot vertical drop. It's so steep the park service installed an 80-foot chain, a third of the way down the trail, to assist hikers. Betty tried to convince us that we weren't prepared for the hike by pointing out that we didn't have gloves, we weren't wearing long pants, and we didn't have the recommended gallon of water each. But we insisted on trying anyway. We thought, "It's a short hike, how hard could it be?" Also, when someone tells Karen she can't do something, it only makes her want to do it more.

Hikers are required to get a backcountry permit and listen to an orientation talk before attempting this hike. Betty prepared our permit, and then got out her notebook with the orientation script. She began to take us through the orientation: what plants we would encounter (Stinging Nettle and Poison Ivy were my favorites), how to use the chain, etc. About three minutes into the orientation, Karen wandered off to look at postcards. Ranger Betty stopped her presentation, whistled to get Karen's attention and motioned her back. This only deepened Betty's concern about us (mostly Karen).

Once Karen was with us again, Betty went over the animals we might encounter on the hike. She turned her notebook to a page with a picture of a black bear and a mountain lion. She first pointed to the mountain lion and said, "If you see this one, there's nothing you can do, so I'll tell you about the bear instead." Already, we felt more confident. Betty told us about a black bear that frequents the trail, and what to do if we came across him. After the orientation, we signed the backcountry permit and were free to do the hike.

On the trail, we quickly learned why ranger Betty tried to discourage us. The beginning of the trail was nearly vertical. We struggled in several places, trying not to fall and slide on our butts down the canyon, and we hadn't even gotten to the chain yet. After a quarter of a mile, we called it quits and climbed back up. We had to use our hands to pull ourselves up the trail, grabbing tree trunks and roots. The hike lasted about as long as the orientation.

Part of the deal with backcountry permits is you have to turn them back into the visitor center when you finish the hike so they know who to go looking for (rescue) at the end of the day. I snuck into the visitor center hoping to slip the permit to the cashier in the bookstore and leave before Betty saw me. But as if on cue, Betty came around the corner as I reached the counter. I handed her the permit, and silently blamed Karen by tilting my head toward the parking lot. Betty could see her standing out there, fixing her hair in the reflection of our car's window. There was no reason to let Betty think we're both lame.

From the visitor center, we hiked the Flat Oak Loop, and then drove the rim road stopping at many of the overlooks. The canyon is very steep and narrow. The views from the overlooks are impressive, but because of the steepness of the canyon, hikes are either flat (along the rim) or nearly vertical (to the river). The rest of our hiking today was along the rim.

It occurred to me as I looked into the canyon that most national parks are defined by what's there: a mountain, a lake, or the wildlife. But BCoftheG National Park is defined by what's not there; a thin, but incredibly deep, chunk of the high plateau is missing. The Gunnison River carried it away. Because of the steepness of the canyon, it's a small park in terms of land that can be used for recreation, and there's not much close by. We stayed in the town of Montrose, 13 miles away, which was the closest lodging we could find.

The canyon was a spectacular sight, especially today when it was clear and sunny. But, unless you hike down to the river, it doesn't take long to see the park. We felt we did everything we wanted to in a few hours.

By the way, Karen and I decided the name of the park is too long, so we've shortened it to BCoftheG. Tomorrow we're stopping in Telluride for the night on our way to Mesa Verde National Park.

Your friend,
Matt

~.~.~.~.~.~.~

From: **Matt Smith**
Subject: **#7 – Mesa Verde National Park**
Date: **July 26, 2010**

Dear Bob and Sue,

The drive south from Telluride on Highway 145 this morning was spectacular; around every turn, there was a scene of red cliffs and dark green forest against a brilliant blue sky. We even saw a black bear by the side of the road. Ten miles east of Cortez, Colorado, in the southwest corner of the state, we came to the entrance of Mesa Verde National Park.

Today was a bonus day for us. We weren't expecting to get to the park as early as we did. We drove straight to the Far View Visitor Center and signed up for tours of Balcony House and Cliff Palace. We also got tickets for tomorrow's Mug House and Long House tours. Our timing was perfect. There was just enough time to TCB before driving to Chapin Mesa for the Balcony House tour.

TCB is short for *taking care of business*, not to be confused with *doing your business*, which is Karen's euphemism for going to the bathroom. Specifically, on our parks trip, TCB means: 1) Taking our picture in front of the park sign; 2) getting a copy of the park map and newsletter; 3) stamping our passports; and 4) buying four postcards (one for each of our kids and one for us). The only other requirement to make a park visit *official* is to do an activity like a hike or ranger-led tour.

Cliff dwellings are the main attraction at Mesa Verde. There are more than 600 of them in the park, but most are not open to the public. The Pueblo Indians constructed them from about the years 550 to 1300, although the golden age of cliff dwelling in the area was from 1100 to 1300. Archeologists can tell that the majority of cliff dwellers left abruptly at the end of the 13th century, probably as a result of a 24-year drought and the stress of over-population on the mesa. Most of the dwelling sites are located under eroded areas beneath cliffs; this protected the inhabitants from the weather and from one another.

In 1888, two cowboys reported finding cliff dwellings on the mesa, and, from that moment, interest in the area grew quickly. Eventually, concerns about artifacts being removed and the potential for damage to the archeological sites led to the establishment of the park in 1906.

Balcony House was our first tour today. Our group met in the parking lot for an orientation talk with Jenny, the ranger who was our guide. She explained what we would see, and warned us of the physical requirements of the tour. To enter Balcony House, each member of the group would have to climb a 32-foot wooden ladder. It sounded scarier than it was. Later, I asked Jenny if there had ever been accidents on the ladder, or if anyone ever needed to be rescued from Balcony House. I was surprised when she said that more than once a person with a heart condition climbed to the top of the ladder, then after stepping into Balcony House, died of a heart attack.

Jenny led us down a steep set of stairs built into the cliff adjacent to Balcony House. At the bottom was a locked gate. Before unlocking it, she turned to the group and said, "This is the last chance for anyone to chicken out gracefully. If you get to the ladder, and don't want to climb it, everyone will have to wait while I walk you back to this gate and let you out." There were no chickens in our group.

Inside the gate, a paved path led us to a spot just beneath Balcony House, and to the foot of the access ladder. It was wide enough for two people to climb side-by-side. I imagined we would go up one at a time, but the ladder was tall enough for several of us to climb at the same time. Looking up, I was relieved to see only a couple of skinny kids above me – 60-pounders at the most. If they fell, they weren't likely to take mc with them. Everyone on our tour made it up the ladder without incident. There were no falls or heart attacks.

Balcony House was a medium sized cliff dwelling; it had 40 rooms and two kivas. Some rooms were a few feet deep and wide, probably built for storage, while others looked large enough for a family to sleep in. A kiva is a room where communal or religious gatherings took place. They are usually round, with a floor several feet below ground level, with a place to make a fire.

Balcony House faces east; it would have been a cold place to live in the winter. Because of the way they built it into the cliff, it was an easy place to defend, but a hard place to get into or out of in a hurry. Our exit included crawling through a narrow 12-foot tunnel. A big person would not be able to get through. Another reason for the orientation talk before the tour was to give Jenny a chance to size up the group – literally – and to encourage anyone who might be too big to make it through the tunnel to sit this one out. Once through the tunnel, we climbed another ladder; then we scrambled back up to the mesa using the handholds and toeholds carved into the side of the cliff by the original cliff dwellers.

Usually, we don't like guided tours, but this one we enjoyed. Besides, going on a ranger-led tour is the only way to see most of the major cliff dwellings in the park. The park service does this to protect the sites from damage by visitors. Even the smallest wear-and-tear, multiplied thousands of times over the years, can do serious damage to the sites.

After a quick lunch and a visit to the Chapin Mesa Museum, we got in line for our afternoon tour. Cliff Palace is the largest cliff dwelling in North America. It's a magnificent sight from the trail just below the parking lot. From a distance, it looks fake, like an architect's model, until a tour group files in to give it a sense of scale. I can only imagine what those cowboys thought when they first saw these houses.

Cliff Palace was much easier to get into than Balcony House. It only required climbing a couple of short ladders, and there were no tunnels to crawl through. With 150 rooms and 23 kivas, the park service estimates that 100 people lived at Cliff Palace. Karen wanted to stay all afternoon, but the rangers kept us moving. There were more tours scheduled after ours.

With the balance of the afternoon, we hiked the 2.5-mile Petroglyph Point Trail, which goes past one of the largest and best-preserved petroglyph panels in the Southwest.

A petroglyph is a design – often prehistoric – carved into rock; not to be confused with a pictograph, which is a design drawn or painted onto the surface of a rock.

The petroglyphs were clearly visible in the bright afternoon sunlight: spirals, hand prints, zig zags, big horn sheep, human stick figures – one with both arms overhead, another with its right arm up and left arm down. Standing in front of the panel, it was exciting to think that another person once stood in that same spot, in the case of these petroglyphs no fewer than 700 years ago, scratching their design into the rock. It's as if the person just stepped around the corner a few minutes ago.

On the petroglyph trail we met Paula and Gary from Indiana. Later at the Far View Lodge, we ran into them again and drank a beer together. They told us about all the parks they've visited; it was an impressive list, even more so considering they drive to them all – they don't like to fly. We told them about our plan to visit all 58 national parks; they were enthusiastic and encouraging. It's fun to connect with other fans of the parks. It gives us the energy to keep going. Bob and Sue, it's not too late for you to join us.

Your friend,
Matt

~.~.~.~.~.~.~

From: **Matt Smith**
Subject: **Mesa Verde day two**
Date: **July 27, 2010**

Dear Bob and Sue,

The park newsletter describes the Mug House Tour as a "strenuous two-hour, three-mile round-trip hike that includes... steep drop-offs, switchbacks, and scrambling over boulders." That's code for "if you have to rock back-and-forth several times to build up enough momentum to get your ass out of your car, don't sign up for this tour." It's a weed out tactic. The tour is a ranger-led "limited-time-only hike" that the park just started offering to test the level of public interest; this morning we took the 10:00am tour.

There were nine of us on the hike, including the two rangers. We were happy to visit this remote cliff dwelling with such a small group. It was sunny and cool, a perfect day for a hike. From the parking lot, we walked about a quarter of a mile along the paved road where we found the trail to the cliff dwelling. We then left the road and walked down a trail through the scrubby, desert-like landscape, watching for rattlesnakes that sometimes sun themselves in the open. After dropping down a few hundred feet in elevation, the path leveled, and then followed the contour of the cliffs until it reached Mug House. When explorers first entered these ruins, they found three mugs hanging in one of the rooms, as if the residents forgot them when they left in a hurry; that's how the site got its name.

The ranger leading the tour had done her homework on Mug House. She and her husband are seasonal rangers, and teachers during the rest of the year. She showed us how archeologists could tell that various sections of the complex were built at different times because of the methods and materials used. She also explained how the cliff dwellers would recycle building materials; when they built a new complex, they got much of their building materials from tearing down older dwellings. This was all thoughtfully prepared and presented in a three-ring binder with plastic page protectors for each exhibit.

Karen and I enjoyed the Mug House tour very much. Being in a small group and a couple of miles away from the road gave it an intimate and authentic feel. In that setting, we could imagine what it was like for the early explorers of this area when they stumbled across these ruins. Hopefully, the park will continue to offer these backcountry tours.

By noon, we were back at the parking lot where we began. Nothing about the hike seemed as strenuous as the newsletter suggested. There was just enough time to eat lunch in our rental car and do a self-guided tour of Step House before our 1:00pm Long House tour.

A tram from the parking lot took our Long House tour group of 40 a few miles along a paved path to a staging area. Long House was the most picturesque dwelling we visited, partly because the lighting was perfect when we were there. The site faces west, and when the afternoon sun hit it, the red stones against the green vegetation make it a striking scene. When the late 19th century explorers discovered these ruins, they were jumbles of stones; centuries of silt obscured most of what was beneath. Now, they've been carefully unearthed, but many of the walls remain in mid crumble, their stair-step edges suggesting where the complete walls once were. The park service has made modest repairs to some of the structures, but nearly everything visible at the cliff dwellings is from the period of the Pueblo Indians.

Long House was beautiful, but the ranger leading the tour was a bonehead. If he only pointed and grunted the tour would have been more enjoyable and educational; a huge difference from the tour this morning.

Most rangers we encounter in the parks are dedicated, enthusiastic, and do a great job on the tours. This guy must have slipped through the screening process. At the beginning of the tour, he chose a 12-year old girl from the group, and played "let's pretend you're an Indian girl and you're getting ready for your wedding." (The Pueblo Indians married young 700 years ago.) She had to choose a boy from the group to be her husband, which was awkward and kind of creepy. The rest of the tour involved asking the two of them questions like "what food would you serve at your wedding?" while the rest of us stood around listening to them guess wrong answers. The only thing I hate more than audience participation is guessing games. If the ranger wants us to know that the Pueblo Indians ate beans, corn, and squash, then JUST TELL US! The tour was painful and inappropriate, but the site was beautiful. They should make this a silent tour.

During one of the guessing sessions, I instinctively stood up; I had to get away. Karen looked up and whispered, "Where are you going?"

"Back to the car, I wasn't invited to the wedding." She grabbed my leg and said, "You're not going anywhere." She was right. There was no way out. We were a few miles from the parking lot, and the tram would not be back for another 45 minutes. I just had to tough it out.

After the Long House tour, we drove back to Far View Lodge. Mesa Verde is a beautiful park to drive through. It's a plateau ranging from 7,000 to 8,000 feet in elevation. Juniper and pinyon trees normally cover much of the park, but nine sizable forest fires over the last 100 years have wiped out many of them. A ranger told us that the re-growth cycle for juniper trees after a fire is about 250 years. At 400 years, the juniper and pinyon tree forest gets so thick it's susceptible to a major fire – usually caused by lightning – and so the cycle continues. Two fires in the year 2000 burned more than 28,000 acres in the park. We could still see the impact of those fires today as we drove through the park.

As we were driving to the lodge, a heavy thunderstorm blew in. It was perfect timing. We'd finished our day of tours, and welcomed the cool break. We ate at the lodge restaurant for the second night in a row. It was fantastic: Indian rugs on the walls, professional wait staff, and interesting menu items. I ordered the Poblano Rellenos that Karen ate last night. It's hard to find that kind of authentic southwestern cooking in Seattle.

Your friend,
Matt

~.~.~.~.~.~.~

From: **Karen Smith**
Subject: **#8 – Great Sand Dunes National Park**
Date: **July 28, 2010**

Dear Bob and Sue,

Walking from the parking lot onto the sand at Great Sand Dunes National Park was like stepping onto a beach, minus the ocean. There were people in swimming suits lounging in beach chairs, toddlers running around in diapers, and kids building sand castles and throwing Frisbees. It didn't seem like we were in south central Colorado.

In the spring, Medano Creek runs between the parking area and the eastern edge of the dunes. In May, there can be surge flows. Sand creates small dams upstream in the creek, and when the water breaks through, waves up to 12" high flow downstream. In wet years, with high runoff, people float, surf, and skimboard down the waves. We heard that the creek area is crowded during these weekends, causing lines of traffic and overflowing parking lots. The creek bed was dry today, but the beachgoers didn't seem to mind.

The Great Sand Dunes are the tallest dunes in North America. Rising in front of the Sangre de Cristo Mountains, they're a dramatic sight. We stopped at the visitor center first, and then set off to hike to the top of one of the dunes, about a 700-foot rise, *in the middle of the afternoon.* This was a serious lapse of common sense. In the summer, you should avoid the dunes during the afternoon. The ranger at the visitor center told us this, but we ignored her advice. The air temperature is brutally hot, and, of course, the sand gets even hotter. The surface temperature on the dunes can reach 140 degrees. We were also starting at a high elevation, 8,200 feet, which meant we were breathing heavily just walking through the parking lot.

Minutes into the hike, the wind started blowing sand into our eyes and faces; it stung our bare arms and legs. It was all very painful. We had to close our eyes to keep the sand from blinding us. The sand stuck to our sweat, which for me was pretty much everywhere. Walking was slow and difficult. With every step, our feet would sink and our shoes filled with sand. We tied our shoelaces as tight as possible, but the sand found a way in regardless. Eventually, there was no room in our shoes for our feet and toes to move. Every few minutes, we had to take off our shoes, balance on one foot – because it was too hot to place the other foot on the sand – and dump out the sand. There was no way to keep the sand out.

Occasionally, I would pry open my eyes to see where I was going. I could barely make out the shape of Matt's body ahead in the sandstorm. I did my best to keep up with him, but I was miserable. The only thing that kept me going was envisioning how much younger my face was going to look with the top layer of skin sandblasted off.

The sand dunes kicked our asses. We didn't make it to the top. On our way back to the car, we saw people having way more fun than we were. They were sand boarding and sledding on the dunes, dragging everything from snowboards to cookie sheets with them. Some were also dragging their dogs. They must not have seen the signs warning that dogs shouldn't be on the dunes after 11am in the summer because their paws will burn on the hot sand. Dogs can't tell their owners when their paws are on fire.

We learned a few hard lessons today. Our negative experience wasn't because it's a bad park; it was due to our poor planning. Matt says I'm his "research assistant." He should fire me. I wish we would have allowed ourselves another day to spend in this park. The mountains and forests surrounding the dunes are beautiful, and there are some great hikes we missed. And of course, we should have hiked the dunes in the early morning or evening.

Tomorrow morning we're heading to Lawrence, Kansas to be with Matthew on his birthday. Along the way, we're planning to visit a couple of national park *units*: Bent's Old Fort National Historic Site and Fort Larned National Historic Site. Then, if we have time during our stay in the Kansas City area, we'll go to Independence, Missouri to visit the Harry S. Truman National Historic Site. Even though these sites aren't named *national parks,* we still enjoy visiting them when we can, so long as they have a stamp for our passports.

Your friend,
Karen

~.~.~.~.~.~.~

From: **Matt Smith**
Subject: **Travel day – to Holbrook, Arizona**
Date: **August 10, 2010**

Dear Bob and Sue,

Bob, you will appreciate this (because you're cheap like me). At 5:54am this morning, we took the No. 218 bus from the Issaquah Park and Ride to the International District in Seattle, where we caught the light rail to SeaTac airport. The total cost for the two of us was $6.50. That's one-tenth the cost of a taxi and way cheaper than parking at the airport.

We flew to Las Vegas where we picked up a rental car for the week. Our plan is to drive to Petrified Forest National Park, then to Grand Canyon National Park and then back to Las Vegas to celebrate Karen's 50th birthday this weekend.

On our way east to Holbrook, Arizona, we stopped in Flagstaff. Downtown Flag (Flag is what the locals call Flagstaff) has several decent outdoor gear stores. I found a backpack that I'd been looking for, and as I took it to the cashier, Karen reminded me that she had officially banned me from buying any more backpacks. (I just bought one last month, and have a couple of others.) I explained to her, "I can't have just one backpack. They're all different sizes and made for different activities." She said, "You mean like purses? Why didn't you say that in the first place? Now I get it. A backpack is your man-purse."

I started to tell her that she didn't know what she was talking about, *and* that she doesn't have authority to ban me from doing anything, but she was already gone. She was looking through the backpacks to see if there was one that matched my hiking boots.

Earlier, when we were exploring the town, we'd stopped in the Lumberyard Brewery for a beer. Since we didn't know what restaurants we'd find in Holbrook, we headed back to the brewery and ate an early dinner. Flagstaff has everything we like in a city: it's a college town, high in elevation, with good breweries and endless outdoor recreation opportunities. We could live here.

When we finished dinner, we drove to Holbrook and checked into the Travelodge. It's an older motel that looked sketchy on the outside, but the room was nice and clean (and inexpensive). The person who checked us in was extremely helpful; he gave me a map of the area and showed me the quickest way to get to Petrified Forest National Park. If we're ever in Holbrook again, we would stay here. Karen went to bed at 8:30pm, (7:30pm pacific time). That's a new record.

Your friend,
Matt

~.~.~.~.~.~.~

From: **Matt Smith**
Subject: **#9 – Petrified Forest National Park**
Date: **August 11, 2010**

Dear Bob and Sue,

When we got to the Petrified Forest National Park Visitor Center, I noticed that their passport stamp was misshapen and hard to read. I was hoping all the park stamps would be the same size, style, and quality so they would look orderly when I frame them together after our parks trip is complete. That's just OC, right, no D? This didn't seem to bother Karen. I said to her, "You didn't even notice that the stamp looked different from the others. That's the opposite of OC. There should be a name for *that.*" She said, "There is. It's called *normal.*"

I don't think so.

From the visitor center, we hiked about a half-mile to the Painted Desert Inn. It was an interesting hike because of the amazing views of the surrounding Painted Desert. The colors were incredible. The inn is no longer structurally stable enough to allow overnight guests. Now, it's a national historic landmark, and functions only as a museum and bookstore. You can look in the windows of the original guest rooms; they are small and primitive.

There's a fantastic petroglyph of a mountain lion displayed inside the inn. The ranger in the gift store said that during construction of the inn, workers building the road flipped over the rock and found the petroglyph on the back. It makes me wonder how many great petroglyphs are out in the desert that will never be found.

Ten miles to the south of the inn is Blue Mesa. It gets its name from the bluish bentonite clay on the mesa. We hiked the one-mile Blue Mesa Loop; there we saw lots of petrified wood, but mostly in small pieces. Karen thinks the park should be renamed Petrified Pieces National Park because there is no forest; all the petrified wood is laying on the ground in pieces. I'm not bothered by this fact. Now who has the OC?

The Puerco Pueblo ruins, just north of Blue Mesa, are the remains of a 100-room pueblo (occupied between 1,200 and 700 years ago). Close to the ruins, we saw several petroglyphs near the paved trail. My favorite was one of a large bird with a baby in its beak. Not a baby bird, a baby human. No one knows why the bird has a baby in its beak. Karen is sure the bird was bringing a baby to a family, rather than carrying a baby away. I'm not so sure.

We drove to the Rainbow Forest Museum in the southwest corner of the park. Behind the museum, we walked through an area with giant logs of petrified wood. The name of the trail is, surprisingly, the Giant Logs Trail. It takes visitors through one of the best-preserved areas of petrified wood in the park. The size and number of logs was amazing. Karen was more impressed with these specimens but still wouldn't call it a forest. This area once had many more times the number of large, petrified logs than it has today. Before the area became a national park, prospectors hauled away train carloads of petrified wood. Much of it was ground up for use as industrial abrasive. That's a real shame; I wish I could have seen this area before that happened.

We wrapped up our visit early; we had a long drive to get to the Grand Canyon where we're spending the night.

Your friend,
Matt

~.~.~.~.~.~.~

From: **Matt Smith**
Subject: **#10 – Grand Canyon National Park**
Date: **August 12, 2010**

Dear Bob and Sue,

Yesterday on the way to the Grand Canyon, we stopped at the Cameron Trading Post because we'd heard it had a huge selection of Navajo rugs. It's on the Navajo Indian Reservation and has been an active trading post for nearly one hundred years. The parking lot was full of tour buses, motorcycles and cars with out-of-state license plates. Their rugs were fantastic but out of our price range, so we left empty handed.

Along the road from the trading post to the park's east entrance there were roadside stands selling Navajo art and crafts. We stopped at a couple but didn't buy anything. It was so windy that the pottery on the tables wobbled constantly. I kept imagining having to buy an entire table of vases because we were standing there when a strong gust came by.

Our first stop inside the park was the Desert View lookout. The sun was setting, and the light was perfect. It was the golden hour. The views were amazing. It's the Grand Canyon; what can I say? Any description would be inadequate, so I'm not even going to try. It's a must-see wonder.

We drove along the canyon rim, stopping at a few more overlooks. The Grand Canyon is overcrowded this time of year. We'd like to come back when there aren't so many visitors and when it's cooler. The rims of the canyon actually get a fair amount of snow in the winter. I imagine on a sunny day the colorful rock walls of the canyon dusted with snow are a magnificent sight.

Our last stop yesterday was the Grand Canyon Village where we ate dinner in the El Tovar Hotel bar. The El Tovar Hotel is a prime example of a style of architecture called National Park Service Rustic. It opened in 1905 and sits at the edge of the south rim of the canyon. It's a classic lodge complete with dark log siding and animal heads in the great room. We tried to get a reservation to stay overnight in the hotel, but it sold out months ago, and we were too late in making our plans. Instead, we're staying at the Best Western just outside the southern entrance to the park.

Before we finish our parks trip, we're planning to come back and hike rim to rim. This morning, however, we just wanted to do a half-day hike. We got to parking lot E in the Village at 7:45am and were hiking down Bright Angel Trail before 8:00am. There wasn't a cloud in the sky.

You want to get on the Bright Angel Trail early. A park concessionaire uses this trail to take people down the canyon on mules. They don't slow you down so much as they leave presents along the trail. Early in the day there's less mule shit to step around.

The hike to the canyon floor on Bright Angel Trail is about seven miles. Today, we were hoping to hike four miles down, but when we got to the three-mile rest stop at 9am, it was getting so hot we decided it was a good time to turn around. Since the hardest part of the hike is going uphill, we wanted to make sure we'd have enough energy to make it back. From our rest stop, we had 2,000 vertical feet to climb to get back to the top of the canyon. We rested for 20 minutes, and then started our return.

There's an abrupt attitude change when you switch

directions on a steep hike. On the downhill, everything is right with the world. Steps are effortless, and views are spectacular; you greet every passing hiker with a smile and, "Good morning!" Karen might even convince me to hold her hand and laugh now and then. But the way up is a trudge. Every other breath is a gasp. Your aching legs feel thick and heavy, and all you want to say to passing hikers is, "No, it's not a good morning. Stop smiling, and get out of my way before I pass out."

Hiking up the canyon, there's no bailing out; you have to make it to the top to get out. Time slows, and you lose perspective on how much farther you have to go. But, on long hikes, we've found a reliable method of determining how close we are to the parking lot by looking at passing hikers. The first sign that we were getting close to the top was when we passed a husband and wife with two small children. The kids looked to be about four and six years old. The four-year old was making himself dizzy by twirling in circles with his arms straight out, the father trying to keep him from spinning off the side of the canyon, while the mother consoled the six-year old who was sitting hunched over, arms crossed and with tears running down his cheeks. That's as good of a one-mile marker as there is on a trail like this.

A short distance past the happy family, we stopped to take a drink. We were both sweating heavily and glad we'd brought plenty of water. I looked at Karen and said, "Nice red underwear." There was no response, just a confused look on her face. "Your white shorts are completely see-through." Karen sweated so much that her hiking shorts were transparent. That may explain why no one passed us on the way up the trail.

I dug an extra t-shirt out of my backpack, Karen tied it around her waist, and we continued our death march to the top. Finally, I looked up to see a woman coming toward us wearing shiny gold flip-flops, designer jeans that were tight enough to be body paint and a black t-shirt with the words "Wine Tester" spelled out in bright red sequins. That was a sure sign we were less than a quarter of a mile from the car.

We reached the top of the canyon well before noon. As soon as we were off the trail and on flat ground, we regretted not having gone farther down the trail. We had plenty of energy left. The park service warns people not to attempt hiking down to the bottom of the canyon and back up in the same day, but everyone needs to know their own fitness level and adjust that advice accordingly. Families with small children and wine testers certainly aren't going to make it, but a down-and-back hike in one day is doable for people in good shape. Still, I wouldn't try it in August (especially hiking with someone who's about to turn 50). Tomorrow we're driving to Las Vegas to celebrate Karen's birthday, and then next week we're off to Alaska.

Your friend,
Matt

~.~.~.~.~.~.~

From: **Matt Smith**
Subject: **#11 – Glacier Bay National Park**
Date: **August 18, 2010**

Dear Bob and Sue,

Alaska is big. Things here are on a different scale than in the lower 48 states; Glacier Bay National Park is about the size of Connecticut, yet there are four national parks in Alaska that are even bigger.

It was easier than we thought it would be to get here. The flight from Seattle to Juneau was two and a half hours, and from Juneau to Gustavus the flight was 14 minutes. Four minutes into our flight to Gustavus, the pilot asked the flight attendants to prepare for landing; I was timing it. By late afternoon, we were sitting on the deck of Glacier Bay Lodge, having a beer and looking out over Bartlett Cove. I asked our waitress if Bartlett Cove was named after President Bartlett. Karen interrupted by saying, "Ignore him." Well, she can ignore me, but I got us to Alaska. Seeing Alaska has been at the top of Karen's wish list ever since we moved to Seattle, and now we're here.

The town of Gustavus has 346 permanent residents and an airport large enough to land a 737. The federal government subsidizes the airport as part of its Essential Air Service program. There's no other way a town this remote could support such a large airport.

At the airport, we boarded a Glacier Bay Lodge school bus along with the other guests. Our driver gave us the nickel tour from the airport to the lodge. He stopped briefly in town, which the locals call the "intersection" where there's a gas station, pizza place and art gallery. A couple of miles past the intersection we came to the Glacier Bay National Park boundary and the park sign. This is one of the few sections of the road from the airport to the lodge that's not heavily treed. It's called the moose flats because moose often stop there to feed. (Actually, there are moose feeding all over this area. However, at the flats they're easier to see because there are fewer trees hiding them.)

"There are always moose here," the driver said. "When I drove past here ten minutes ago, there was a moose standing right by the park sign." Fifteen faces pressed against the windows; the bus tilted to the sign side of the road. Everyone who comes to Alaska wants to see a moose. There was no moose.

We ate dinner at the lodge, and afterwards walked down the pier to the docks along the water. It had been a cloudy day, but while we were walking along the docks, the sun came out. It was refreshing to feel the sun on our faces. There's a park sign at the end of the pier that welcomes visitors who arrive by boat. We asked a passerby to take our picture in front of it. The sun was in perfect position.

We're excited to be in Alaska, finally. Tomorrow we're

taking an all-day boat tour of Glacier Bay.

Your friend,
Matt

~.~.~.~.~.~.~

From: **Matt Smith**
Subject: **Glacier Bay day two**
Date: **August 19, 2010**

Dear Bob and Sue,

Standing in line this morning to board our boat it was raining and in the mid 50's; August here feels like October in Seattle. I had to maneuver my way around a pregnant woman pushing a stroller to get one of the last tables by the windows. As soon as we settled in one of the crew gave us plastic, souvenir coffee cups with no-spill lids. I nervously left Karen in charge of our table while I went to fill up our new cups with coffee. I was worried she would invite another couple to share our table while I was gone. When I got back I was relieved to find that we still had the table to ourselves.

Ten minutes into our tour the captain spotted a sea otter. He slowed down while the passengers crowded to the otter side of the boat. There was chatter in many different languages, and everyone took pictures or videos. This was our first wildlife sighting of the day. As the boat pulled away, I wondered if we would see more otters. Was that the lone otter or would there be others? In the next 30 minutes we saw hundreds of otters. If anyone had fallen overboard they could have walked across otter stomachs all the way to shore without getting wet.

Otterfest was only the beginning of our wildlife sightings. Our next stop was just off South Marble Island where sea lions rested on rocks trying to dry out. The biggest ones got the highest spots where they could dry out the quickest. There was a clear pecking order, and everyone knew his place. The slightest nudge from a smaller sea lion below brought a loud growl and showing of teeth from the one above. The youngest ones were in the water, each looking for a place to climb ashore without getting a chunk taken out of his hide.

At a tidal inlet just past Tlingit Point, we spotted two pair of grizzly bears on the beach. I always thought grizzlies weren't afraid of anything, but after watching these bears, it's clear they're afraid of one another. One pair was fishing in a stream close to the shore, until the second pair ran them off.

Our national park ranger guide, Jane, corrected me by saying these are brown bears. *Grizzlies* are a type of brown bear found inland and in the mountains. It's confusing because another species of bear, a black bear, can be brown, which doesn't make it a brown bear, it's just a black bear that's brown. Karen likes cinnamon bears, because she likes the sound of the name. Cinnamon bears are usually black bears, but brown bears can also be cinnamon – in color. The way to tell them apart is that grizzlies have a distinct shoulder hump and smaller ears than black bears.

The wildlife sightings continued. We spotted humpback whales off Willoughby Island. On Gloomy Knob, we saw mountain goats high on the cliffs through our binoculars. Across the bay, on Gilbert Peninsula, a whale carcass had washed onto the beach. Jane explained that animals had been taking turns feeding off the carcass for several months. There were no animals feeding on the carcass when we went by. I'm guessing an animal needs to get pretty hungry before it starts in on a whale carcass that's been lying there for three months.

We saw many bald eagles, and countless other birds. Jane explained in detail the fascinating nesting and feeding habits of the birds we saw. I don't remember any of their names. We were standing close to Jane when she said, "Now, if you are keeping a life list of birds, be sure to write down the 'such and such' bird that we just saw." A life list of birds?

Who keeps a life list of birds? I turned to Karen, and in a panicked voice said, "Karen, do you have my life list of birds? I can't find it. You had it last, remember?" Karen caught Jane's eye, tilted her head toward me and said, "Ignore him. He's an idiot."

A massive cruise ship was making its way out of Johns Hopkins Inlet as we headed toward the entrance. Johns Hopkins Glacier dumps into the bay at the end of this inlet. Two hundred years ago, Glacier Bay didn't exist. A glacier extended all the way to where the town of Gustavus is today. Since then, the glacier has receded more than 60 miles. Johns Hopkins Glacier is a remnant of the original glacier that once covered the area that is now the bay.

At the head of the inlet, the captain eased the boat to within a half-mile of the glacier. The passengers again crowded to one side of the boat. The captain slowly spun the boat 360 degrees, so everyone got a turn at being in front. He obviously had done this before.

Up to this point in the tour, there was a constant din of conversation from the passengers, but as we stood together looking at the glacier, everyone was silent. Every couple of minutes, thunder would roll across the water and over our boat. House size chunks of ice were breaking off the glacier and falling into the bay. The water around us was turquoise. Through my binoculars, I could see a torrent pouring out from beneath the 170-foot tall wall of ice. Even on cool summer days, a tremendous amount of ice melts.

A raft of brown ice chunks was floating in front of the glacier. The ice looked dirty. Jane explained over the public address system why we had to keep our distance from the glacier; those spots on the ice weren't dirt, they were *seals*. They use this area as a breeding ground, and boats the size of ours must stay at least a quarter of a mile away.

I fell asleep on the boat ride back from the glacier. I had just eaten lunch, it was raining, and the sound of the boat's engines made me sleepy. The last words I remember hearing before falling asleep were Jane's over the public address speaker saying, "If you fall asleep now it will be the most expensive nap you'll ever take." The tour cost $185 per person. I had a good nap, but dreamt I lost my life list of birds.

Your friend,
Matt

~.~.~.~.~.~.~

From: **Karen Smith**
Subject: **Glacier Bay day three**
Date: **August 20, 2010**

Dear Bob and Sue,

In the park, there are bear warnings everywhere. Matt and I were nervous about hiking by ourselves, so we did something we never do. We signed up for the daily ranger-led group-hike. Matt worries he will get stuck with slow walkers or loud talkers, but luckily today we were the only ones who showed up. We had a private tour of the Bartlett River Trail with ranger Kevin Richards. The park service closed the trail a few days ago because a brown bear charged a hiker along the river. Kevin had bear spray with him, but I wondered if park rangers pledge an oath promising to defend and protect park visitors, or if a bear charges us, it's every man for himself. Matt always tells people that he doesn't have to run faster than the bear, just faster than me. In case of a bear encounter, ranger Kevin might be my only hope.

The Bartlett River Trail meanders several miles along an intertidal lagoon. Then, it cuts through the forest before ending at the Bartlett River estuary. We didn't see any bears, but maybe that's because the bears saw us first, or heard us. Kevin kept a steady conversation going all through the hike. We spent three hours with Kevin: the first two hiking the river trail and the last hour in the lodge talking about our parks trip.

From the stories he told us, it sounded like he's been to most of the 58 national parks. He wrote out hiking suggestions for many of the parks in California and Utah. Kevin's enthusiasm and passion for the parks made us even more excited to visit them all.

After lunch, we rented well-used bikes at the lodge and rode eight miles into Gustavus to sightsee and buy beer. We figured if we bought a six-pack of beer at the market, it would be cheaper than paying $5 for a beer at the lodge bar. The ride was flat and easy, except for a small incline near the lodge. A worker at the lodge told us that moose have chased bikers along the park road. I was a little nervous about whether I could out pedal a moose if we ran into one. Visitors to Alaska are always worried about bear encounters, but moose injure more people each year than bears. They tell you to watch for signs that the moose is upset. If its ears are laid back and hackles are up, it's likely to charge. Neither Matt nor I know what a hackle is; we just hope that if a moose raises his we'll be able to spot it.

When we got to the market – the only one in town – we searched up and down the aisles for beer. I could see Matt walk slowly at first and then speed up as reality set in. He circled the store twice, but there was no beer. I finally asked the 16-year old stocking the shelves if the store sold beer. He loudly told us the only place that sells beer is the town liquor store, open from 4–7pm each day. It was 2:30pm. Everyone in the store was looking at us. It felt awkward to leave without buying anything, so $12 later we had a bag of blue corn chips, a cherry ChapStick, a rubber bouncy ball, a moose shaped Christmas ornament, a Snickers for Matt, and a purple Pixie Stix for me.

Since we had 90 minutes to kill, we sat on the porch swing in front of the market, eating our candy and swinging back and forth like a couple of 80-year olds. There was a scale next to the swing for weighing nails. Matt weighed all the things we had bought, and then everything in his pockets. It started to rain. I felt like we were in an episode of Northern

Exposure.

We entertained ourselves by watching the locals come and go. An elderly native woman walked past us and into the store. She then came back out empty-handed and sat on the porch with us. When Matt went over to our bikes to tighten my wobbly handlebars she sidled up to me. She whispered, "Guess what? I saw a white moose while walking to the store today. I've never seen a white moose before. I came to buy a Pepsi, but I don't have enough money."

I gave her the three dollars I had in my pocket, mostly because it was the right thing to do, but partly because I don't ever want to be on the bad side of a native woman who's seen a white moose, be it real or imagined. I figured I was buying myself curse insurance for the price of a Pepsi.

As the rain let up, we rode our bikes down to the water's edge by the public docks and walked along the beach. Gulls were circling and landing by something thrashing in the water. We pulled out our binoculars and could see it was a sea lion wrestling a halibut. The halibut was *huge,* but the size and strength of the sea lion was even more impressive. The sea lion was clearly winning. Sea lions may look lazy and awkward when they're sunning themselves on the rocks, but in the water, chomping on a halibut with his mouth open and teeth flashing, this one looked fierce.

At 4:01pm we peddled to the liquor store. We bought a six-pack, paying double what we would at home, and stuffed the bottles into our backpacks. Riding back to Glacier Bay Lodge, we again carefully looked for moose by the moose flats. We didn't see any there, but a mile farther down the road, a moose suddenly stepped out from the woods. Not a white moose, but still he was spectacular: huge, dark, and shiny. We stopped about 50 yards away and looked at him. The moose looked back. He seemed very sweet and gentle, but there was no way we were going to try to ride past him. After a few minutes, cars came down the road, and the moose disappeared back into the woods.

After dinner, we walked the forest loop by the lodge. At

the end of the loop, when the sun was almost down, we saw a moose and her baby eating by the side of the road. The mother moose was wearing a bright orange tracking collar with "Number 2" written on it. Even though there were people watching them and taking pictures, both mother and baby seemed calm. Their ears weren't back, and there was no sign of hackles.

Hiking, biking, beer, and moose – what a great day. Oh yeah, and about that beer: the beer that we rode 16 miles to get so we could save some money? Between the bike rentals and the cost of the six-pack, each beer ended up costing about $8.

Your friend,
Karen

~.~.~.~.~.~.~.~

From: **Matt Smith**
Subject: **Out of Gustavus**
Date: **August 21, 2010**

Dear Bob & Sue,

We had all day to kill in Gustavus, as our plane to Anchorage didn't leave until late afternoon. Karen and I rented bikes again and rode to the only restaurant in town. We sat outside and ordered a large pizza. Once the pizza came, the owner's dog, Shorty, was our friend. Shorty never begged, but I fed him some sausage pizza anyway. Just about the best thing that can happen to a dog is for a stranger to give it sausage pizza. I felt proud of myself for making Shorty's day, until the woman at the next table coaxed him over and started petting him. When the waitress came around, the woman asked if it would be okay to give him a scrap of pizza crust. The waitress said, "Oh no, he's not supposed to have pizza. He'll get sick."

"Check please!"

Our flight out of Gustavus was an hour and a half late departing. It was the last Alaska Airlines flight out of Gustavus for the season. Every "guys week in Alaska" fishing group booked the same flight. Each group had boxes of frozen fish they were taking with them on the flight. The TSA crew struggled with processing the mass of cargo and passengers.

The pilots and flight attendants used the extra time to take pictures of themselves in and around the plane. All the passengers watched from the boarding area. We could see them through the wall of glass separating us from the tarmac. Each time they posed, we cheered mockingly. The crowd was getting restless; the flight was already an hour past its scheduled departure time. One flight attendant would pose sitting in the cockpit, with her head stuck out the open window, then with much wriggling about another flight attendant would appear a few minutes later, waving to the camera.

Down on the tarmac, they took turns having their picture taken while sitting inside the cowl of the plane's engine. Three of the crew sat inside the engine while another crewmember took their picture. I'm not sure the 737 was designed to hold the weight of three people sitting *in* the engine.

When it was finally time to take off, I no longer worried about the engines. I was just glad to be going.

Your friend,
Matt

~.~.~.~.~.~.~.~

From: **Matt Smith**
Subject: **Travel day – to Copper Center, Alaska**
Date: **August 22, 2010**

Dear Bob & Sue,

This morning Karen and I almost hit a moose while driving to a grocery store. It scared the bejesus out of me. We turned a corner, and he was right there, standing by the side of the road eating leaves that were sticking through a chain-link fence. I drove slowly past trying not to spook him into running in front of our car. He (or she) is one of a few hundred moose who roam Anchorage in the summer. That number increases to one thousand or more in the winter. A couple of hundred city moose die each year: cars hit them, they starve, or they die of illness. The State of Alaska says that a live moose belongs to the state, and a dead moose belongs to whoever owns the property it's on. In Anchorage, if a moose dies on your property it's your problem, and since they can weigh more than a thousand pounds, it's a pretty big problem. It can cost close to $300 to have a moose retrieval company drag a moose carcass off your lawn. That's if you know it's there. Sometimes people don't realize they have this problem until the spring thaw reveals the gift nature has left them.

Being Sunday, there wasn't much traffic on our three-hour drive from Anchorage to Copper Center, a small town just outside Wrangell-St. Elias National Park. Copper Center has a population of about 450, including the nearby native village of Kluti Kaah. We're staying in Copper Center because it has a new lodge, and it's close to the park and the new Wrangell-St. Elias Visitor Center. (FYI, Wrangell-St. Elias National Park is nowhere near Wrangell, Alaska.)

The Copper River, which flows past Copper Center, is famous in the lower 48 states for its salmon. One of the most rugged rivers in Alaska, it begins at Copper Glacier deep inside the park on the northern edge of the Wrangell

Mountains. The river defines the western border of the park as it flows south toward the Gulf of Alaska. Every May, around the 15th, the first salmon of the season return to the river: Copper River Kings and Sockeyes. In some years, commercial fishermen catch more than a million Copper River salmon. (The commercial fishing happens south of the park boundaries near the mouth of the river.)

By the time we reached Glenallen, a small town just north of Copper Center, it was noon – lunchtime and beer time. We tried to stock up on beer in Anchorage this morning, but in Alaska, it's illegal to sell beer before noon on Sunday. We headed straight for the grocery store, but after searching in vain for beer, we were told by the store clerk that the town was dry. Yikes! My research assistant should have learned this before we got to the Edge of Nowhere, Alaska. We contemplated eating pizza at the restaurant across the street, or Thai food from the trailer at the end of the block, but decided on driving to our hotel, the Princess Lodge, in hopes they were serving lunch, and that Copper Center was not dry like Glenallen.

Princess Lodge is owned by Princess Cruise Line. They bus their cruise passengers to the hotel and set them up with activities like river rafting, fishing, and flightseeing.

We checked in and took our luggage to our room. It smelled like bad perfume. I thought about asking for another room, but there were two busloads of new guests arriving, and I was too hungry to stand in a long line. Karen gets concerned when I mention that our hotel room smells. She knows what usually follows: she has to get off the bed, put her shoes back on, gather her things that are thrown around the room, drag them all the way back to the front desk, stand there embarrassed while I tell the manager our room smells, drag her stuff to another room, and wait while I decide if the new room smells. I spared Karen this time. I opened a window and we went looking for food.

After we ate lunch at the lodge and took care of business

at the visitor center, we drove 20 miles north to the historic Gakona Lodge to check it out. Karen read an article about the lodge, and was interested in seeing it. (Her real interest was their Trading Post, even though she had nothing to trade.) Built in 1904, it's one of the few remaining roadhouses left in Alaska. The original roadhouse had living quarters, a kitchen/dining room, a few private rooms, an upstairs dormitory and a store. In the early 20th century, there were roadhouses located every 20 miles or so, the distance a person could reasonably travel in a day without a car. Only a couple of the original roadhouses in Alaska are still around today; most of the others have burned down.

Inside the lodge's Trappers Den Tavern, we met Greg and Val, the owners. He was bartending and she was cooking dinner. Everyone in the bar was friendly. We heard some interesting viewpoints from the locals about living in Alaska. A guy at the bar told us that residents resented the federal government setting the rules about what can and can't be done within the park boundaries. His point was that locals were using the land long before it was made a national park and they should be allowed to continue to use it as before. I told him that I had a different perspective; I felt the national park land belongs to us all, and the park service is stewarding it for us and for future generations. He said he met the park superintendent recently on a float trip, and she echoed my opinion. Despite his complaints, I could tell he was appreciative of the work the park service does to preserve the land and create access for people like himself who love to spend time there.

He told me how he enjoyed fishing on the Copper River. He went on to describe how he feels when he's in the park, going to Copper Lake in the winter, and how pristine the area is, especially covered in snow. As he started to tell me what it's like to see Copper Glacier, and to know it's the birth of a river, his voice trailed off. He couldn't continue. Here was a man, hardened by 30 years of living in Alaska, choking up about his experience in the wilderness. He said he and his buddies were going back to Copper Lake in March, and invited me to go with them.

We drove back to the Princess Lodge and ate dinner. Afterward, Karen and I sat by the two-story window in the great room, watching Mt. Drum slowly change colors as the sun went down. It was a great place to sit quietly and enjoy the sunset. Two women plopped down next to us, neither of them looking at the incredible scene out the window. They talked loudly about the weather in St. Louis, who was hosting bridge tonight back home, and how the Cardinals were doing this year. I've never understood why people spend so much time, energy, and money to travel to a distant place, and then wish they were home.

When our loud neighbors pulled out pictures of their grandchildren and starting talking baby talk, I stood up, turned to Karen and said, "That's it." We were tired anyway and needed to get a good night's sleep, so we walked back to our room and called it a day. Tomorrow we're driving into the park, just the two of us.

Your friend,
Matt

~.~.~.~.~.~.~

From: **Karen Smith**
Subject: **#12 – Wrangell-St. Elias National Park**
Date: **August 23, 2010**

Dear Bob & Sue,

On our way out of the hotel this morning, we were surprised to see that all the other guests had set their luggage in the hallway right outside their door. Apparently, a cruise company employee picks up the luggage from the guest's door, and transports it to the next hotel room (or cruise cabin) where they will be staying that night. Having someone else cart your luggage all over Alaska clearly gives you permission to bring multiple big-ass suitcases and over pack them. I'm a little bit jealous. For as long as I've known Matt, he's had a strict "You pack it, you carry it" rule. No exceptions. If I ever left my luggage outside our door expecting him to transport it to our next destination, I'd be going commando for the rest of the trip.

Today we visited Wrangell-St. Elias National Park and Preserve. It's the big kahuna of the national parks with more than 13 million acres. It's the size of six Yellowstones.

Four major mountain ranges meet in the park, including nine of the 16 highest peaks in the United States. The east boundary of the park runs along the Canadian border; on the other side is Canada's Kluane National Park. Just one of Wrangell-St. Elias' glaciers, the Malaspina Glacier, is larger than the state of Rhode Island and 2,000 feet thick in places. Because of the park's sheer size, vast mountain ranges, and limited road access, it's impossible to see the entire park and grasp its enormity unless you fly over it. Unfortunately, we're only driving into the park on this trip.

There are only two roads into Wrangell-St. Elias, and both of these dusty dead-end roads are unpaved and occasionally impassable. Before starting out on either of them, it's advised to have a high clearance vehicle, a full tank of gas, a tire jack and full-size spare tire, flares, automobile insurance, a jumbo-size bag of animal crackers, and enough water to last for a couple of days. Nabesna Road, on the north side of the park, is a 42-mile stretch of road originally built by the Alaska Road Commission in 1933 to connect the Nabesna Mine to the port in Valdez. There are no services or communities along the road. Mainly it's just an access into the park for people who want to camp, hike, fish, and hunt.

Hunting is not allowed in most national parks, but there are exceptions in some of the Alaska parks, including Wrangell-St. Elias. When the park was created in 1980 by the passage of the Alaska National Interest Lands Conservation

Act (ANILCA), compromises were made. Local residents are allowed to subsistence hunt and gather food to feed their families inside the national park. The national *preserve* section of Wrangell-St. Elias allows anyone with a gun and an Alaska state hunting license to sport hunt. The definition of a national preserve is, ironically, areas in which Congress has permitted continued public hunting, trapping, oil/gas exploration, and extraction. Until this Alaska trip, Matt and I thought national preserves *protected* the land, its resources, and the animals that lived there. I guess the word *preserve* threw us off.

Today we took the other road into the park, the infamous McCarthy Road, which starts on the east side of the park at the town of Chitina and runs for 60 miles to the towns of Kennecott and McCarthy. Kennecott is a former mining town restored and maintained by the park service. When copper was discovered in the area in 1900, the Kennecott Mining Company built the mines and the company town of Kennecott. Because alcohol and prostitution were forbidden in Kennecott, people in the nearby town of McCarthy sensed a lucrative business opportunity and built a bar and a brothel. Business was brisk, and McCarthy quickly grew. The Copper River and Northwestern Railway reached McCarthy in 1911. By 1938, however, the copper deposits in Kennecott Mountain were exhausted, people abandoned the towns, and the railroad discontinued service that year. McCarthy and Kennecott became ghost towns nearly overnight, and the population fell to almost zero until the area became a national park.

The park service website calls the road to McCarthy "An Alaskan Adventure!" People who have driven it say it's the worst road in America. It usually takes three hours to drive the length of the road one way. Other hazards can make it longer: heavy rain, giant potholes, washboard ruts, and large, sharp rocks. The road follows the abandoned railroad track, and you can see evidence of that when you cross the bridge at Mile 17. It was originally built in 1910 as a railroad bridge and is still used today to get cars and trucks across the raging Kuskulana River, 238 feet below.

Five miles into the drive, Matt determined that we were averaging about ten miles per hour, so at that rate it would take six hours to get to McCarthy. Eventually, the road smoothed out, and we were able to make it up to 35 miles an hour. It felt like we were flying. We didn't see any wildlife from the road, but there were great views of the surrounding mountains. When we got to the rickety narrow bridge over the Lakina River, there was a state road worker on each side, stopping every car. They told us that the bridge would close at 5pm, and whatever side of the bridge we were on at that time was the side we would be on until the bridge reopened at 9:00am the next morning. Thank you, good to know.

McCarthy Road ends at a parking lot where you have to leave your car, walk the final quarter of a mile, and cross a footbridge over the Kennicott River to get to McCarthy. On the other side of the footbridge, you can walk to McCarthy or take a shuttle to Kennecott, five miles away. When we got out of the car, we saw a shuttle van sitting on the other side of the footbridge and assumed it was the shuttle to Kennecott, which runs every half hour. I could see Matt's head swiveling back and forth, judging the distance to the shuttle against the baggage he had with him – me. He said, "We can make it!" Then he sprinted, shouting, "Run, Karen, run!" We ran like maniacs, waving and yelling, "Wait, wait!" to the shuttle driver. We got there just in time, panting and sweating, and piled in with the other passengers. The van pulled away, two minutes later it stopped in McCarthy, and everyone got off. Matt and I looked at each other and laughed. We ran like crazy people to catch a half-mile ride when we could have easily walked. Ten minutes later we boarded a different shuttle that took us to Kennecott.

Kennecott was buzzing with construction activity. Listed on the National Register of Historic Places in 1978, and designated as a National Historic Landmark in 1986, Kennecott is considered the best remaining example of early 20th Century copper mining. Many of the buildings in Kennecott were abandoned for 70 years. The National Park

Service had to identify which buildings to stabilize or rehabilitate, and which ones could not be saved. Their goal was to protect the town's historic integrity, while rehabilitating a few buildings for the park service and the public to use. The Recreation Hall, used for educational programs and community events, was completed in 2004. The General Store and Post Office serves as the visitor center. It looks today like the general store must have looked 100 years ago, complete with canned goods on the shelves. Other buildings are currently receiving repairs to roofs, foundations, and walls. The stabilization work, which can only be done during summer months, is expected to take many years.

Inside the Kennecott Visitor Center were rubber molds of animal tracks. There was a wolf, black bear, and brown bear. The mold of the black bear paw was impressive, larger than Matt's hand. I picked up the mold of the brown bear (grizzly) paw. It was monstrous, like what I imagine a dinosaur paw would be. I shuddered to think of coming into contact with an animal that large in the wilderness. When we left the visitor center to begin our hike, I took the package of salmon jerky that I had in my backpack out and threw it away. If bears that large were in Wrangell, I didn't want to hike through the woods smelling like a giant piece of smoked salmon.

As we hiked from Kennecott to Root Glacier, a four-mile round trip, we could hear the land to our left cracking and moaning. We couldn't figure out what the noise was. The sound was coming from what looked like a gravel patch, which was a mile wide and several miles long. We didn't realize it was part of a glacier until later when we saw layers of ice underneath the gravel and grit. The trail took us to the edge of Root Glacier where we stood and gazed at the vast expanse of packed snow and ice. It was tempting to walk out onto the glacier, but we didn't have the right equipment or training. There are many things in Alaska that can kill you; a glacier is one of them.

Crevasses and icefalls can make glaciers deadly. A

crevasse is an open break or cut in the surface of the glacier. You could fall in and never be seen again. Toward the end of the summer, crevasses are at their widest, and they are covered with the least amount of snow. Snow bridges form on top of crevasses and add to the danger because they look solid, but they're just a thin covering over a deep hole. One wrong step and you could break through. An icefall is the steep part of a glacier that often looks like a frozen waterfall. Glaciers are always moving slowly, which causes stress and cracking within them, and blocks of ice can break off and tumble. Sometimes an entire section of the icefall front collapses; you don't want to be standing too close when that happens. At Kennecott, there are wilderness guides who provide visitors with the proper equipment and take them out onto Root Glacier. Since Matt and I were on our own, we were happy to admire it from a distance.

After we got back to the visitor center, we took the shuttle to McCarthy and strolled through the tiny town before returning to our car. The park literature says that McCarthy is the "last remaining remote intact community of individuals inside a national park." This community of about 50 residents includes a couple of hotels, a saloon, gift store, liquor store, and a hardware/grocery store. The buildings were historically restored to look like they did 100 years ago.

It was a long three-hour drive back on the McCarthy Road. I'd been looking forward to eating the other bag of smoked salmon jerky we left in the car, but as I pulled the top of the bag open, it exploded and salmon jerky flew everywhere. Some of the pieces went into the air-conditioning and heating vents. Whoever rents this car in the future will curiously find themselves craving smoked salmon. Coincidentally, about that time we saw a bear on the road. We tried to get a picture, but he was too far away. He disappeared into the forest before we could pull closer.

Once out of the park and headed back toward Copper Center, we stopped for dinner at a local pizza restaurant. The place was empty except for two other people who also sat in the bar. On my way to the bathroom, I walked through the main room of the restaurant, which was once a garage, and almost tripped over a man who looked to be 100 years old, in his pajamas, and asleep in a lawn chair in front of a giant TV. When I came back to the bar I told Matt what I saw, but he didn't believe me. A few minutes later, we heard a loud, "I can't get this remote to work!" Matt turned around to see Mr. Pajama Man, with a dirty Santa Claus beard, standing at the bar waving the remote. The owner muttered something and went off into the garage area with the old guy, returning a minute later still muttering.

We ordered a sausage and jalapeno pizza like we always do. The pizza came out on a rusted, dented and what may have been a panning-for-gold pan. The sausage looked like chopped hotdog, and the jalapeños weren't on top of the pizza, they were cold and in a separate bowl. The owner of the restaurant, Vicky, kept calling them "ha-la-peen-as." She said, "I never know how many ha-la-peen-as people want on their pizza, so I just leave them on the side." After she left Matt said to me quietly, "Wouldn't that be true for *any* pizza topping?" (Matt was so amused with the way she pronounced jalapeños that he kept using the word in conversation as often as he could, and mispronouncing it the way she did.) It was the worst restaurant pizza we'd ever eaten; we've had worse freezer burned pizza at home, but that would be an unfair comparison. Not wanting to hurt Vicky's feelings, I tried to eat my fair share, but I couldn't. I looked around to see if there was a dog we could feed it to under the table. In Alaska, it seems there's always a dog hanging around these local restaurants and taverns. No dog. I glanced hopefully back at the old man in his pajamas. He was asleep again.

Vicky kept walking by our table, making comments like "You're sure not eating very much." Matt and I finally managed to choke down a piece and asked her to wrap up the rest "for later." When we got back to our hotel room, we put the rest of the pizza in our trashcan. Whoever checks into this room tomorrow is going to think the room smells like hotdogs and ha-la-peen-as.

Your friend,
Karen

~.~.~.~.~.~.~

From: **Matt Smith**
Subject: **Driving to Denali**
Date: **August 24, 2010**

Dear Bob & Sue,

Every road sign in Alaska has bullet holes. Even the new ones; the manufacturers must send them from the factory with a starter hole or two. I realized, as I was driving along the highway today, that the Alaska state flag is a blue road sign with bullet holes in the pattern of the Big Dipper.

We had three options for getting to Denali. First, we could backtrack toward Anchorage then turn north on Parks Highway (Parks Highway is named after George Parks, former governor of the Alaska Territory; it's not named Parks Highway because it leads to Denali National Park, which it does.) Our second option was to go north from Copper Center on Highway 4 and then turn west on the Denali Highway (which is named after Denali). This looked to be the most direct route, however, the Denali Highway is 135 miles in length and more than 100 miles of it is unpaved. After driving the 60-mile unpaved McCarthy Road yesterday – twice – I couldn't pull the trigger on that option. Third, we could drive to Fairbanks and then turn south on the Parks Highway, following it to Denali. That's the route we chose.

The scenery on the drive to Fairbanks was beautiful; the highway crosses the Alaska Range of mountains. There is so much wilderness in Alaska that it's easy to imagine there are entire mountain ranges that no one has explored. Very few cars were on the highway, and in the middle of the range, we stopped to take pictures of glaciers that were just a mile or so from the road. Alaska is a beautiful place.

We knew we were getting back to civilization when we came to a nice little town north of the mountains that had three gas stations, two liquor stores, and a road sign with no bullet holes. The sign was in a school zone; instead of bullet holes it had paint gun splatters. Seriously, I'm not making this up.

In Fairbanks, we stopped for lunch, and then continued south toward Denali. The drive south from Fairbanks to Denali was not as interesting as the drive this morning. For much of the way, trees block the view from the highway, making it impossible to get a sense of the surrounding country.

South of Fairbanks, Karen was car weary and slaphappy. We passed a billboard for Skinny Dicks Halfway Inn; this became her entertainment for a good 50 miles. She worked "Skinny Dick" into our conversation as many times as possible. I was relieved when we passed a dead animal on the side of the road hoping it would break the pattern. Karen said nothing for about two minutes then asked me if I thought Skinny Dick had killed that animal with his car. I muttered, "Please Lord, let Denali be over the next hill."

By late afternoon we were at the entrance to Denali National Park. We took care of business, and picked up our bus tickets for tomorrow; we're taking a bus 66 miles to the Eielson Visitor Center in the center of the park.

Your friend,
Matt

~.~.~.~.~.~.~

From: **Matt Smith**
Subject: **#13 – Denali National Park**
Date: **August 25, 2010**

Dear Bob & Sue,

Our shuttle bus to Eielson Visitor Center left at 8:30am. The trip took four hours one-way. Usually we avoid organized tours, but the general public is not allowed to drive past the ranger checkpoint at mile 15 of the park road. If you want to see anything beyond that point, you have to take a bus or walk.

We only had one day scheduled to go into the park, and we didn't want to miss our bus. All the shuttle times were sold out, so taking a later bus was not an option. People started lining up 20 minutes early for each bus.

While we were in line, an older man (older than us) walked out of the transit building and past the lines for the buses. He stood in the middle of the road and shouted, "Where's our bus!" Then he shouted toward the transit building for his wife, "Nancy!" A minute later, he shouted again, "Nancy!" Finally, Nancy came out; she was struggling to put on her coat and wrestling a large bag of items she purchased at the gift shop. "Nancy, where's our bus!"

"I don't know where our bus is!" (I don't think they were aware they were shouting.)

"Well it's supposed to be right here!"

The old guy walked over to the worker who was coordinating the loading of buses. He shouted, "Where's our bus!"

"Sir, what bus do you have tickets for?"

"Eight o'clock!"

"It's 8:20 sir." The old guy looked at the worker like he didn't hear him. "Your bus is probably already gone, sir."

"Well it's supposed to be right here! Nancy! Where's our bus!"

"I don't know where our bus is!"

This went on for a while. I'm pretty sure they spent the rest of the day in the gift shop.

There are two types of buses that go into the park: tour buses (that are narrated with lunch provided) and shuttle buses. We took one of the shuttle buses, which are not narrated, but our driver shared some interesting park information with us. Once the shuttle bus is past mile marker 15, you can get off wherever you want and then catch another shuttle later. To allow for this, they save a few empty seats on each bus. The busses run about every 15 minutes.

Some people take the shuttle into the park, get off and hike for hours, and then come back to the road and catch the next shuttle that comes by. The shuttle buses are for people who are more self-sufficient; you bring your own food and water and plan your own itinerary. It was nice for me not to have to drive, so I could look out at the scenery and wildlife instead of the road.

Once we passed the ranger checkpoint, we felt like we were really in the park. Everyone on the bus was looking for wildlife, except the couple in the row across from us. They were eating. They ate continuously. The wife would pull out a sandwich bag full of nuts, eat one nut, give her husband one nut and then put the bag away. She'd get a granola bar out, take one small bite, give it to her husband, so he could take one small bite, and then put it away. She'd rummage around for another bag, eat one carrot and put it away. Non-stop. Apple slices, potato chips, sandwiches, cookies. I never saw them eating the same thing twice, but they were always eating. They never looked out the windows.

About an hour into our trip, John, our bus driver, stopped when he spotted a bear. It was a mother bear with two cubs. They were maybe a half-mile away up the hillside. I'm glad Karen and I both brought binoculars on this trip. In Alaska, you need binoculars or a good telephoto lens on your camera to see much of the wildlife. The bears were grizzlies, smaller than the coastal bears that live close by the ocean. The coastal bears have evolved into much larger animals because of their diet of salmon. The bears in Denali are mostly vegetarian; berries are their main food.

The park ranger we spoke with at the visitor center had a relaxed attitude about the bears in the park. She said if we don't bother them, they won't bother us. This was much different from the bear warnings we got in Glacier Bay, where bear spray is advised on all hikes, and trails are frequently closed because of bear activity. Still, if you ever run into a grizzly bear in the wild, the main difference to remember is the larger bears can kill you in about two seconds while it takes the smaller bears about three seconds. In total, we saw ten bears today; three sightings of a mother with two cubs and one lone bear.

The park road past mile marker 15 is gravel, but well maintained. The main reason it takes four hours to get to Eielson is because of the stops for wildlife sightings and bathroom breaks. At our first bathroom stop, we overheard a woman complaining to John, our driver. She said, "Can we skip the bathroom and wildlife stops? I just want to get there." John was very polite but explained that people come to the park to see wildlife and no, we can't skip the bathroom stops. I wondered where she thought "there" was; we were "there."

Very soon after we pulled out of the rest area, John stopped the bus in the road. I could hear the complainer exhale loudly. There was a wolf pup in the road ahead. John thought the pup was born this spring. He wasn't very big, but he had huge paws. We all looked for the other members of the pack, but couldn't find them. I'm sure they were very close by.

I looked over at the couple who had been eating to see if they showed any interest in seeing the wolf pup. They were both asleep with their mouths open.

John the driver looked like he was about 70 years old. He told us at the beginning of the trip to yell, "Stop!" when we saw wildlife because the engine noise was loud, and he couldn't hear us unless we yelled. This started a very annoying pattern of "Stops!" that lasted all morning. There were many false alarms and sightings of animals so far away we would have needed the Hubble telescope to see them. At a curve in the road, the bus came very close to the edge of a cliff. I was sitting in the window seat on the cliff side of the bus. Looking straight down, I couldn't see any part of the road, only fluorescent cones that once marked the edge of the road, which had fallen several hundred feet to the bottom of the valley. I was hoping no one would yell, "Stop!" at that moment; it wouldn't be a good time to frighten or distract John.

When we arrived at the Eielson Visitor Center, we ate our lunch outside. Sadly Mt. McKinley wasn't "out." Because of frequent cloud cover, only about 30 percent of visitors to Denali see Mt. McKinley. So many visitors miss seeing the mountain that inside the visitor center, on a large window that frames a view of the mountain, the park service drew the silhouette of Mount McKinley. There is a spot on the floor where you can stand, and if your eye level is just right and you look at the drawing on the window, that's where the mountain would be.

After lunch, we hiked the Alpine Trail behind the visitor center. The hike was a 1,000-foot elevation gain and one mile long. At the top, there was a 360-degree view of the park. The hike was steep, but it felt good since we'd been sitting all morning. We got some amazing pictures at the top.

Because of our hike, we missed the return departure of our original bus, so we had to catch another shuttle back to the park entrance. However, one of the shuttles broke down, so the people who would have been on it were now also waiting to get on another shuttle. We had to put our name on a waiting list, and wait through several buses to catch a ride. There were about 30 people in our same situation standing around with us.

Everyone was relieved when finally an empty bus arrived that could take us back. The waiting list "manager," who clearly was having a bad day, started calling out names to board the bus. He called out, "Kim, party of three." No response. He yelled louder, "Kim!" Again, no response. He looked around the parking lot and in the visitor center, then came back to the bus. One more time he called out, "Kim!" Suddenly, we heard voices and saw hands waving out of the windows of the broken down bus. The Kim family had been sitting in the back of the broken down bus ready to go. Everyone, including the Kims, laughed, which broke the tension. The manager waved them over to the new bus; he shook his head and said, "Now *that* was funny."

The shuttle makes fewer stops on its way back to the park entrance. The bar is higher for wildlife sightings in the afternoon because everyone is bus weary. Park regulations say you must stay at least a quarter of a mile away from large wildlife. But, for practical reasons, if a bus stops and wildlife approaches it, the bus doesn't have to back up.

On the way back to the entrance, our bus came around a blind curve and about 100 feet in front of us was a group of Dall sheep in the road. The bus driver stopped the bus and turned off the engine. We sat there for about 15 minutes as the sheep ate and ambled toward our bus. They walked right past the bus, and then down the mountainside. We had a front row seat. It was fun to see them so close; usually you see mountain sheep as tiny specks miles away on a cliff.

It was a great day in the park; I'm sure we'll be back someday. Tomorrow we head south to Seward, Alaska.

Your friend,
Matt

~.~.~.~.~.~.~

From: **Karen Smith**
Subject: **#14 – Kenai Fjords National Park**
Date: **August 26, 2010**

Dear Bob & Sue,

It's nice to start the day with the smell of three-day old smoked salmon jerky. As we left for Seward bright and early in our rental car, the smell came blowing out of the heating vents. When the salmon jerky bag exploded in Wrangell-St. Elias, salmon bits flew into crevices so small that the only way to get them out would be to dismantle the dashboard. Good thing it's a rental.

Kenai Fjords National Park is one of only three national parks in Alaska that you can drive to. About 100 miles south of Anchorage, it covers 1,760 sq. miles of the Kenai Peninsula near the town of Seward, the park's headquarters. Kenai Fjords National Park was created in 1980 to protect the scenic and environmental integrity of the Harding Icefield, its glaciers and the coastal fjords, islands, and peninsulas of the Kenai coast.

We didn't see much of that scenic beauty today when we arrived in Seward; it was dreary, raining, and the clouds were low. After checking into our hotel along the harbor, we walked to the Information Center down the street. Matt struck up a conversation with a ranger, asking her about other things to do in the park besides the boat tour. (We're doing that tomorrow.) The ranger asked if we were bird watchers. Matt said, "No." There was an uncomfortable silence; Matt felt like he needed to explain, "We don't have anything against birds; we just aren't that interested – we don't have a life list of birds." A woman looking at postcards next to me overheard the conversation and started laughing at Matt. If I had a nickel for every time...

We drove to the Exit Glacier area, the only part of the park accessible by road. Exit Glacier is open year-round, but once it starts snowing, usually in mid-November, the road is closed to cars until weather permitting in May. During those months, you would need a snow machine or dogsled to get there, unless you want to snowshoe or cross-country ski the 8.6 miles from Seward Highway to the Exit Glacier parking lot. Exit Glacier is a half-mile wide river of ice, one of 30 glaciers flowing outward from the 700-square-mile Harding Icefield. There's a hiking trail that goes to the edge of the glacier, as well as a strenuous four-mile trail up to the Harding Icefield.

As soon as we entered the park's boundary, we stopped and took our picture in front of the Kenai Fjords National Park sign. Every national park sign is unique, and most reflect something special about their park, either on the sign itself or in the local materials used to build it. In its current condition, the Kenai Fjords sign appears to be welcoming visitors to a shooting range. The decrepit condition of the sign shocked me – it had peeling paint and what looked like bullet holes. As the first thing visitors see when they enter the park, you can't underestimate the importance of the park sign. We may seem like geeks because we're thrilled when we see a park sign, but we're not the only ones. Many people have told us that they get excited when they're driving into the park and first glimpse the sign; for others, it brings back memories of childhood vacations.

We strolled through the Exit Glacier Nature Center looking at the exhibits, and checked out the Alaska Geographic bookstore. When we got back to the car, Matt realized he mistakenly picked up a Bear Safety brochure instead of the park map. He went back in to get his own map because I will no longer share mine. We decided early in our parks trip that in order to avoid unnecessary bickering we should get two maps and newsletters at every park. Matt puts the unopened, pristine map and newsletter away in his file, and I'm free to do with mine whatever I like: wrinkle it, tear it, stain it, use it as a sun shield on long car rides, level wobbly tables in restaurants, re-fold it incorrectly, or use it as a napkin. Matt calls my maps "biohazards." So, I'm not sharing.

Back in our hotel room, Matt told me about his Photo of the Day Contest. I couldn't help but laugh. It was just so cute and slightly pathetic. Matt is the one who takes the photos; Matt is the only one who enters photos into the contest, and Matt is the one who decides which photo is the winner. The way it works is this: he downloads all the day's photos onto his laptop. He looks through them and then selects the top three. He moves the three finalists onto his desktop, studies them again, thinks about it for awhile, and then chooses a winner which gets to appear in the "Photo of the Day" spot on our website.

I mentioned to him that I'd like to be one of the judges of the Photo of the Day, but his feelings were hurt because I laughed at him. He said, "I don't think you're the kind of judge we're looking for at this time."

Who's "we?"

After walking through Seward's downtown and not finding any place that met all Matt's dining requirements – no bright lights, no bad live music, no strong smells of cleaning fluid, no Formica eating surfaces and no screaming children – we ended up back in the harbor area at the bar of a seafood restaurant.

We sat at the bar and ate seafood chowder. It was fantastic. The bartender turned to the guy sitting next to Matt and asked, "How big?" The guy replied, "187 pounds." That was the weight of the halibut he caught today. I guess that's a good catch; he had the biggest steak on the menu in front of him and was eating like he hadn't seen food in a week.

After one beer and chowder, we called it a night; we have a long day tomorrow with the boat tour.

Your friend,
Karen

~.~.~.~.~.~.~

From: **Karen Smith**
Subject: **Kenai Fjords boat tour**
Date: **August 27, 2010**

Dear Bob & Sue,

We have good news and bad news to report about our boat tour of Kenai Fjords National Park. The bad news is the weather today was rainy and foggy, and since we'd already bought non-refundable tickets, we were going no matter what. The good news is that often when it rains there are seas of 15–20 ft. and 30–40 mph winds, but today the ocean was calm, so we weren't puking over the side of the boat. That's where they ask you to puke so you don't clog the toilets. They call it "feeding the fish."

The best way to see a big chunk of the park and its wildlife is by boat. There are several boat tours to choose from, all run by private concessionaires. We went with the eight-hour cruise, which included lunch and an all-you-can-eat salmon and prime rib dinner on Fox Island with a park ranger presentation. There was, however, no park ranger on board our boat. Our tickets cost $164 each, which we thought was pricey. It seems like that price would be out of reach for most families, which may explain why there were so few children on board.

We didn't see any whales or bears today, but I'm sure they were out there. At some spots, it was too foggy to see anything farther than 50 feet from the boat. We did see Dall's porpoises, Steller sea lions, harbor seals, and sea otters. We saw a sea otter close to our boat eating an octopus. It was creepy watching it tear off arms of the octopus and eat them like stalks of celery. Otters are the largest members of the weasel family, but they are adorable (when they're not ripping apart the other animals) floating around on their backs. A ranger told us the cutest thing: to keep from drifting apart when they sleep, sometimes they hold paws.

The highlight of the tour was seeing the Aialik Glacier, the largest tidewater glacier in the park, which comes off of the Harding Icefield. It's hard to describe how tiny the boat suddenly seemed when the engine stopped, and we were bobbing next to the immense blue cliff of ice that was cracking and falling into the sea with thunderous sounds.

Even though the weather was bad, the boat was warm, the seats were comfortable, and we would have just settled back and enjoyed looking out the window except – the captain wouldn't stop talking. Since there wasn't a park ranger on board, he was our tour guide. On our Glacier Bay boat tour, ranger Jane was informative while still being professional and respectful of where we were, a national park – a wilderness area. The captain of our boat today *really* liked the sound of his voice. Now, I agree enthusiasm is good, but he came off like a cheesy Las Vegas lounge performer – on an eight-hour shift. There was nowhere on the boat we could go to get away from the sound of his voice. "Allrighty folks, now sit tight and hold on to your seats! You are about to see (his voice drops to a dramatic whisper) a—black—billed—magpie."

The captain was clearly a birder. He maneuvered the boat in and around the Chiswell Islands, home to countless birds: horned and tufted puffins, thick-billed murres, black-legged kittiwakes, and auklets to name a few. The captain was explaining the nesting habits of the tufted puffin when he stopped, handed his microphone to some unlucky passenger and made him say, "Picture perfect puffins" ten times fast. Spit flew, and Matt got out his iPod and headphones to drown out the sound.

The last straw came at the end of the tour as the boat was making its way toward Fox Island for dinner. "Do you want to add a half pound of crab to your all-you-can-eat salmon and prime rib dinner for $8?" They asked us that question when we bought our tickets online, and they asked us again when we picked up our tickets this morning at the boat dock. No thanks. We were already planning to eat $164 worth of salmon and prime rib. Still, the Captain got on the loudspeaker to let us know that this was our last and final chance to purchase this incredible deal. Only $8.00! He added, "This is Alaskan crab, not Russian crab." On top of being annoyed, we then wondered what the difference was between Alaskan and Russian crab.

Then he left the wheel and went around the boat. He stopped at every table to make a personal plea to add a half-pound of crab to the all-you-can-eat salmon and prime rib dinner. What I wanted to know was, while the captain was hawking crab, who was steering the boat?

The rest of the boat tour was enjoyable, despite having missed out on the Alaskan crab (not Russian crab). The lodge on Fox Island was beautiful, and the food was excellent. We stuffed ourselves with salmon, but when the boat dropped us back at the Seward dock it was only 6:00pm, so we went back to the same bar as last night for more seafood chowder.

The bartender recognized us and said, "You missed all the excitement last night." After we left, a black bear lumbered down the pier outside the restaurant and walked beside the boats, sniffing and poking around. Then he walked along the deck right outside the windows of the restaurant. The restaurant called the police, and they took the bear away. They had to put him down; he was a repeat offender, and this was his final strike.

Matt was tired by the end of the day. Maybe it was the Dramamine he'd taken earlier, or maybe it was the effect of our long trip and a lot of driving. He said to me, "Trying to visit all 58 parks in such a short time feels like being in a hotdog-eating contest. We're just trying to shove them down as fast as possible. We need to enjoy the journey and not make it a race." I agreed.

Tomorrow if the weather improves, we're planning to hike to Exit Glacier, and possibly the Harding Ice Field. After that we'll head toward Anchorage.

Your friend,
Karen

~.~.~.~.~.~.~.~

From: **Matt Smith**
Subject: **#15 – Crater Lake National Park**
Date: **September 6, 2010**

Dear Bob and Sue,

After Labor Day, it's walkers and strollers season in the national parks. Families with school-aged children have wrapped up their summer vacations, and it's just old people and babies (except for us). It's the perfect time to start a 13-park road trip. Yesterday we drove from Issaquah to Roseburg, Oregon. I had to reserve a motel room in Roseburg because Crater Lake Lodge was sold out.

A couple of years ago, also in September, we stayed at Crater Lake Lodge for the first time. I reserved a room with a view of the lake. A friend of ours who had stayed here before told us there is nothing better than looking out over Crater Lake while lying in bed. When we got to our room though, I was surprised to see we had a view of the parking lot instead of the lake. It wouldn't have bothered me much, except we paid *extra* for a view and we should get a view – or a discount.

I put our bags on the bed and then stood in the center of the room looking at the parking lot. Karen said, "Isn't this room great? Let's go for a walk." She was trying to keep me from OCDing over not having a view of the lake. It wasn't going to work. She went over to the window, opened it, leaned her body halfway out and looked to the left and the right. When she came back in she said, "There it is. See? You can see the lake if you lean out the window and look over there. Now let's go for a walk."

I tried to let it go. I really did. The walk along the crater rim was stunning; it was a beautiful fall evening, Karen even said something about it being so romantic, but I just had to talk with the front desk about our room without a view.

The manager was at the front desk when we got back from our walk, so I explained to him about our room not having a view of the lake. He looked up our room number and said, "I see here that you *are* in a room with a view of the lake."

I replied, "It's actually a view of the parking lot. You have to lean out and look to the right to see the lake."

The manager said, "Well, some rooms do have a better view of the lake than others but you can still see the lake from your room, correct?"

I said, "If we're being technical about it, you have to put your head *outside* the room to view the lake. So no, you can't see the lake from our room." I may have been stretching the truth to make my point, but still, the room did *not* have a view of the lake.

The manager looked down at the computer screen behind the counter, and after way more keystrokes than could possibly be necessary to check if there were any other rooms available with a view of the lake he said, "I'm sorry there are no other rooms available, with or without a view: we're sold out tonight."

"What about tomorrow?"

There was silence, and again a lot of keystrokes. "You're in luck. Tomorrow we have another room with a view that you can move to. But, you will have to check out in the morning and check back in in the afternoon."

This was enough for me to claim victory so I took it.

The next morning, we checked out of our parking lot view room, put our bags in the car and headed out for the day. First we drove the rim road and then came back to the snack bar for a quick lunch before hiking Mount Scott. It was an unusually warm day and the hike wore us out, so afterward we decided to first stop in the great room of the lodge for a beer before checking in.

It took what seemed like forever to get a waiter's attention to place our order, and even longer for the beer to arrive. Maybe I was delirious from the heat of the hike, but when the beers arrived they looked small: smaller than usual. I knew right away that we would soon be ordering another round, so before the waiter left I placed the order. A confused conversation then ensued whereby our waiter asked Karen if she also wanted a beer and/or another. I'm not sure exactly what was said, but a couple of minutes later he brought us four more beers. Small though they may have been, chugging three beers each on an empty stomach and after a hot, strenuous hike made us very relaxed. I would say even a bit light-headed.

We paid our bar bill and went to the front desk to get the keys to our new room. The woman at the front desk seemed befuddled when I explained that we had checked in yesterday and checked out this morning, but were only switching rooms so now we were checking back in. I had to explain this at least a couple of times. Eventually she handed us two sets of keys and sent us on our way.

I handed one set to Karen and we headed toward the elevator. The plastic key fob had a white "508" printed on it. I wanted to take the stairs, so I told Karen I would meet her on the fifth floor. She got on the elevator and I climbed the stairs, wishing I had taken the elevator. The last exit was at the fourth floor, so I exited into the fourth floor hallway and proceeded to look for another set of stairs leading to the fifth floor. After about five minutes of searching, I met Karen at the elevator doors on the fourth floor. She said, "The elevator only goes to the fourth floor. What kind of room did you get us? Did they put us in the attic?"

Together we searched for an access to the fifth floor without luck. We took the elevator back down to the lobby and asked a bellboy how to get to the fifth floor. (He really was a boy: he looked like he was 14.) He said, "The hotel doesn't have a fifth floor." I said, "Well our room key says 508." I handed him my key and he laughed. He said, "508 is part of the address of where to mail the key if it's found. It's the P.O. Box number. You're in room 314. See here, where it says '314'?" In my defense, the ink had worn off the embossed 314, *and* I had just chugged three beers on an empty stomach after a hot, strenuous hike. Did I mention we were also at 7,100 feet altitude?

We went back to the elevator, took it to the third floor and found room 314, still with some difficulty. Karen got to the door first and used her key to open it; I was right behind her. Just as she entered the room, she stopped and jerked backwards. I ran into her and almost knocked us both to the floor. Karen said in a startled tone, "Oh! I'm sorry" and pushed me back into the hall. She slammed the door and we both ran down the hall toward the elevator. I didn't know why we were running until Karen said, "There was a man and a woman in bed and they were naked."

"OK, but why are we running?"

"They looked angry. I think they may come after us."

"Naked?"

Karen nervously hit the elevator down button repeatedly until the doors opened. A minute later we were back at the front desk for the third time since our beerfest, explaining to the previously befuddled front desk clerk what had just happened. She took our keys and said, "Well, these aren't your keys Mr. Smith. You're not in room 314; you're in room 212." She handed us keys to room 212; I took them and paused.

Karen was in a hurry to get to our room and hide from the naked couple. She had turned to walk toward the elevator but stopped when she saw I wasn't coming along. I said to the clerk, "Now, does this room have a view of the lake?" Karen stomped. She rarely stomps. But, even though they are rare, I know what a stomp means: "This is not the time to be a dick."

We made it to room 212 before the naked couple found us. Our new room, by the way, had a spectacular view of the lake. The next morning we sat in bed, door securely bolted, looking at the lake while drinking coffee. It was well worth the trouble of switching. I made sure to point out to Karen that sometimes my OC pays off. Sitting there looking at the magnificent blue lake, she agreed.

On this trip, I hadn't told Karen that I'd reserved a room at a motel instead of a hotel. Karen isn't a big fan of motels where the front door of the room opens to the parking lot. She makes me sleep on the side of the bed closest to the window, so "the bullets will hit me first" when the shooting starts.

So, you can imagine how uncomfortable she was last night, as we were unloading our car outside our room, and she found herself standing next to a man with no pants. We think he was staying in the room next door. He was searching for something in the trunk of his car for a very long time, with nothing on below the waist, nothing. He was wearing a dress shirt and the tail covered most of his business. He must have been looking for his pants.

No bullets or naked men came into our room last night, so we were well rested this morning for our drive to Crater Lake. We got to the park about 10:30am. There was not a cloud in the sky, but a haze from an active forest fire hung in the air. It was a small fire, but it had been burning for a couple of weeks and was not actively being suppressed.

We entered the park through the north entrance and drove east on the rim road around the crater stopping at several overlooks. On a sunny day like today, the color of the lake looks unreal; it's a stunning blue. Crater Lake is one of those places like the Grand Canyon that everyone should see at least once in their lifetime. Staying at the lodge is also something everyone should do; stargazing on the back patio of the lodge while looking over the lake is awe-inspiring.

Just to the east of the crater is Mount Scott, the highest point in the park at 8,926 feet. There's a five-mile round-trip hike to the summit where a lookout tower sits. It's a moderate hike with an elevation gain of 1,250 feet. We parked near the trailhead and hiked to the summit.

I have a small voice recorder that I carry with me almost all the time. It's easier to use the recorder than to write notes, especially while on a hike. Halfway to the summit of Mount Scott, Karen took my voice recorder from me. She wanted to make a formal complaint for the record.

Her complaints were numerous: a) She feels that when we go on strenuous hikes, which she called "death marches", I falsely promise to go slowly and stop for rest breaks. b) I never stop to take in the beauty of the surroundings. c) I ignore her gasping and wheezing. d) Finally, I never look back to make sure she is okay, or that a bear hasn't gotten her.

Bob and Sue, this is your fault, of course. Whenever we go for hikes with you, Karen notices how you hold hands the entire way. She thinks *we* should hold hands on our hikes, and kiss every now and then. You guys are getting me in trouble.

I got the recorder back from Wheezy, and we made it to the summit. The views were amazing. We had a good view of the fire from the summit. It wasn't large, but it put out a large amount of smoke. The lake was almost mirror flat; the only ripples were the ones made by the tour boat going to Wizard Island.

After the hike, we made peanut butter and jelly sandwiches in the back seat of our car. We realized before this trip that we could save money by not eating in restaurants and snack bars for every meal. Also, when we were here last time, I had a bad experience with my lunch from the snack bar. I was halfway through my sandwich when the top piece of bread fell off. There was an iridescent rainbow on my roast beef. I like rainbows as much as the next guy, just not on my meat. In defense of the snack bar, I don't think the meat was spoiled. I never got sick, but still...

We finished lunch and drove the rim road toward Crater Lake Lodge, then out of the park through the same entrance we came in this morning. Tonight we're staying at Homewood Suites in Medford. We've never stayed at a Homewood Suites before, so we didn't know that dinner was included in the price of the room. The woman checking us in told us that dinner would be served from 5:30–7:30pm, the menu was hamburgers and hotdogs, and as always, free beer and wine. Karen said, "It's our lucky day. They have our two favorite things, beer and free."

Your friend,
Matt

~.~.~.~.~.~.~

From: **Matt Smith**
Subject: **#16 – Redwood National Park**
Date: **September 7, 2010**

Dear Bob and Sue,

Karen is a banana smuggler. On our drive from Medford, Oregon to Arcata, California today, we stopped to hike in Redwood National Park. At the California border, I lied to the agriculture inspector who asked if we had any produce in our car. I said we didn't, but Karen had a banana in her purse. I tried to get it from her before we got to the inspection station, but she said she would "never give it up." By lying to the inspector, I became an accomplice. I don't even like bananas.

Karen tried to justify her actions by saying bananas aren't produce. Then she gave me her personal guarantee that her banana didn't have any diseases or insects, *and* it posed no danger to California's agriculture industry. As soon as we pulled out of sight of the inspection station, I made her eat it, so we would be legal again. I should have turned her in at the border.

Karen always has a banana with her when we travel. She says it's the perfect travel fruit; it will always be clean on the inside when she's ready to eat it. A few years ago we were in London and took a day trip to Windsor Castle. The Queen was in residence, so security was tighter than normal. The guards searched Karen's purse. Can you guess what they pulled out? A banana. They put the banana on the conveyor belt to be X-rayed. The guards gathered around and laughed as the banana slid beneath the X-ray curtain. One of the guards said, "Look, the bananer's going to see Mum."

Once across the California border, we entered what we thought was Redwood National Park. At the Prairie Creek Visitor Center, we found a person who we thought was a volunteer ranger, and asked his suggestion for a two to three-hour moderate hike in the national park. He gave us an unpleasant look and asked, "Why do you want to hike in the *national* park?" That seemed like an odd question. I explained how we're visiting all the national parks, and we would like to hike in Redwood National Park. He rolled his eyes and said, "OK, but the trails in the state park are *much* better." He gave us a map and highlighted several hikes we should consider. They were all in the state park. Later we realized that Prairie Creek Visitor Center is in one of the units of Redwood State Park that are clustered around Redwood National Park.

There seems to be a strained rivalry between Redwood State Park and Redwood National Park. A national park ranger told us that when the law was passed to create the *national* park it called for all the state park land along the coast in northwest California to be included in Redwood National Park. The state wasn't happy about this so not all the old state park land was included in the national park. We didn't get a clear answer when we asked how the state was able *not* to comply with the federal mandate. Now that California is having budget problems, they want the federal government to help with resources to manage Redwood State Park. At least that's what we were told. We just wanted to take a cool hike among the coastal redwoods, not get in the middle of a senseless squabble between government agencies.

Regardless, we made sure that at least part of our hike went through the national park, so we're *official*. From the Prairie Creek Visitor Center, we hiked west into the park then looped back north along Prairie Creek. There was an overcast sky and it drizzled off and on while we hiked. The trail was spongy, like the trails in the rain forests of the Pacific Northwest. It felt like home except the trees were much larger here.

Around every bend, a new stand of redwoods impressed us with their size. Each time I stopped to take pictures of the massive trees, I was disappointed when I looked at the images in my camera. It's difficult to capture their size with a point-and-shoot. A mature redwood had fallen across the trail and a maintenance crew had cut a section out of the downed tree to clear the path. Karen stood next to the cross section while I took her picture. Having her there for scale made it easier to tell how enormous the tree was.

On the way back to the visitor center, our trail passed by a parking pullout along the Newton B. Drury Scenic Parkway. There were several buses parked there when we walked by, but none of the passengers had walked more than 50 yards from their bus. That's a shame: the best part about hiking in the park is getting away from other people and being quiet among the peaceful, big trees.

After the hike we continued driving south on Highway 101. Around the area of Elk Meadow, we saw a herd of elk – lying in a meadow. Cars had stopped and people were standing along the side of the road watching them and taking their picture.

If we had more time we would have driven farther into the park and hiked more, but the weather was still lousy and we wanted to get to Arcata where we're spending the night before it got dark.

Tomorrow we're driving to Redding, California and will visit Lassen Volcanic National Park the next day.

Wish you guys were with us.

Your friend,
Matt

~.~.~.~.~.~.~

From: **Matt Smith**
Subject: **#17 – Lassen Volcanic National Park**
Date: **September 9, 2010**

Dear Bob and Sue,

We had no wildlife sightings today in Lassen Volcanic National Park; we saw lots of squirrels, but Karen said they don't count as wildlife. She gets frustrated when I repeatedly stop our hikes to take pictures of small animals, like squirrels and lizards. We agreed that from now on there would be a two-pound minimum weight requirement for any animal to qualify as a wildlife sighting. If I see an animal below that weight, I've agreed not to shout, "Karen, look!" And, I will only stop to take their picture if I can do so without Karen having to break her stride. Birds are exempt from the weight minimum. If there's any doubt whether an animal meets the two-pound requirement, I will be the sole judge.

When we woke up this morning, it was a gloomy day. Karen suggested we go back to bed, skip the park, and tell everyone we visited it anyway. She said, "No one will know. If someone asks us what the park was like we'll say, 'The trees and mountains were beautiful, it was a magical place, yada yada yada.' You can move some of your squirrel pictures from the other parks into the Lassen file folder and no one will ever know we didn't go." Later she said she regretted her suggestion and asked me not to tell anyone. I assured her it would be our secret.

It took more than an hour to drive from Redding to the

southwest entrance of the park; we got to the Kohm Yah-mah-nee Visitor Center about 9:00am. The park and the visitor center are open year-round, but because of the amount of snow Lassen receives each year, the main park road past the visitor center is usually closed from October through June, sometimes as late as July. The temperature was 36 when we arrived, with frost in most places and a couple inches of snow at the higher elevations. The snow would be gone within an hour after we arrived, but we were able to get a few good photos before it melted.

Our first hike was the Bumpass Hell Trail, which has the largest concentration of hydrothermal features in the park: boiling mudpots, fumaroles, and steaming pools. It looks like a small version of Yellowstone. The sun broke through the clouds as we got to the boardwalk that allows you to walk over the thermally active areas. With the cold temperatures, bright sun, and steam coming out of the ground, we got some great photos.

A *Good Morning America* cameraman (Burt) was there with a park ranger filming a segment about the park for the show. He asked if he could interview us about our impressions of the park. It took Karen about two seconds (maybe three) to brush her hair and put on lipstick using the back of her 68-cent bottle opener as a mirror. He said we might be on *Good Morning America* in a few weeks when they air the story. I hope in our first and most-likely last media interview we don't look like complete morons.

After finishing with Burt, we headed to the Lassen Peak trailhead parking lot. Lassen Peak is the southernmost active volcano in the Cascade Range. It exploded in 1915, and that eruption was the last one in the Cascades until Mt. St. Helens blew in 1980. The trail to the top of Lassen Peak is 2.5 miles one way. The summit provides spectacular views of the 1915 devastated area, but we only got to see part of the view. The park service closed the trail just past the halfway point to allow maintenance crews to work on stabilizing the upper half.

We then drove to the Summit Lake South campgrounds,

and from there hiked two miles to Echo Lake, the first lake on the Cluster Lakes Loop. We were surprised at how beautiful and pristine the park was; a park that we'd never even heard of a year ago. Karen called it a "hidden gem." It's every bit as spectacular as the more popular national parks, but without traffic jams and crowds of people. We nearly had the place to ourselves.

Driving north on the main park road we left the park through the northwest gate, and headed back to Redding where we're staying again tonight. Tomorrow we're driving to Yosemite.

Your friend,
Matt

~.~.~.~.~.~.~

From: **Matt Smith**
Subject: **#18 – Yosemite National Park**
Date: **September 10, 2010**

Dear Bob and Sue,

Yosemite has been on Karen's "must see before I die" list for a long time. Her head was hanging out the window as we entered the park from the northwest, at the Big Oak Flat Entrance. We stopped and took our picture by the park sign, and then drove into the valley for our first look. After everything we'd read and heard about this "crown jewel" of the park system, we wondered if it would live up to the hype. Yosemite Falls was dry, (as I guess it usually is in September), but even without the famous waterfall spilling over the canyon walls, the valley was every bit as spectacular as promised.

Today was our "getting the lay of the land day," which is what we do when we arrive in a park for the first time late in the afternoon. We take a look around, check out the food and beverage offerings, or lack thereof, take care of our park business and get suggestions from the park rangers about hikes to do the following day(s).

We drove through a giant parking lot in the middle of the valley. After squeezing into a parking spot between a couple of big-ass RVs, we walked past the bus stop and the lines of people waiting for the shuttle and continued on the paved path to the Yosemite Valley Visitor Center. It was surprising to see that Yosemite Village is a small city with lodging, restaurants, grocery store, deli, gift shops, post office, museum and a medical clinic. There were people everywhere.

We walked to the Ahwahnee Hotel to check it out. We have reservations there for our last night in the park. After I coaxed Karen out of the gift shop, we had a drink outside on the patio overlooking the back lawn. The weather was perfect – mid-70's and sunny.

Tonight we're at the Yosemite View Lodge just outside the west entrance to the park. We had a mishap on our hotel room balcony a little while ago. While opening a beer, I dropped my 68-cent bottle opener. It bounced off our deck and landed on the roof of the room below us, out of reach. Fortunately, we have two backup 68-cent bottle openers, so we didn't have to try to bite the caps off. The best $2.04 I ever spent. Another good value was the $1.98 Spork I bought for Karen. A Spork is a spoon, knife, and fork all in one utensil. Karen cried when I gave it to her.

We're excited to hike and to see more of the park. Tomorrow we're headed up to the Tuolumne Meadows area.

Your friend,
Matt

~.~.~.~.~.~.~

From: **Matt Smith**
Subject: **Yosemite day two**
Date: **September 11, 2010**

Dear Bob and Sue,

When we got to the parking area next to Lembert Dome this morning, there were six deer in the meadow across Tioga Road. A couple of small ones were head-butting each other and kicking up dirt. It was fun to watch them play. Even Karen thought they were cute. Early in our parks trip Karen said that deer aren't binocular-worthy because, "We see them at home all the time, most of the time dead along the side of the road." She said she would look at them if they come close enough to see with her naked eye.

Today we hiked to the Glen Aulin High Sierra Camp, our longest hike so far on this trip, 12.5 miles. The trail to Glen Aulin follows the Tuolumne River, which dumps into the Hetch Hetchy Reservoir 20 miles downstream. We hiked through alternating areas of shaded, cool forests and sunny patches of bare granite. The river was low, as it usually is in late summer. In several places, there were hikers jumping into the cold water. In the spring or early summer you couldn't do this without the current sweeping you down the river and over dangerous falls.

Stapled to the markers along the trail were signs asking people to be on the lookout for a missing hiker. He failed to return to his camp when he said he would and was now several days late. About six miles into our hike, at a junction of two trails, rescue workers were questioning everyone who came by, trying to gather clues that might help them find the hiker. As crowded as these popular national parks can be, the wilderness is still vast, and people can get lost and disappear.

When we reached Glen Aulin, we were surprised to find a camp in the middle of the wilderness that provides tent cabins with real beds, hot showers, and gourmet meals. Karen thought this might be the perfect way for her to "ease into the whole camping thing." She said she'd probably *love* to camp if she didn't have to carry a tent and a sleeping bag on her back, sleep on the cold, hard ground, eat freeze-dried food, and pee in the woods. We were ready to sign up when she found out that the tents are dormitory style; you're assigned to a tent that sleeps either four women or four men. Goodnight John-Boy, goodnight Mary Ellen, goodnight Grandpa.

On our hike back to the car, the mule train that supplies the Glen Aulin camp passed us. Karen felt sorry for them. She said they looked sad, especially the little black one at the end of the train who was having trouble keeping up. I told her, "Of course they look sad, they're carrying hundreds of pounds of supplies on their backs so people like you can sleep in the wilderness in comfort and be fed gourmet meals."

After hiking back to our car, we drove 90 minutes to the Evergreen Lodge close to the Hetch Hetchy entrance of the park. We're staying here for two nights. The lodge was built in the 1920's to cater to the Hetch Hetchy Dam construction workers. Over the decades, various owners have added on to the resort. In the last ten years, the lodge has been renovated, and 75 new cabins were built. We're staying in one of the nice new cabins. My favorite spot in the complex is the tavern, which has 90 years of character, a big-screen TV showing college football, and beer.

We just finished a great dinner and plan to hang out here, write down our notes from the day and download our pictures. Our hike today was beautiful and the weather perfect. We're glad we planned for several more days in Yosemite.

Your friend,
Matt

~.~.~.~.~.~.~

From: **Karen Smith**
Subject: **Squirrels between our toes**
Date: **September 12, 2010**

Dear Bob and Sue,

We're back in the Evergreen Lodge tavern, and no, we haven't been here since last night. That wouldn't be a bad thing; they have sweet potato fries, and it's a great place to hang out. There's a wedding reception taking place in the courtyard off the restaurant, but at least a dozen of the male guests are here in the bar watching Sunday Night Football and cheering loudly. We're placing bets on whose wife stomps in here first to drag her husband away. The groom looks a little pissed off too. We can see his face through the window as he spins his mother around to a bad rendition of *You Are the Sunshine of My Life.*

Day three in Yosemite started with a drive to Glacier Point. It was a beautiful drive, but it's a long distance from the Evergreen Lodge, and it took much more time to get there than we thought due to winding roads and traffic. Glacier Point sits 3,214 feet above Yosemite Valley, providing great views of the entire valley, Half Dome, and El Capitan.

Glacier Point was crowded with visitors today, many with expensive cameras. It's always fun to watch people take pictures of themselves in weird poses. There was a park ranger stationed at the point, and visitors were taking their picture with her like she was a celebrity. A man with an elaborate camera on a huge tripod was taking pictures of the valley. He would point to a location and an assistant would carry the camera to that spot and set up the camera and tripod. The man would approach the camera; he would take the picture and then point to another location. The assistant would move the camera and tripod for him again. Very odd.

Starting at the Glacier Point parking lot, there's a 4.8-mile hike that leads down to Yosemite Valley. Matt wanted to do the hike, but we hadn't checked the park's shuttle schedule, so we weren't sure if we could get back to our car after the hike. I'm glad we didn't try it. I don't like hiking straight down; it bothers my knees. (I just sounded really old, didn't I?)

From Glacier Point, we drove seven miles to the trailheads for both Sentinel Dome and Taft Point. The trails were crowded, but Matt was able to shoehorn our car into the last available parking spot. There were amazing views on both trails. The elevation of Sentinel Dome is 8,122 feet, and from there it's possible to see the Sierra Nevadas, Half Dome, Clouds Rest, Tenaya Canyon, and The Giant Staircase. From Taft Point, there's a great view of Yosemite Valley and across the valley floor to El Capitan and Yosemite Falls (when it's flowing). One of the first things you see when you reach Taft Point is the Fissures. These are huge cracks in the granite with sheer 3,000-foot drop-offs and no guardrails. Not for the faint of heart.

There was a small squirrel poised on a rock at the edge of one of the fissures. It was motionless; it looked like a statue. Matt spent ten minutes trying to get just the right picture of it, even though we agreed that we would not stop a hike to photograph small animals.

As we reached the Fissures, we caught up with a youth group of about 50 teenagers hiking together. There didn't seem to be an adult in charge. They were obviously having fun, but there was some serious grab-assing going on: throwing rocks, spitting, pretending to push someone off a cliff. It made Matt very nervous, so we turned around before we got to Taft Point. He didn't want to spend the rest of the day giving interviews to the park police if one of the teenagers ended up at the bottom of the 3,000-foot drop. Matt said he was glad to see that natural selection is still alive and well, but he didn't want to be an eyewitness to it.

This afternoon we drove into Yosemite Valley and walked to Curry Village. We were surprised by the endless rows of cabins and tents. There's a pavilion in the village with a fireplace and free Wi-Fi where we were able to access the Internet. *Inside* the pavilion, squirrels were making themselves at home, scampering under the tables and between people's feet looking for food. It creeped me out. I couldn't concentrate; they kept popping up everywhere, so I left. I felt it was safer to wait for Matt outside, taking my chances that I could be crushed under tons of granite rock falling from Glacier Point like it did in 2008, than being in there with the squirrels.

Tonight is our last night at the Evergreen Lodge; tomorrow we're staying at the swanky Ahwahnee Hotel. Before we check in, I need to scrape the mud off my hiking boots and scrub the toothpaste off my suitcase.

Your friend,
Karen

~.~.~.~.~.~.~

From: **Karen Smith**
Subject: **Yosemite day four**
Date: **September 13, 2010**

Dear Bob and Sue,

This morning we checked out of the Evergreen Lodge and drove into Yosemite Valley; it was a perfect day for hiking in the valley. We parked in Curry Village and hiked the Mist Trail up to the top of Vernal Falls. I know you've done this hike many times, and Hannah did it when she was three, but that steep granite stairway with more than 600 steps was a killer. At the top of the falls, we continued on the trail to Clark Point and then back down to Curry Village. The round-trip hike ended up being 6.5 miles. We'd heard that the Vernal Falls hike is one of the most popular hikes in Yosemite, but we weren't prepared for the mass of oddly attired humanity; we saw more than one set of high heels on our way up the granite stairs.

What got me through the hike was my excitement about staying at the Ahwahnee Hotel tonight, the grand daddy of the historic park lodges. Even though it's wildly expensive, we figured it's one of those places we have to experience at least once in our lifetime. Based on what you've told us and the pictures we've seen, we agreed that it's worth the splurge for one night.

Hoping to get the most bang for our buck, we tried to check in at 1pm. Our room wasn't ready, so we hiked from the Ahwahnee to Mirror Lake, which was a 3.5 mile round trip. The Mirror Lake trail was covered with horseshit and urine puddles to the point of disgust. Did I mention the flies? Having to share a hiking trail with horses is pretty common in the national parks and usually not a problem if you watch where you step. This was more than a nuisance; it was like hiking through a giant litter box. "Leave no trace" apparently doesn't apply to horses. Either the horses need to wear diapers, or someone needs to follow behind and clean up after them. I'm definitely writing a letter to the superintendent.

We were able to check into our room around 4pm. It was a nice room, but I don't think it's where they put the Queen of England when she stayed here. Before we went back downstairs, we thought the other hotel guests would appreciate it if we washed the dust, dirt and horse manure off our legs. Matt went first. When it was my turn, I took off my socks and shoes and stood in the tub in my clothes and turned the faucet on. *Someone* had pulled the little shower knob thingy up, so when I turned the water on, the shower, not the tub faucet, came on full blast. Not only did it scare the shit out of me, it soaked my clothes, my hair and my make-up. Good thing for Matt I started doing yoga, because instead of yelling, I do deep yoga breathing first. Then I yell. I could hear Matt in the bedroom laughing so hard I thought he might stop breathing altogether.

While I was drying my hair and reapplying my makeup, the bathtub was taking a long time to drain, and the dirt, dust, and horse manure turned the remaining stagnant water into a lovely brown soup. I was willing to let it take its sweet time, but Matt said, "There's no way we're paying a million dollars for a room with a bathtub that doesn't drain." He called housekeeping and made a few friends.

We sat in the solarium before dinner and ate cheese and crackers, and drank beers from our cooler, which wasn't as tacky as you're probably imagining (we left the spray cheese and Saltines at home). Later we ended up eating dinner in the bar instead of the dining room because the dining room has a dress code and we didn't bring nice clothes with us on this trip. For us, a nice restaurant is a gourmet pizza place.

The Ahwahnee dinner dress code is what they call *resort casual*: "Gentlemen are asked to wear collared shirts and long pants, and ladies are asked to wear dresses, skirts, or slacks and blouses." This was a red flag for us, not just because they have a dress code, but also because they used words like gentlemen and ladies. It didn't sound like our kind of place, so we ate chili in the bar, which was more like a snack bar than a bar-bar. It had bright lights and kids. After dinner, we sat in the Great Lounge, shared a bottle of wine and read.

Our two observations of the Ahwahnee are: the hotel is incredible; the price is prohibitive. We're glad we experienced it, but we feel no need to stay here again. We would highly recommend that park visitors spend some time here since they don't have to be a hotel guest to eat in the dining room, hang out in the bar, or sit in the common areas. Next time we're in Yosemite, which hopefully is with you guys, we'll bring books, snacks, and beverages, spend some time in front of the massive fireplace, and then head down the road to a hotel that's half the price.

Your friend,
Karen

~.~.~.~.~.~.~

From: **Matt Smith**
Subject: **#19 – Kings Canyon National Park**
Date: **September 14, 2010**

Dear Bob and Sue,

Our bill for staying at the Ahwahnee Hotel in Yosemite last night was $521.59. That was just the room charge for a one-night stay. For that price, we decided everything in the room not nailed down was "complimentary." So, expect a package in the mail from us containing pretty much everything in the room that wasn't nailed down: shower cap, sewing kit, two paper coasters, a pen with teeth marks, and two pieces of stationary with matching envelopes (sorry, one has a coffee stain ring, my fault). We wanted you to have these items as our thanks for recommending the Ahwahnee Hotel. We even included the personal note from Priscilla our roomskeeper just in case you want to contact her and ask if there is anything else we could get for our $521.59.

I was going to send you the Bible from the nightstand, but I wasn't sure if that would trigger some form of eternal damnation. It says on the inside cover that it was put in the room by the Gideons. I think they would want you to have it. I asked Karen her opinion. She said, "I have three words for you: do not under any circumstance steal the Bible." She was very convincing, so I hid the Bible in our bag of groceries, and made sure she carried the bag out of the room when we left. As I thought about it more, I realized she was right; it would be wrong to steal a Bible. I'm glad I wasn't the one who took it.

On our drive out of Yosemite, while searching for a granola bar for breakfast, Karen found the Bible under the Tostitos Organic Blue Corn Chips. She was *not* happy. She insists we leave it in our next hotel room. I tried to reason with her, "Why would we leave it in another hotel room? I want to send it to Bob and Sue; they might actually put it to good use."

She said, "No, if we leave it in Fresno then it's like we didn't really steal it, we just moved it, a hundred miles. God will go easier on us."

Who's "us?"

A two-hour drive south of Yosemite Valley put us in Fresno, where we turned east and drove another hour to Kings Canyon National Park. Kings was established on October 1, 1890 as General Grant National Park, that date being six days after Sequoia National Park was created. This makes Kings the fourth oldest national park, behind Yosemite (also established on October 1, 1890), Sequoia, and Yellowstone (est. 1874). In 1940, General Grant National Park was enlarged and re-named Kings Canyon National Park. Sequoia and Kings Canyon National Parks have distinct areas of land, but the park service manages them as a single entity. Now you know more than you ever wanted about when these parks were established.

Kings has two units. The west unit encompasses the Grant Grove and Redwood Mountain Groves of Sequoia trees.

It's much smaller than the unit to the east, which features the park's namesake, Kings Canyon. In 1873, John Muir visited the canyon, and wrote about how similar it was to Yosemite Valley. (By the way, Kings Canyon is more than 8,000 feet deep.) So, we were excited to see the canyon, but an active forest fire was creating heavy smoke along Highway 180, the only way to get there.

Instead of driving into the forest fire, we explored the west unit today. The main attraction in the west unit is the General Grant Grove, about a mile from the visitor center. The grove contains the General Grant Tree, which was named after Ulysses S. Grant in 1867. It's the second largest tree in the world right after the General Sherman Tree, which lives just down the road in Sequoia National Park.

The Sequoia trees were stunning. Coastal Redwoods are taller, and Bristlecone Pines live longer, but Sequoias are the largest trees on the planet by total volume. Their most distinguishing feature is a trunk with very little taper. One hundred-eighty feet off the ground, General Grant's trunk is still 13 feet in diameter. By comparison their branches look small, but they too are massive; single limbs can grow to be 12 feet in diameter. My camera couldn't capture how massive these trees are; you need to stand at their base and look up to appreciate their size.

Busloads of tourists crowded the paved trail through the Grant Grove. I was standing close to the parking lot with my head stretched skyward looking at an impressive specimen when a woman stood right next to me and began yelling to her friend who was 100 yards down the trail. I shushed her. She looked at me and then began yelling even louder before my shhhhhhhh even ended. It was an impressive display of rudeness. Karen interrupted my deep inhale as I prepared to tell my new hiking buddy to not yell in my face again.. "Making friends are you?" Karen told me that I was not the noise police, which was a shock since this whole time I thought I was. I was outnumbered *and* surrounded; the rude yelling lady on one side and the still-pissed-off Bible stealer on the other. So I moved on.

Later, Karen and I hiked for several miles in the Redwood Canyon area of the park, also in the west unit. It was a great hike. We saw huge Sequoias, and there were very few other hikers to shush or swear at. Along the trail, we saw massive pinecones. The ranger at the visitor center told us these particular pinecones were from Sugar Pine trees, and they're the largest pinecones in the world. I wanted to put a few in my backpack, but Karen reminded me that it's against the rules to take anything out of the park. I'm married to the enforcer.

We'd seen enough large trees for one day, and were anxious to find a new home for the Gideon's Bible, so we drove to the Homewood Suites in Clovis, California (just east of Fresno). We were just in time for their free dinner, beer, and wine. It was lasagna night. We also did a couple of loads of laundry. Free food, beer, and a washer and dryer that work; we could live here.

Your friend,
Matt

~.~.~.~.~.~.~

From: **Karen Smith**
Subject: **#20 – Sequoia National Park**
Date: **September 15, 2010**

Dear Bob and Sue,

Matt's OCD flared up today when we visited Sequoia National Park. At home, he's made 58 hanging files, and with his label maker he's neatly labeled each one with the name of a national park. (Yes, he has a label maker. I had one too, in the sixth grade.) He keeps his park files in alphabetic order in his filing cabinet. I'm not allowed to go into his filing cabinet because he says I "won't put anything back where it belongs."

All the stuff we collect in the parks: maps, newsletters, trail descriptions, etc. goes into Matt's park files. He got a little freaked out because Sequoia and Kings Canyon have the same map and newsletter. At the Lodgepole Visitor Center in Sequoia, we were talking to a ranger about hikes in the park when the ranger asked if we needed a copy of the park map and newsletter.

I said, "No, that's okay, we already have them."

Matt corrected me and told the ranger we needed them.

I said, "What? We just got both of them yesterday in Kings."

Matt said, "No, we don't have those anymore. We need the map and newsletter, thank you."

The ranger looked confused and slowly handed him a copy of each.

We moved away from the ranger and Matt said to me, "I have a file for each park, so I need a map and a newsletter to put in the Sequoia file."

"Can't you just put all the stuff from Kings and Sequoia in the same file?"

"I could, but if I needed to find something later, which park name would I look under?"

"You could look under both park names, how long would that take?"

"You have a point, but then I would only have 57 files instead of 58, and there are 58 national parks."

"And that's a problem because...?"

"Because, then I would only have 57 files instead of 58, and there are 58 national parks."

I thought for a minute that I was in a scene from the movie *Rain Man*. "And you don't think you have a disorder? That's OC with a capital D."

"No, OCD would be asking the park service to create a separate map and newsletter for Sequoia National Park," he replied.

This is what I live with.

When we get home, I'm going to hide his Lassen Volcanic National Park file and see how long it takes him to notice.

Your friend,
Karen

~.~.~.~.~.~.~

From: **Matt Smith**
Subject: **#20 – Sequoia National Park**
Date: **September 15, 2010**

Dear Bob and Sue,

It's worth the trip to Sequoia National Park to see the big trees; without the park's protection, they would all be gone. In the 1880s, a group of investors were amassing claims to the land where the Sequoia groves sit today, and building roads into the mountains to carry the logs to the sawmills. They would have cut down every one of the big trees if no one had stopped them. That's why, in October 1890, the park was created, to protect the big trees from being lost forever.

But still, many of the largest trees were cut down, often for foolish reasons. In 1853, a 25-foot diameter Sequoia was leveled to make a *dance floor* to attract tourists. In 1854, a profiteer destroyed a tree named the "Mother of the Forest" by removing its bark, which was then re-assembled as a traveling exhibit.

Not to be outdone in the category of stupid, the U.S. government decided their official exhibit at the 1893 Chicago World's Fair would be made from a section of a Sequoia. They cut down one of the largest Sequoias on the planet, ironically named the General Noble Tree – ironic because it was named after John Noble, the Secretary of the Interior at the time, the guy in charge of protecting America's natural resources – and made an exhibit out of a 30-foot section of its trunk. The exhibit was hollow and had a spiral staircase inside that visitors could climb to the second story. Why did they choose a Sequoia? Because, they wanted to convince the public back east that the big trees existed.

After the World's Fair, the exhibit moved to Washington D.C., but a few decades later it was gone. The government said it was "misplaced" in the 1940s. So to prove a point – that Sequoias exist – they cut down one of the best examples, a tree perhaps 2,000 years old, and within a few decades lost it.

It all sounds like a rant until you stand next to one of these magnificent trees and imagine a jackass with an axe in full backswing.

Today the largest tree in the world is General Sherman; it lives in the Giant Forest a few miles from the Lodgepole Visitor Center in Sequoia National Park. Sherman is nearly 50 feet *shorter* than the Mother of the Forest was when they stripped its bark. Karen and I hiked through the Giant Forest and stood in front of General Sherman. The paved path gives visitors easy access to the big trees, which means it gets crowded in the summer, especially when tour buses fill the parking lot. We took a side hike on the Congress Trail, which was less crowded, and a bit more challenging than the paved path. There we saw other named trees: the Senate, which is a cluster of Sequoias each of impressive size, and the President, a close rival to General Sherman in total volume. If you want to see big trees, Sequoia and Kings Canyon National Parks are the places to see them.

We stayed overnight at the Wuksachi Lodge in the park and ate dinner in their dining room. The food was very good. For our parks trip, this was a rare romantic dinner; the lights were low; there was a tablecloth and a candle on the table. We had appetizers, salad, an entrée, and a shared dessert; we even ordered a bottle of red wine. This wasn't our usual meal of blue corn chips and Coors Light while sitting at a picnic table at the edge of a parking lot.

It was still early when we finished dinner, so we went to

the gift store next to the dining room to look around. I was flipping through a book titled *Who Pooped in the Park* when something caught my eye. Next to a bin of chipmunk finger puppets was a display of personalized pocketknives; maybe it was the wine, but they fascinated me. What a clever idea, the knives each had a name – Ashley, Brad, Cody – branded on one side and "Sequoia National Park" on the other. There was even an image of a Sequoia tree burnt into the wooden casing. I searched every peg of the display and then made my way to the checkout counter; I laid four knives down. Karen came up behind me when she saw that I was trying to get the salesperson's attention.

"Buying some knives are you?" Karen asked.

"Yes I am."

"What do you have here, a 'Matt,' a 'Justin,' a 'Bob,' and a 'Tammy.' Who is Tammy?"

"That one's for Sue."

"For Sue?"

"I wanted to buy a 'Sue' but the Sue peg was empty. Tammy was the next closest name. I didn't want Sue to feel left out."

Before the salesperson could ring me up, I looked down and Tammy was gone. So was Karen; she was putting Tammy back on her peg.

Bob, look for a package from me in the mail, and tell Sue it's Karen's fault that I didn't get her anything.

Your friend,
Matt

~.~.~.~.~.~.~

From: **Matt Smith**
Subject: **#21 – Death Valley National Park**
Date: **September 16, 2010**

Dear Bob and Sue,

There's no easy way to get from Sequoia National Park to Death Valley National Park. As the crow flies, the park boundaries are no more than 30 miles apart. But to get to the visitor center, we had to drive around the south end of the Sierra Nevadas and through the Panamint Range.

After seven hours of driving, we reached the park sign at the west entrance of Death Valley National Park; it was 2:30pm and the temperature was 82 degrees. We drove into the park on Highway 190. The first few miles were flat and uninteresting, but soon the road in front of us dropped in elevation revealing sweeping views of the Cottonwood Mountains to the east. I was surprised at how beautiful the mountains were. They had no snow and very few trees, but the colors of the exposed rock made them remarkable. We stopped several times to take pictures of the mountains. Unfortunately, it was impossible to capture the dramatic views with my small camera.

By the time we reached the Furnace Creek Visitor Center at 3:50pm, the thermometer on the side of the building read 111 degrees; the elevation at the visitor center is 196 feet below sea level. We did our park business, but it was too hot to hike. We know September isn't a good time to see the park, so we're planning to come back in the winter when the temperature isn't in the triple digits. Today was just a drive through.

Two and a half hours later, we were checking into the Mandalay Bay hotel in Las Vegas where we're spending the night before driving to Zion National Park tomorrow. The woman at the hotel's registration desk told us the mini-bar items in our room were on a weighted tray. If we picked anything up off the tray our credit card would automatically be charged for the item.

Just as she had told us, sitting next to the TV in our room was a tray with a cord running out from the back; it was no doubt connected to the hotel's mini-bar inventory control system. From a safe distance, Karen and I leaned over the assortment. We were more interested in how the device worked than what was for sale. I contemplated what would happen if we accidentally bumped something off the tray. What if I tripped on the way to the bathroom in the middle of the night? Would we be leaving here with $378 worth of candy bars, cashews and single-serve screw off bottles of wine? We agreed to stay clear of the tray; all pillow fights, yoga stretches, bad dancing and general flailing around were restricted to the other side of the room.

Karen lingered over the tray. Between the Peanut M&Ms and the stubby can of Pringles was a shiny box with the words "Love Box" printed in red on top. She studied it intently.

I said, "Please don't touch the Love Box. If you do, we're going to be charged for it."

In a belligerent tone, she said, "I'm not going to touch it. Why would I touch it?" I went into the bathroom to brush my teeth. When I came out, Karen was sitting on the bed holding the Love Box. It was killing her to know what was inside. She shook it, smelled it and even tried to open it, but she was unable to because the box had a safety seal. That makes sense, right? The hotel needs to know when someone has been in the Love Box. I looked at the price list; the Love Box cost $16.80. Karen carefully put it back on the tray. I don't know if the hotel will charge us for the Love Box, but if they do, I want my $8.40 of love.

Your friend,
Matt

~.~.~.~.~.~.~

From: **Matt Smith**
Subject: **#22 – Zion National Park**
Date: **September 17, 2010**

Dear Bob and Sue,

Springdale got one of Karen's highest ratings for a town: "darling." I don't exactly know what *darling* means, but it makes Karen sound like my grandmother when she says it. Springdale, Utah is a three-hour drive northeast of Las Vegas. When we arrived at noon today, the temperature was in the mid-90s with not a cloud in the sky.

We parked at our hotel and took the free Springdale Shuttle to the Zion Canyon Visitor Center. After taking care of business in the visitor center, we took the park shuttle to the Zion Lodge, a few miles north on the park road. In 1997, the shuttle system was established to eliminate the area's nightmarish traffic and parking problems. The town of Springdale also has a shuttle system. The Springdale Shuttle stops at six locations in Springdale, and the Zion Canyon Shuttle loop stops at eight locations in the park. It's easy to hop on and off either, and the wait is usually never more than five to ten minutes for the next shuttle.

Since we got to the park earlier than planned, we had time to do some hiking. From a shuttle bus stop along the park road, we hiked to the Upper Emerald Pools, and then to The Grotto, about 3.5 miles total. Zion Canyon was an incredible sight today. The contrast of the red sandstone canyon walls against the blue sky and the green vegetation was stunning. The park shuttle took us from The Grotto to the visitor center, and from there we walked the couple of miles back to our hotel, checking out dinner options along the way.

Tomorrow we plan on hiking The Narrows, which is a section of the Virgin River that is a slot canyon, an especially narrow canyon where the opposing walls can be as close as 25 to 30 feet from each other. Much of the hike is in the river, which requires more preparation than usual. We need to plan on everything getting wet: clothes, camera, backpack – and everything in the backpack.

The Narrows can only be hiked when the river is low enough to be safe, which usually begins late summer. Since it's a slot canyon, there's no place to climb if the water rises quickly. Even if it isn't raining in the canyon, a thunderstorm 20 miles away can cause the river to rise dangerously. The forecast for southwestern Utah tomorrow is for clear weather. We should be okay.

There are several outfitters in Springdale whose main business is renting gear for this specific hike: water shoes, water socks, and walking sticks. We've spoken with several park rangers about the best footwear for hiking in the river, and they all said that water shoes don't provide enough support for a long hike. They recommended that we wear our hiking boots or thick-tread tennis shoes in the water. We're going to wear the hiking boots we brought with us.

I bought a waterproof Pelican case for my camera at one of the outfitters. I already have a large dry bag to carry our lunch and other stuff that we don't want to get wet. Trekking poles are a must on this hike; we brought our own from home. I think we're ready for The Narrows.

Your friend,
Matt

~.~.~.~.~.~.~

From: **Matt Smith**
Subject: **Zion day two – The Narrows hike**
Date: **September 18, 2010**

Dear Bob and Sue,

This morning we didn't get the early start I wanted, but we were early enough to beat the weekend crowd. We took the bus to the farthest stop north in the park, the Temple of Sinawava. Running north from the bus stop is a one-mile paved trail called the Riverside Walk. At the end of that trail, we started our hike in the river. It was 9:30am and the temperature in the canyon was in the 70s.

Even though all the trail descriptions say that the river *is* the trail, we kept looking for a path. We stood there, at the river's edge, not sure exactly where to go. Pretty soon it dawned on us that there were no choices, the canyon walls at that point were a couple of hundred feet apart. If there was a trail, we would have seen it. The only direction we could go was up river.

For the first 50 yards, we walked on the bank, trying not to get our feet wet. A couple of times we had no choice, so we tiptoed through shallow sections of the river that were a few inches deep. I tried to step past a deep spot and my foot slipped. The water came over the top of my ankle high hiking boots. Wow! The water was cold, even at the end of summer.

I looked up the canyon and saw it was narrower where we were headed. There were places with no riverbank at all. Karen and I looked at each other, and it finally sank in, *the river is the trail.*

There was no use putting it off. I intentionally stepped my other foot into the ankle deep water, and started walking down the center of the stream. Soon, I was knee-deep and struggling to keep my balance. We couldn't have done this hike without our trekking poles.

Looking back at Karen, I could see that she was still negotiating with the river. She was standing in ankle deep water, and looking at the options in front of her. Finally, she followed my lead and waded into the middle of the stream.

Once our shoes were thoroughly soaked, and we were wet up to our knees, we felt a sense of release. We forgot about trying to stay dry, and started enjoying the hike. When we stopped looking down at the river and began looking up at where we were going, we noticed the incredible views.

The light in the canyon was amazing. There was no

direct sunlight where we were because of the time of day and because we were at the bottom of a narrow canyon. Light reached the river by reflecting off the 2,000-foot high canyon walls. The sky reflected off the river; the river reflected light back onto the walls of the canyon. There were infinite shades of color, subtle and dramatic at the same time. The scene in front of us changed from moment to moment. Every bend in the river revealed another stunning view.

My waterproof case was clipped to my backpack at chest level. I was glad I had it. Without it, my camera would have gotten soaked. I was also glad that I brought a dry bag on the hike. Before the hike, I'd taken everything out of my backpack, put our essentials in the dry bag, and then placed the dry bag in my backpack. Even if I went under, our lunch and extra clothes would stay dry.

We kept making our way up river. There were places where it was too deep and swift to walk through. Fortunately in these spots there was just enough riverbank for us to climb around the deep sections. There were a few spots, though, where we weren't sure we would be able to make it any farther up river.

At one of these spots I was ahead of Karen. I was trying to find a way forward that didn't involve the river going above my waist. The water was swift and smooth; it tugged at my legs. I couldn't see the river bottom. With my trekking pole, I tested the depth around me. In every direction it seemed deeper than where I stood, including from where I just came. How could that be? The next step brought the river to my waist. I took a deep breath instantly; I hoped to keep the boys dry for the entire hike. So much for that idea. I took another step, and another deep breath. Easing my hiking boots over what felt like slippery bowling balls, I secured each foot before lifting a trekking pole off the riverbed. One foot then one pole. I remembered the ranger telling us yesterday, "Keep at least three points firmly planted at all times."

I continued easing my way up the river. Karen was somewhere behind me. I didn't hear a yelp or scream, so I assumed she was still mostly above water. I began to think that maybe I would make it to a shallow spot without going under. A few more steps and I was dry, standing on a boulder in the middle of the river. I turned toward Karen. She was moving through the waist-deep section I just came through. She almost went down, caught herself, then another near fall. Between wobbles, she looked up at me with a smile and mouthed the words, "I love this."

We hiked about 4.5 miles up the river from where we first entered the water. There was never a point where we were forced to turn back because the river was impassable, only places where it was challenging to keep from going in over our heads. Neither of us got dunked. We won a small victory over the river.

While we were still hiking up river, a solo hiker caught up with us. He was soaked and carrying a wooden hiking pole about six feet tall. His backpack was running like a faucet. When he got to within 30 feet of us, he slipped and went completely under the water. Before I could think about helping him, his head came up. His mouth was wide-open taking in a big breath. He walked another ten feet and went under again. He'd gotten comfortable with letting the river win; it looked like he'd been going under all morning. As he walked passed us, he smiled and said, "How's it going," as if we were passing each other coming out of a Starbucks. He was having a great hike.

The sun was at its highest point about the time we stopped to rest and eat lunch. It was one of the few times on the hike we were in direct sunlight. It felt good after being in the cool water. After lunch, we turned around and started back toward home.

We saw very few people during the hike until we got to within a mile of the Riverside Walk on our return. Being a weekend and a hot sunny day, the river attracted a crowd. What was a peaceful, secluded hike turned into a crowded noisy scene. This didn't bother us; we had a great hike and were tired and satisfied. All we could think about was plowing through the crowd to get to the bus and back to our hotel room, so we could collapse.

The last quarter mile of the hike was crazy. There were people in the river unprepared to be there. We had sturdy shoes and trekking poles, and *we* almost went under a hundred times. How did these people think they were going to make it up river? Karen almost had a heart attack when we passed a man carrying a baby who looked to be about six-months old. He was holding the baby close to his chest and straining to look over the baby's head to see where to put his foot next to keep from falling. We had to look away and just keep moving. Many, many people were in the river with expensive cameras around their necks. We're sure that at least a few of those cameras went under today.

The prize for the strangest sight went to the old guy in the middle of the river, water halfway up his legs and with no shoes on, with a walker! Yep, I saw my future right there. Just because you need a walker doesn't mean you can't hike in the river. Good for him.

We rode the bus back to town soaked and sitting butt to butt with people who were dry and wondering where we had been. It felt good to get back to our hotel and into dry clothes. The temperature on my keychain thermometer read 100 degrees. I took our socks and hiking boots and laid them in the sun on the sidewalk outside our room. I pulled the insoles out so they would dry faster. As hot as it was, I thought they would dry enough to be wearable by tomorrow. Forty-five minutes later, they were bone dry, inside and out.

We were too tired to look for a place to eat dinner. Last night we ate carryout pizza in our hotel room. There was plenty left for dinner tonight, but no way to heat it; our room doesn't have a microwave. Karen, without hesitating, took the leftover pizza out of the small refrigerator in our room and went outside. She placed the pizza, still in its foil, on the dashboard of our car and shut the door. After about 15 minutes in the car, the pizza was warm and ready to eat. This is one of the many reasons I married her.

Your friend,
Matt

~.~.~.~.~.~.~

From: **Karen Smith**
Subject: **#23 – Bryce Canyon National Park**
Date: <u>**September 19, 2010**</u>

Dear Bob and Sue,

On our way into Bryce Canyon National Park, we stopped to take our picture by the park sign like we always do. While Matt was setting up the camera on our mini tripod, we heard a crackling sound like a fire. Climbing to the top of a small hill next to the sign, we were shocked to see a forest fire burning 100 yards away. It wasn't a large fire -- the burnt area was about the size of a football field -- but it was startling to see the park on fire! We ran to our car to drive to the visitor center to report the fire as a ranger pulled into the parking lot. In a panic, gesturing wildly, we told him about the fire. As he picked lint off his sleeve, he said, "Yeah, thanks, we know about it. We let the little ones burn themselves out."

We drove to the visitor center anyway; we had to get the stamp, buy postcards and change our underwear. Then, after consulting the map, we headed toward the area called the amphitheater. The first mile past the visitor center took us through an ordinary landscape, with no sign of the magical place that lay just east of the main park road. We turned off at the sign for the lodge and parked in one of their parking lots. As we walked toward the rim of the canyon, I felt the same anticipation that I felt the first time I walked to the edge of the Grand Canyon. And the view into this canyon did not disappoint. It may not have the size of the Grand Canyon, but its every bit as jaw dropping.

Until this trip, I had never heard of Bryce Canyon NP, or the hoodoos that make it famous. It's hard to describe a hoodoo because each is a unique sandstone rock formation taking the shape of a spire, a steeple or castle wall. They reminded me of the Magic Rocks crystal growing kit I had as a kid. Standing on the rim, facing east, the view from north to south is spectacular, hoodoos as far as the eye can see. After taking a million pictures, we hiked down into the amphitheater and did the Navajo/Queens combination loop, a total of three miles. It was 70 degrees and sunny, but very windy.

Struggling back up to the rim (I could feel every foot of the 8000 ft. elevation), we walked along the rim trail from Sunrise Point to Sunset Point. We watched crowds of foreign tourists, most of them speaking French or German, take pictures of themselves in various poses: balancing on the narrow edges of precipices, dangling over the rim hanging on to a tree root, and other feats of stupidity.

Before we headed out, we went to look at Bryce Canyon Lodge, which sits about 200 yards back from the rim. Built in 1924, it's the type of historic park lodge that we love to stay in: stone facade, massive log beams and a very cool, steeply pitched roof with a rippled shingle pattern. Unfortunately we'd been trying for months to get a room or cabin there, with no luck. We asked again at the reservation desk if they had any cancellations, but the answer was still no.

We drove back to our hotel in Bryce Canyon City, located just outside the park entrance. Coming from Springdale, which is one of the cutest little towns on the planet, Bryce Canyon City was disappointing.

It's not obvious now, but the "city" has historical roots. In 1916, when tourism around Bryce Canyon was just beginning, Ruby Syrett built a lodge and cabins at this location. Syrett's business, Ruby's Inn, grew rapidly once the area became a national park in 1928. The community of Ruby's Inn officially became Bryce Canyon City in 2007 and the Syrett family still owns the land and businesses. It's a company town: one of the Syretts is both the company's board president and the mayor, a majority of the 138 year-round residents are members of the Syrett family, and nearly all the adult family members are employees of Ruby's Inn or its adjoining properties.

Situated on both sides of the highway leading into the park, the city consists of an RV park, a general store, some fake looking old-time western shops and several restaurants, all clustered around two hotels. There's the Best Western Plus Ruby's Inn, not to be confused with the Best Western Plus Bryce Canyon Grand Hotel across the street. Completing the picture are acres of asphalt filled with cars, trucks, motorcycles and busses.

When we asked the hotel desk clerk about a good place to have dinner, he gave us his best sales pitch to buy tickets for Ebenezer's Barn and Grill Cowboy Music Show, located in a building across the hotel parking lot. Tempting, but instead we picked up sandwiches at the Subway just outside town. We spent the rest of the evening back at the rim of the amphitheater watching the sun set. Matt had a very confusing conversation with a tourist who asked him if the best place to watch the sunset would be Sunset Point or Sunrise Point. Do you stand at Sunset Point to watch the sun set? Or does the sun set over Sunset Point and therefore you should stand at Sunrise Point to see it? We still haven't figured out which is correct.

Matt came up with a possible business opportunity for the four of us. He thinks we should buy some land just outside Bryce Canyon City, build a hotel and call it *Rudy's* Inn. He thinks we could give Ruby a run for his money. I think he just wants to be the president *and* the mayor.

Your friend,
Karen

~.~.~.~.~.~.~

From: **Matt Smith**
Subject: **#24 – Capitol Reef National Park**
Date: **September 20, 2010**

Dear Bob and Sue,

The first half of our day was spent back in Bryce Canyon. We hiked from Bryce Point to Peekaboo Loop, Navajo Loop, Wall Street and then back to Bryce Point along the Rim Trail. The entire hike was a six-mile round trip. Peekaboo Loop gets its name from the small natural arches along the trail that frame views of hoodoos in the distance. There isn't another place that I can compare to the Bryce Canyon Amphitheater. The colors, the light, and the unusual rock formations are one-of-a-kind.

After our morning hike, we drove to the south end of the park and hiked the Bristlecone Loop Trail. Bristlecone pine trees are among the oldest living things on the planet; many are more than 3,000 years old. It's amazing they can live so long in this harsh climate and at such high altitudes (this trail was at 9,100 feet elevation).

We ate our lunch amongst the Bristlecones, and then drove two hours to Capitol Reef National Park just outside Torrey, Utah. Capitol Reef is long and skinny, running mostly north and south for 60 miles. In many places, it's only a few miles wide. One of its main features is the 65-million-year-old Waterpocket Fold in the southern half of the park. It's an odd geological formation with a jumble of cliffs and canyons. The park also has many examples of ancient human activity (petroglyphs) and more recent human activity, the abandoned Mormon settlement of Fruita.

We took care of business at the visitor center a few miles inside the park along Highway 24. I was interested in finding out where we could see petroglyphs in the park. There's a clearly marked pull-off along Highway 24 where we could walk to see some, but I wanted to know if there were any others. I asked the ranger at the information desk, "Are there any other petroglyphs in the park besides the ones on Highway 24?"

He said, "Yeah, lots."

"Can you tell us where they are?"

"No."

"You can't tell us where they are?"

"No, I can't."

I think this ranger was more comfortable with trees and rocks than with people. I switched to open ended questions.

"Why can't you tell us where the petroglyphs are?"

"Because people will vandalize them if they know where they are."

That was a fair response. But did we look like the kind of people who would draw boobs and wieners next to ancient petroglyphs? Maybe Karen.

The ranger began to warm up to us. He pulled out a map and showed us where a couple of petroglyph sites were farther down the highway. He said, "I think it's okay to tell you about these." He looked at another ranger standing next to him and asked, "Isn't it?" She didn't say a word; she just shook her head quickly back and forth.

"Oh well, you didn't hear it from me."

The area where the visitor center is located is called the Fruita Historic District. It's named after a Mormon settlement that started in 1880. The settlers planted orchards that now have about 2,700 trees. The last residents moved out in 1969, and the National Park Service now maintains the orchards. There was a sign on the desk that read, "Orchards #1 and #18 open 9/20."

"What does that mean, 'Orchards #1 and #18 are open?'" I asked the ranger.

"There are 22 orchards in the park, and when the fruit is ripe they are open to the public for U-pick. It costs a $1 a pound, and you pay by the honor system. Orchards #1 and #18 are apple orchards, and they're open today. Number 8 will be open tomorrow."

After taking care of business in the visitor center, Karen

and I picked apples. Well, I picked the apples, and Karen rejected most of them. She said they had wormholes. I told her that we could eat around the wormholes, but she was worried the worms would still be inside. Instead, she threw the apples to the two deer that were hanging around waiting to eat the ones we dropped. I tried to get Karen to pet one of the deer. She said, "No, they're dirty and probably have deer ticks." She really isn't a big deer fan, unless it's a baby.

In Torrey, we checked into the Best Western. Our room is nothing special, but the view out our window is incredible. I suggested to Karen that we go to a different orchard tomorrow and pick apples again. She replied, "God help us." She pointed out that we couldn't possibly eat all the apples I already picked. She said, "You just want to pick apples because it's fun." I'd forgotten that we're not here to have fun. Tomorrow we'll hike in the desert instead.

Your friend,
Matt

~.~.~.~.~.~.~.~

From: **Matt Smith**
Subject: **Capitol Reef day two**
Date: **September 21, 2010**

Dear Bob and Sue,

The weather was perfect this morning. It was sunny and in the 60s. We hiked the Chimney Rock loop and Spring Canyon trail in Capitol Reef National Park for a total of 8.5 miles. We didn't see another person on the hike. The canyon was beautiful. The trail was a dry riverbed through a deep canyon with red rock walls. It was obvious that fast moving water once ran through the canyon; the rocks were smoothed over like those from a mountain stream. Some were black volcanic rocks. The contrast of the black and red rocks was striking. It looked like a landscape architect planned the color scheme in the canyon. We looked for petroglyphs as we hiked but didn't see any.

After the hike, we drove to the roadside petroglyph viewing area along Highway 24. It was an unfortunate example of how people will deface ancient petroglyphs if given the chance. One of the thousand-year-old sheep drawn on the rocks had a cartoon voice bubble over its head letting the world know "Amanda luvs Josh." This is why the park rangers won't tell visitors where the petroglyphs are.

Despite Karen's objection to me having fun, we picked apples again today; this time in orchard #8. The apples were better today than yesterday. They were bigger and had no wormholes. There were no deer today, just RVers walking their dogs and watching us try not to fall off the three-legged fruit picking ladders.

We stopped and talked with a couple that lives full-time in their RV. In the summer, they drive all over the country, staying for a week or two at a time in one place then moving on. In the winter, they park their RV in the desert of Arizona along with thousands of other RVers, and hangout in the warmer climate until the weather improves up north. That lifestyle sounds tempting, but I would want to test-drive it for a season or two before selling everything and moving into a house on wheels.

Most people just drive through Capitol Reef National Park. It's difficult to get to many regions of the park because of the park's odd shape. This may not be as popular as the other Utah national parks, but the Fruita Historic District is a welcome relief from the surrounding desert. It has an oasis feel to it with plenty of trees and some nice RV campgrounds. It would be a pleasant place to spend a few more days and explore if we had the time, but we don't. Tomorrow we go to Moab.

Your friend,
Matt

~.~.~.~.~.~.~

From: **Karen Smith**
Subject: **#25 – Arches National Park**
Date: **September 22, 2010**

Dear Bob and Sue,

Wind and erosion have carved more than 2,000 natural sandstones arches in Arches National Park. The park service considers any opening larger than three feet in all directions an arch; anything smaller is just a hole. (I know this sounds like something Matt made up, but it's true.) Matt was confused. "They're all holes," he said. "Why are the big holes more important than the small holes? And why do they call a big hole an arch? It's just a hole – that's big."

I said, "Because Big Hole National Park would be a stupid name." That seemed to satisfy him.

This morning, we drove from Torrey to Moab, where we will be visiting both Arches and Canyonlands National Parks over the next four days. We went straight to Arches, five miles north of Moab, and took care of our park business. When we talked to a park ranger about signing up for the ranger-led Fiery Furnace hike, he told us that they were sold out through Friday, and there were only two spots left on Saturday. He said this hike is so popular that it usually fills up weeks in advance, so we were lucky to get the last two reservations.

It was not noon yet, but the sky was turning dark. Rain was on the way, so we decided to do a quick hike to Delicate Arch, which is only a three mile round trip. Towering 80 feet, Delicate Arch is one of the highlights of the park. It's billed as the most beautiful and most photographed arch in the world. It's an icon in Utah; it's even on the Utah state license plates.

We took a short side-trip on the way to Delicate Arch to view a Ute petroglyph panel depicting horses and a bighorn sheep hunt. It was one of the best petroglyph panels we've seen. Someone carved this hunting scene into stone hundreds of years ago, but the bright color of the underlying sandstone was still crisp and clear against the dark surrounding rock. Matt was sure these petroglyphs were made more recently; they looked a little too Disney to be ancient.

Petroglyphs can be dated by measuring the age of the rock varnish on the surface of the carved figures. Rock varnish is darker than the underlying stone and is caused by oxidation of elements in the stone. Once fresh rock is exposed – like it is when a figure is carved into the stone – new rock varnish begins to form. By measuring the age of the oxidation on the figures, the age of the petroglyph can be determined.

The hike to Delicate Arch was easy, although we got slightly lost for about five minutes. There was a group of older hikers right behind us. We accidentally led them down the wrong trail with us. They thought we knew where we were going. Even though you can *see* the arch from miles away, if you're not careful to follow the cairns, you won't be able to *get* to the arch. We had to backtrack a bit, find the cairn that we missed, and continue down the correct path. Our followers grumbled. Every few minutes we could hear them behind us asking one another, "Are we sure we're going the right way?" Matt wanted to lead them astray again, this time on purpose, for doubting him, but I nixed that idea. I wanted to get to the arch and back to the car before it started raining.

Delicate Arch lives up to its billing; it's a beautiful sight. They say this hike competes with Devil's Garden as the best hike in the Park. We'll be checking out Devil's Garden on Friday.

After the hike, a huge thunderstorm rolled in, so we hung out in Moab and visited art galleries and outfitters. Moab is packed with people; every hotel in the city is sold out. Our hotel desk clerk told us that it's busy like this nine months a year. The city's main industry is outdoor adventure. Everywhere you look, there are signs for hot air balloon tours, jeep tours, river rafting, bicycle tours, rock climbing and canyoneering, scenic flights, skydiving, and horseback riding. The next adventure we have planned is to navigate the beer menu at the Moab Brewery.

Your friend,
Karen

~.~.~.~.~.~.~

From: **Matt Smith**
Subject: **#26 – Canyonlands National Park**
Date: **September 23, 2010**

Dear Bob and Sue,

Canyonlands National Park is near where Aron Ralston got his arm pinned between rocks and had to hack it off with a dull knife to free himself and save his life. I assured Karen that if she got her arm stuck today in Canyonlands I wouldn't need to hack; I always carry a knife sharpener in my backpack. There would be no 127 hours wasting away in the desert; we'd be back in time for dinner.

The northern section of the park is a 45-minute drive from Moab. The Colorado and Green rivers meet in the center of the park forming a "V" shaped plateau. This section of the park is called the "Island in the Sky" because the canyons of the rivers – one to the east and one to the west – have left a high plateau in the center. It's like two Grand Canyons coming together in the middle of the park.

Today we hiked in the Island in the Sky section of the park. After stopping at the visitor center and getting hiking tips from a ranger, we set out at 9:15am on the Lathrop Trail. We hiked from the park road to the rim of the canyon overlooking the Colorado River to the east. It rained heavily yesterday, but today was sunny and in the 60s. When we started our hike, the trail was muddy, but drying quickly. The colors of the vegetation and rocky landscape were brilliant because of the recent rain; it was a spectacular morning.

About an hour into the hike, I noticed hoof prints on the trail. I was taking a picture of the prints right at my feet when I looked up to see a bighorn sheep standing like a statue 20 feet from me. He walked a few yards away from us, and then stood there for a few seconds staring at Karen and I. Suddenly he snorted, and took off like a shot, running away from us. He must have finally caught our scent. With my camera, I got a good video of him running away. Karen said, "Wow. He's a good runner."

I said, "They're all good runners. The slow ones get eaten."

We kept hiking along the Lathrop Trail expecting to see more wildlife, but we didn't. We saw other fresh prints in the soft, sandy mud that looked like paw prints of a cat – a *big* cat like a mountain lion. I kept imagining that it was following us. We would be easier to bring down than a bighorn sheep.

When we reached the edge of the canyon, the hike dropped a couple of hundred feet below the rim and snaked along the canyon wall. To one side of the trail we could see for dozens of miles to the southeast, following the path of the

Colorado River. The morning sun was in our eyes, but the overlook to the river was still amazing. Through my binoculars, I could see Jeeps in the distance driving the backcountry roads down by the river. A couple of miles later, we turned back. At the car, my GPS said we hiked 8.5 miles.

Karen didn't like the fact that there wasn't a single flush toilet in this section of the park. There were only outhouses at the visitor center, and because the smell was overwhelming Karen opted to take care of business outside while we were hiking. She really has come a long way since we started this journey: carrying her own backpack and peeing in the wilderness.

A few miles farther south on the park road (Highway 313), we parked and walked to Mesa Arch. Mesa Arch is one of the most beautiful arches in Utah. I think it's on par with Delicate Arch. We were shocked to see people climbing on top of it: dancing, jumping up and down and posing for pictures in stupid positions. In Arches National Park, the park service doesn't allow people to climb on the arches, but in Canyonlands they do. Not sure why. It's too beautiful a formation to have people crawling all over it.

Mesa Arch was crowded, and many of the people there traveled a long distance to see this particular arch. They didn't want to wait all day to take a picture of the arch without someone standing on top of it holding his crotch. When the group that had been messing around on top of the arch finally moved on, I started to take a picture. But before I was able to, a woman sat in the middle of the arch to have her picture taken. No big deal – except she wouldn't leave.

She sat there with her head resting at an angle in her hand while her husband took her picture countless times. Besides the fact that it's just plain wrong to pose for a picture with your head resting in your hands, there were a dozen people waiting to take a quick picture of the arch. The woman could clearly see that she was holding everyone up, but she stayed there and kept changing poses. We gave it ten minutes, and then started back toward the car. Many other people gave up also. I have a message for the park service, "Rope this one off!"

After lunch, we did two more hikes, Upheaval Dome and Murphy Point. In total, we hiked more than 14 miles today. We had extra energy, so we kept going. I like it when we hike that much during the day because then I can eat as much pizza as I want at night. We're going to Zax for dinner. They have an all-you-can eat pizza buffet.

Back in Moab we needed to find a store to buy aloe vera gel for Karen's sunburned legs. She forgot to put sunscreen on them, and they got fried. She called them her "fried chicken legs." That sounds good; maybe tomorrow we'll get fried chicken instead of pizza.

Your friend,
Matt

~.~.~.~.~.~.~.~

From: **Matt Smith**
Subject: **Arches day two – Devil's Garden**
Date: **September 24, 2010**

Dear Bob and Sue,

We woke up today happy that it was Friday, but didn't know why. Every day is Friday for us. But we're still happy it's Friday.

We went back to Arches National Park today to do the eight-mile Devil's Garden hike. The trail leads to eight arches, the farthest being the Double O Arch. The hike got progressively harder as we went. We found ourselves scrambling over slick rocks and walking on narrow ledges with steep drop-offs. It was very windy, and the wind made parts of the hike even more intimidating.

There was a section of the hike that went over the ridge

of a rock formation called a sandstone fin. The initial step onto the fin was only a couple of feet high, but as the trail climbed, the flat surface where we could walk became narrower and the drop-offs on either side became deeper. At a point where the flat top of the fin was only a few feet wide, the drop-offs on either side were a couple of hundred feet. Finally, we had to step from rock to rock to get to the other side of the fin, so we could get back down to level ground. The steps across the rocks were only a couple of feet apart, but it was unnerving because the wind was gusting. We leaned into the wind to keep from being blown off the fin. Had the wind stopped suddenly, we could have fallen in the other direction. We got through that section without any problems, but I find it hard to believe the park service lets anyone do that hike without so much as a permit.

We saw bighorn sheep tracks on the trail, but didn't see any sheep. After seeing one in Canyonlands yesterday, we keep expecting to see another. You need to be on the trail early for the best wildlife viewing, before the other hikers scare off the animals for the day.

Several miles from the trailhead, we came upon two women sitting by a small pool of stagnant water that accumulated from the recent rains. The pool was about five feet in diameter and was right in the path of the established trail. As we approached the pool, one of the women came up to us and in a nervous tone said, "Watch out for the baby frogs." She directed us a few feet away from the pool, and around to the other side. We could see the tiny frogs hoping around the pool.

A group of six hikers approached quickly from the opposite direction. It took both women to slow them down and keep them from trampling the frogs. Just then, more hikers came from where we came. The women split up again. This is a popular hike, so I'm pretty sure they spent their entire day racing from side to side trying to keep the frogs from being stepped on. I wondered how long they could keep this up; they looked weary. Surely they weren't planning on coming back day-after-day to protect these baby frogs. Eventually they'll have to give up the cause.

After the Devil's Garden hike, we went looking for petroglyphs around Moab. At the information center in town, we bought a guide to petroglyphs in the area, many of which are not in the park. At the edge of town, across the road from the golf course, we saw several interesting petroglyphs. There was a rock wall not far from the end of someone's driveway with 20 or 30 drawings including *Moab Man*. *Moab Man* is a well-known petroglyph from the Fremont period, which puts it at 600 to 800 years old. It was right by the side of the road. I wonder how many are out in the wilderness that no one knows about.

Your friend,
Matt

~.~.~.~.~.~.~.~

From: **Karen Smith**
Subject: **Arches day three – Fiery Furnace**
Date: **September 25, 2010**

Dear Bob and Sue,

The Fiery Furnace is a twisted maze of canyons where hikers frequently get lost and can't find their way out; the trail is not marked. There are only two ways to hike the Fiery Furnace: with a ranger (strongly recommended) or by purchasing a permit. Most permits are issued to professional guides or hikers who have experience with this hike – like park rangers on their days off. Not wanting to get lost in any place with *fiery* or *furnace* in its name, we signed up for a ranger-led tour. The ranger at the visitor center told us the hike was challenging; it involves scrambling over and sliding down rocks, and passing through squeezes. A squeeze is a canyon so narrow that you can touch both sides of its opposing walls as you squeeze through.

There were 20 of us on the hike today, including our ranger, who looked us over carefully and made sure we'd followed the pre-hike instructions: sturdy hiking shoes or boots, at least one quart of water each and a backpack to put everything in so our hands would be free for climbing. She made us introduce ourselves and tell where we were from. It was interesting that six of the people on the hike were part of a singles RV club and knew one another. How well they knew one another, we didn't care to find out.

Our ranger was a botanist and herbalist. She passionately shared local plant information on our three-hour excursion. At one point, when our group stopped to listen to her tell us about a rare plant next to the trail, I inadvertently stood on a tree root that was growing across the path. Big mistake. The ranger scolded me as if I were 12, and then made an example of me in front of the entire group. She said that I just crushed the blood system of this thousand-year old tree, and may have killed it. Out of the corner of my eye, I could see Matt moving to the back of the crowd. He was trying to distance himself from me. Luckily, the ranger hadn't seen me yesterday when I was trying to get the mud off the bottom of my hiking boots by kicking them against a clump of tree roots over and over.

The three-hour hike was challenging in a fun way. There were several tight spots where we had to press our hands and feet against the opposing walls of the canyon to get up or down the trail. Matt became the designated *extra hand,* helping some of the older women (older than me) in difficult places. It was a snug fit; even on the most open parts of the trail the canyons were narrow. When we stopped to rest, we easily lost our bearings; everywhere we looked seemed like the direction we just came from. Without a guide, we would have been lost for days in there. However, being with a guide doesn't mean you won't get lost. Our ranger told us stories of hikers separating from their group – falling behind to take a photo or to briefly explore a side trail – and needing Search and Rescue to find them.

The scenery was spectacular. The area is named the Fiery Furnace not because it's hot, but because of the brilliant red and orange hues made when the sun hits it in the afternoon and evening. The color and light changed constantly as we snaked through the narrow passages. An occasional tree or bush provided stunning green contrasts against the rocks.

Besides the lecture about not kicking tree roots, we learned some other things from our botanist ranger. (Our favorite was that we should drink gin and tonics in the winter because the flavor for gin comes from juniper berries, which she believes prevents colds.) Also, we met interesting people from around the country who are living life to the fullest. John, an 83-year-old full-time RVer, was climbing over rocks and squeezing through holes like a kid. John was a retired trucker who had driven over a million miles during his career.

We rate this hike a nine out of ten. We had to deduct a point because the ranger did something that never fails to annoy us: she played guessing games with the group. As we made our way past countless arches, we played *"Guess what this arch is called?"*

She would point to an arch, and each of us had to guess its name.

"Rainbow Arch, Cupid's Arch, Fairy Arch?"

"No. It's an animal."

"Elephant Arch, Aardvark Arch, Alligator Arch?"

"No. Look closer. It's two of them, and they're kissing."

"Squirrel Arch (that was my guess), Possum Arch, Orangutan Arch?"

"No—it's Turtle Arch."

Of course it is. Matt was muttering under his breath, "How about you just tell us the name, so we don't have to listen to 19 people calling out stupid answers every time we get to another arch."

After the hike, we ate PB&J sandwiches and hiked on our own to a few more arches. We don't know or care what their names were. By late afternoon, Matt couldn't take any more arch pictures or look up any more arch names; he was arched out.

Our first trip to Utah won't be our last. It's an incredible place. We should come back here together sometime. You guys would love the parks. Tomorrow is a travel day; we're going to Baker, Nevada and Great Basin National Park.

Your friend,
Karen

~.~.~.~.~.~.~

From: **Matt Smith**
Subject: **#27 – Great Basin National Park**
Date: **September 26, 2010**

Dear Bob and Sue,

At the start of every trip, I buy a large bag of animal crackers. If there was more nutritional content in them, I could eat nothing but animal crackers for an entire trip. They are my dessert after every meal. It's a good thing we're near the end of this trip; I'm down to only arms and legs in my animal cracker bag.

Today we drove from Moab to Baker, Nevada. It was about a five-hour drive. This was the only day we allotted for Great Basin National Park, so we went straight into the visitor center inside the park, which is five miles west of the town of Baker.

When I stamped my passport, it bothered me that the Great Basin passport stamp was larger than the other park stamps. It's a monster. I'm not sure how that's going to look when I frame my entire passport stamp collection at the end of this journey.

We were surprised to see so many people at the visitor center in line to buy cave tour tickets. I didn't know until we got here that the main attraction is Lehman Cave. I told Karen that I wasn't going into a cave unless it was the *only* attraction in the park. Instead, we opted for a hike in the mountains, so we drove to the Wheeler Peak campgrounds at an elevation of 10,000 feet. On the way up, we saw stands of aspen trees with leaves that had already changed to yellow. That was a strange sight, given that only a few days ago we were cooking our hiking boots in 100-degree heat not far from here.

From the campgrounds, we hiked to the ancient Bristlecone Grove. The Bristlecone Pines in this grove are 3,000 years old. The park service knows this because they've taken core samples from the trunks of these trees and counted the rings. The tree that made our Picture of the Day today is 3,200 years old. It's odd that the oldest living plants on earth grow at such high elevation and are buried in snow for much of the year. Even when they're not buried in snow, they're exposed to high winds and a wide range of temperatures. Another mile or so past the Bristlecone Pines, we came to the foot of Rock Glacier, just below Wheeler Peak. It's the only glacier in the state of Nevada. It's not spectacular in size or to look at, but it's a glacier – in Nevada. It was better than being in a cave.

After the glacier hike, we drove out of the mountains and back to Baker, where there's a brand-new park visitor center. We went inside to see if their passport stamp was *normal* size. It wasn't. I started into a confusing conversation with the ranger about why their stamp was larger than the other park stamps when Karen gave me her "can we go now?" look. Go where? The visitor center was the only entertainment in town.

Baker, Nevada is a tiny town. It's microscopic. Population 68. The motel we are staying at, the Silver Jack, has seven rooms and a stray cat looking for a home. We sat outside, in front the Silver Jack, and drank beers while trying to catch up on email. The motel didn't have a wireless Internet connection, but a restaurant across the street, which had been out-of-business for three months, was still putting out a weak signal that wasn't password protected. In the course of an hour or so, I was able to catch sporadic episodes of signal strong enough to update my email account. By the time we opened our second beer, the stray cat was sitting in Karen's lap. It was staring at her with an "are you my mom?" look on its face. That was not a good sign. I distracted Karen by striking up a conversation with the owner about what was on his dinner menu.

The Silver Jack has a market and a small restaurant/bakery. Thankfully, the food at the restaurant was good since it was the only place to eat in town besides T&D's Restaurant / Lounge / Grocery store across the street. We ate pizza for dinner and a slice of sweet potato pumpkin pie for dessert. After dinner, we walked ten feet to the sitting area and sat on a loveseat amongst stacks of books and magazines while checking out the art for sale on the walls.

Karen liked the Silver Jack; she thought it was charming and authentic. She described our room as shabby-chic. I understood the shabby part, but I'm not sure where she saw the chic.

After dinner, we drove back into the park to look at the stars. This is one of the best areas in the country for stargazing. We parked along the road where we sat on the hood of our car and looked up at the Milky Way. It was amazing – no lights, no people, just us and the brilliant stars.

Tomorrow we're planning to drive back to Issaquah, 934 miles. Must get a good night's sleep tonight. I think Karen is planning to sneak the cat into the car, so she can take him home with us.

Your friend,
Matt

~.~.~.~.~.~.~

From: **Karen Smith**
Subject: **Cannonball!**
Date: **September 27, 2010**

Dear Bob and Sue,

Today was the last day of our current road trip. We had to drive all day to get home from Baker, Nevada. Cannonball!

Since you declined our offer to crisscross the country with us, I thought you might like to know what it's like to be living the dream. A road trip with Matt at the wheel is tiring – for both of us. I made the mistake of saying this to him once. To that he replied, "Really? You're getting tired sitting over there looking out the window, are you? Maybe we should pull off the road and rest until you have enough strength to go on." I think he was joking, but I'm not totally sure.

I started jotting down notes about what it's like to travel with Matt. It's only fair you know these things in case you change your mind, and decide to join us on our next trip.

1. When Matt says "Cannonball!" it means he's not stopping the car until we get there. Of course, we have to stop for gas, so the gas station is where we do all of our business: use the bathroom, stretch our legs, buy snacks, and eat all our meals. Shell, Conoco 76, Flying J Travel Plaza – fine dining at its best. Matt always says to me, "Get whatever you want."

2. Just as I start to read a book, Matt turns to me and says, "Let's visit." Translated this means, "I'm bored, and you need to entertain me." The problem is, when two people are together 24 hours a day, every day, rarely is there anything new to talk about. There's no point in telling him about my day because he's had the exact same day. No matter what the experience, he probably also saw it, did it, felt it, smelled it. There are times when he turns to me and says, "Let's visit" that my mind goes blank.

3. In our boredom, we resort to playing stupid games. Just north of Jerome, Idaho we smelled onions. We were pretty sure the onion smell wasn't coming from us, even

though we'd been on the road for 23 days. Soon, onions began appearing on the side of the road. There weren't many, one or two here and one or two there. This went on for a couple of hundred miles; we played Spot the Onion for hours. When we got to Boise, it was raining onionskins. Eventually, ahead of us, we saw the source. It was an open top produce truck filled with onions. Every time it hit a bump a few onions would pop out. Matt finally passed the onion truck, and that was the end of our fun for the day.

4. If I doze off, Matt wakes me because it's my job to keep him awake. He says, "How can you keep me awake if you're asleep?" When I ask him how he would like me to keep him awake, he says, "Let's visit." I've found that scratching his back helps pep him up, but my arm gets tired after about ten seconds. Whenever I stop, he says his back itches more than when I started, and he goes into this weird spasm. He really should let me drive part of the way, so we can each rest while the other drives. When I offer to drive he says, "OK, as soon I lose feeling in both legs."

Sound like fun? When would you like to join us? We have some long days of driving in Texas coming up in October. How about it? Cannonball!

Your friend,
Karen

~.~.~.~.~.~.~

From: **Matt Smith**
Subject: **Travel day – to Bar Harbor**
Date: **October 11, 2010**

Dear Bob and Sue,

We've been staying at Karen's sister's house in Portland, Maine for the past few days, sleeping on a pullout couch just off the kitchen. Karen's sister has two dogs: a small bug-eyed dog named Henry with a Donald Trump comb-over and a one-year-old German Shepherd named Finn who weighs 85 pounds. Finn is an affectionate dog. Every morning, he jumps in our bed and bites my ears. This morning after I showered, Finn licked my head before I could stop him. All day I smelled like dog spit.

This morning, we drove three hours from Portland to Bar Harbor, where we're staying while we visit Acadia National Park. We ate lunch at a restaurant in town. It wasn't our usual peanut butter and jelly sandwiches out of the back of the car. Today was our "getting the lay of the land day," so instead of hiking we drove through the park along the Park Loop road, around Cadillac Mountain and past Jordan Pond House.

Jordan Pond House is a restaurant inside the park that's famous for its popovers. We ate there years ago, and after having tea and popovers, we bought a popover pan in their gift shop. We thought we would make popovers every day once we were home. We made them once. I suspect most people who buy the popover pan have a similar experience. The popover pan never makes it out of the cupboard except for a final trip to Goodwill. Karen says Goodwill is the graveyard for popover pans.

After the drive through the park, we ate dinner at a local pub, The Thirsty Whale. Then we wandered into the Morning Glory Bakery five minutes before their closing time. The woman behind the counter wasn't happy to see us. She was closing shop and already removed the signs identifying all the baked goods. We pointed to each item one by one and asked what it was. Karen and I both chose a couple of things. When it was time to pay, I asked Karen to fish for change in her purse. I like paying in exact change. Karen always says she has no money, but she can pull endless amounts of change from the bottom of her purse. I paid with six singles, four dimes, two blonde hairs and a Tic-Tac.

After the bakery, we walked through town, took a picture of the six-foot lobster in front of the ice cream store, and went back to our hotel. Tomorrow we plan to hike in the park.

Your friend,
Matt

~.~.~.~.~.~.~.~

From: **Matt Smith**
Subject: **#28 – Acadia National Park**
Date: **October 12, 2010**

Dear Bob and Sue,

This morning we woke up to a cloudy day. We struggled to get going. Karen said, "We're like bears; the cooler shorter days are making us want to hibernate." I asked her if she had put on extra weight to make it through the long winter. She didn't appreciate my question. Apparently, she's the only one allowed to compare herself to a bear.

Our plan for the day was to hike to the top of Cadillac Mountain. On the drive to the trailhead, I could sense Karen slipping into a "let's blow off the hike and go for popovers" mood. I knew if I didn't nip this in the bud, I would find myself in a Bar Harbor gift store shopping for dishtowels with drawings of lighthouses on them. There would be no popovers, or blueberry fudge, or lobster-shaped Christmas ornaments this morning; we were going for a hike.

At 9:30am we parked our car at the Cadillac Mountain trailhead by the Blackwoods campgrounds in Acadia National Park. The lower section of the hike took us through a thick forest. The ground was rocky. Mount Desert Island is mostly a granite outcropping covered with a thin layer of soil. Cadillac Mountain granite is my favorite color of granite, dark red with speckles of black. We saw a lot of it today, of course, hiking to the top of its namesake.

Once we climbed out of the treed section of the trail we started to get better views of the surrounding area. The sun was trying to come out. Occasionally we had good views of the ocean and the portion of the mountain we'd already climbed. Cadillac Mountain is a moderately strenuous hike; it's a 7.5-mile round trip with an elevation gain from sea level of 1,500 feet.

We were both glad we didn't blow off the hike. Since we're trying to visit so many parks in a limited amount of time, we don't have the luxury of waiting for perfect conditions. In Cuyahoga Valley, we hiked in muggy 90+ degrees. In Glacier Bay, we stood in the rain on the boat tour. In Olympic, we hiked along the beach in a cold fog. We have to show up and do it. Overall we've been lucky with the weather; The Narrows hike in Zion could not have been better.

The second half of the hike up the mountain was mostly on bare granite with short sections passing through trees or bushes. There were only a few people on the trail. When we got to the top, the sun came out as if on cue. We had clear views of the entire south side of the island. It seemed like we were alone in the wilderness, until we were startled by a noise that sounded like a bus. We hiked a few more yards and through the trees saw a sightseeing trolley drive by. There, in the middle of the wilderness, at the top of Cadillac Mountain, was a parking lot. A woman strolled past us in gold sequin shoes. She was walking a dog that I doubt could have passed my two-pound test. It had pink bows in its ears. I don't remember seeing them on the hike up the mountain. They probably came on the trolley.

As soon as we started back down the trail, we got the wilderness feeling back. An hour and a half later we were at our car. The morning was a success; we had a great hike, and we didn't buy any useless crap.

With half the day left, we drove to Jordan Pond House and parked so we could walk the carriage roads. The park has 45 miles of carriage roads built by the Rockefellers between 1913 and 1940. John D. Rockefeller, Jr. wanted to travel through Mount Desert Island by horse, so he had the carriage roads constructed as motor-free byways. They are still motor-free today. The roads were carefully planned to follow the gentle contours of the land, so that they disturbed as few trees and hillsides as possible in their construction. There are 17 bridges that are part of the carriage road system. Each is faced with native granite, so that it blends naturally into the landscape. They are beautiful roads; we'll have to come back someday and hike or bike the length of the system.

Today is our last day in Maine. In two days, we fly to Washington D.C., where we will spend a few days with family. Then on Sunday, we plan to drive to Shenandoah National Park, and spend two nights at Big Meadows Lodge inside the park.

Your friend,
Matt

~.~.~.~.~.~.~

From: **Matt Smith**
Subject: **#29 – Shenandoah National Park**
Date: **October 17, 2010**

Dear Bob and Sue,

There were so many motorcycles in Shenandoah National Park today it looked like a Viagra convention. We spent the weekend at my sister Sheila and her husband Carl's house in Arlington, Virginia. This morning, Karen, Sheila, and I drove from there to the park. October is a gorgeous time of year to visit Shenandoah; the temperatures are mild, and the trees are in full fall color. The biker crowd certainly thinks so.

After our ritual at the visitor center, we drove to Matthews Arm Campground and hiked to Overall Run Falls. There was a sign at the trailhead clearly indicating no dogs are allowed on the trail. We saw six dogs in the 6.5 miles we hiked. We saw two other dogs that looked liked they weighed less than two pounds, so we didn't include them in the official count.

About a mile into our hike, I heard a loud snap of a branch. I stopped, hoping we would have a wildlife sighting. Karen and Sheila walked slowly toward me looking into the woods. Sheila whispered, "What is it?" I told them I heard a sound but didn't know what it was. Sheila said, "I hope it isn't a Saskatchewan." I think she meant Sasquatch, but even so, I assured her there were no large Canadian provinces lurking in the woods.

We've been traveling and staying with family for most of the past 12 days. I've enjoyed it, but it's been tiring. Today, when we got on the trail, it felt good to be hiking. I felt like I was home again.

We drove to Big Meadows Lodge where we had reservations for the night. Wanting to get another hike in before dark, we were anxious about how long it was taking to check in. I could hear the man in front of us talking to the hotel clerk.

"Do them rooms have TVs?"

"Yes they do."

"Them TVs get ball games?"

I wanted to interrupt and say "How would she know if them TVs get ballgames, let's move it along," but with the baseball playoffs and Sunday Night Football on tonight I wanted to hear the answer. She didn't know if them TVs get ballgames.

Our room was in a two-story block of 20 rooms that overlook the valley into West Virginia. Sheila's room was one half of a freestanding cabin with a working fireplace and firewood by the front porch. We put our things in our rooms and went for another hike. The trail beside Sheila's cabin connected to the Appalachian Trail about 100 yards into the forest. While hiking along the AT, I thought about all the hikers who successfully through-hiked the entire 2,000 plus miles of the trail, each coming through this very section of trail.

We hiked to the Big Meadow across Skyline Drive then looped back toward the lodge from where we started. A quarter of a mile from the lodge, we saw six deer. Several people stopped to look at them and take pictures. We stopped also; we didn't want to barrel through the scene scaring off the deer and pissing off the onlookers.

While we were standing there being polite, one of the deer raised up on its hind legs. A moment later, another deer went up on its hind legs. They slapped at each other with their front legs like a couple of kids splashing each other in a pool. Then they stopped and loped off into the trees. I'd never seen anything like that before. I could tell Karen enjoyed this rare wildlife display, but she hid her enjoyment because she had earlier declared she wasn't going to get excited about deer anymore.

We ate dinner in the Big Meadows Lodge dining room. Karen and Sheila snuck a bottle of red wine into the restaurant. Their plan was to drink it out of the paper coffee cups they brought from their rooms. Our waiter sniffed out their plan quickly and informed them that guests were not allowed to bring alcohol into the restaurant. They each ordered a glass of wine, and promised the waiter they would keep their wine bottle on the floor next to their purses while we ate. By the end of dinner, the wine bottle was half empty.

After dinner, we walked back to Sheila's room with our half empty wine bottle and unused paper cups. Outside, a lodge employee on a cigarette break saw us and shouted "You are *not* going to drink that wine out of those paper cups. Jesus! Stay right there." He dashed into the restaurant. Ten seconds later he returned and handed us three wine glasses saying, "I can't believe you were going to use paper cups." Now that's customer service.

For about an hour, I tried to start a fire in Sheila's cabin. I never got a fire going; the chimney wouldn't draw. Everything in her room smelled like smoke by the time we left and went to bed.

Tomorrow we're spending another day in Shenandoah. Carl is joining us for a hike.

Your friend,
Matt

~.~.~.~.~.~.~.~

From: **Matt Smith**
Subject: **Shenandoah day two**
Date: **October 18, 2010**

Dear Bob and Sue,

By mid-morning, Carl had arrived from Arlington, and we were at Fishers Gap Overlook: the start of the four-mile Rose River Loop hike. The weather was mild. It was partly sunny with temperatures in the 50's. A mile into the hike, we met two hikers with a Jack Russell Terrier. They asked us if we saw the bear; we hadn't. They said they saw a bear cub a few minutes earlier, on the section of trail we just hiked. The park's literature says Shenandoah National Park has one of the highest concentrations of black bears in the eastern United States.

About halfway through our morning hike, we passed a group of hikers that included a man who looked to be in his 60's. He was wearing a business suit and black dress shoes.

We were at least a couple of miles from the trailhead, but by all appearances, he was enjoying himself as much as the rest of his group. By 12:30pm, we completed our loop by returning to Fishers Gap Overlook; it was lunchtime.

We grabbed the last available picnic table at the Big Meadows wayside. A group of Korean women had an elaborate spread of food laid out across two picnic tables. There was enough food for 20 people. The group consisted of twelve women and one man; he was their bus driver. The women kept hovering around him and putting food on his plate. I caught his eye and he smiled back at me. He knew he had a sweet deal.

Sheila and Carl got to experience our PB&J lunch routine. Carl said he was going "Elvis style" by putting trail mix between his peanut butter and jelly. Carl is on the South Beach Diet. When we finished our sandwiches, Carl disappeared into the wayside snack shop to "find a restroom." He was gone for 20 minutes. I think I saw him eating an ice cream sandwich behind the bundles of firewood.

Our afternoon hike was to Rapidan Camp, a 3.8-mile round trip. Rapidan Camp was President Herbert Hoover's presidential summer retreat. Many of the original buildings are gone, but the Prime Minister's Cabin and The Brown House are still intact and maintained by the National Park Service. The Prime Minister's Cabin has interpretive exhibits inside. The Brown House, a few yards away, is only accessible to the public by way of a ranger-led tour.

I asked the volunteer ranger why it was named The Brown House. She asked me why *I* thought it was named The Brown House. Rather than saying, "If I knew I would not have asked!" I made a lame guess, so we could move on to the answer. She said, "Well, the President already had a White House, so he named this The Brown House." Yep, I felt stupid for asking.

Her husband, who is also a volunteer ranger, gave us a tour of The Brown House. He did a fantastic job telling us the history of the Hoovers and Rapidan Camp. This was one of the most interesting tours we've taken in the national parks. He explained that Hoover did not accept a salary for being President, and he paid for the land and construction of The Brown House with his own money. After leaving office, Hoover donated The Brown House to the federal government for future Presidents to use as a summer retreat. President Franklin D. Roosevelt, who despised Hoover, did not want anything to do with The Brown House. He persuaded Congress to fund the construction – during the Great Depression – of another presidential retreat. Later, President Eisenhower named the new camp after his son David. Camp David has been the summer retreat for presidents ever since.

We've had a great trip to see the national parks in the northeast, but we're ready to go home. Tomorrow we fly back to Seattle.

Your friend,
Matt

~.~.~.~.~.~.~

From: **Matt Smith**
Subject: **Travel day – to El Paso**
Date: **October 26, 2010**

Dear Bob and Sue,

We always get to the airport two hours before our flight time. Today was no exception. (We flew from Seattle to El Paso to begin a three-park trip to Guadalupe Mountains, Carlsbad Caverns, and Big Bend National Parks.) But even when we're early for boarding, the process makes me anxious. I worry someone will cut in front of me out-of-turn; line jumpers should be shot. Karen adds to my anxiety. She's developed an annoying medical condition. Whenever she hears the words, "We're ready to start boarding" she has to use the restroom. I try to get her to go earlier, but she won't. Her response is always the same, "I don't have to go."

As Karen returned from the restroom, the gate agent explained the order of boarding: People with disabilities or in wheelchairs, people over the age of 100, people who act like they're over the age of 100, families with children (children are two-year olds and younger, not fifteen-year olds), in-uniform military personnel, first class, business class, platinum frequent flyer members, gold members, silver members, bronze members, associate members, people who just applied for the airline's credit card five minutes ago, group 1, groups 2 through 10 in that order, and finally, anyone too clueless to figure out how to get into one of the groups already called. We had "group 8" boarding passes. We felt smug as we pushed our way past the five remaining passengers who were lower on the boarding list than us.

I don't like being trapped in a small place, such as an airplane, with a large cross-section of humanity. I think airlines should announce before every flight, "Listen up people. We're all sealed in here together for the next four hours, so try not to be annoying until the flight is over. Once you exit the plane, *then* you can whistle, hum, fart, snore, talk baby talk, take your shoes off and put on as much bad perfume as you want." I think this would make air travel more bearable.

We arrived in El Paso with enough time to pick up the rental car, have dinner (at Carlos and Mickey's) and buy groceries for the week: peanut butter, jelly, bread, water, blue corn chips, peppermint patties, animal crackers and beer.

Tomorrow we're visiting Guadalupe Mountains National Park.

Your friend,
Matt

~.~.~.~.~.~.~

From: **Matt Smith**
Subject: **#30 – Guadalupe Mountains National Park**
Date: **October 27, 2010**

Dear Bob and Sue,

Our mornings begin with coffee. Karen and I agreed that, on the road, we would take turns going to the lobby to get coffee and bring it back to our room. I think "taking turns" means she will get the coffee in our next life. It's not that she doesn't want to get out of bed; she doesn't want the other guests in the lobby to see her first thing in the morning.

The problem is her hair. Every morning she wakes up with a bump of hair sticking up, always in the same spot. It looks like there's a golf ball hiding in her hair. On mornings when it's her turn to get coffee, she disappears into the bathroom to fix it. She wets it, then brushes it, then re-dries it; sometimes I can smell the hair straightener warming up. While she's fixing the golf ball, I get the coffee.

This morning, fully caffeinated and with flat hair, we drove three hours east from El Paso on Highway 180 to the visitor center in Guadalupe Mountains National Park. The sign at the park entrance warns there's no gas available for 35 miles in either direction. This is a remote park.

When we began our parks trip, there were a handful of national parks I knew nothing about, not even their names. This was one of them. Guadalupe Mountains National Park encompasses the southern edge of the Guadalupe Mountain range, including the highest point of elevation in the state of Texas, Guadalupe Peak at 8,749 feet. The park's stated purpose is, "to preserve the rugged spirit and remote wilderness of the American West." The park is not all mountainous; in the southern region the land transitions from the Guadalupe Mountains to the Chihuahuan Desert.

At the visitor center, we asked the ranger for hiking suggestions. She asked in return, "Do you want a challenging hike or a pretty hike?" I answered, "Challenging." Karen answered, "Pretty." I wanted to hike to Guadalupe Peak, the main hiking attraction in the park, but I've learned it's a bad idea to force Karen on a strenuous hike she doesn't want to do. We decided to do the pretty hike in McKittrick Canyon.

McKittrick Canyon is in the far northeast section of the park, so we had to drive another 20 minutes to get to the trailhead. For the first 3.5 miles, the trail was flat and followed a trickle of a stream. We hiked past the point most people turn around, where the trail starts to climb in elevation. Another half-mile up the trail, we were high enough to look down into the canyon from where we'd come. Many of the trees in the canyon were changing colors. It *was* a pretty hike.

Before starting back, we took a break for lunch. We spread our butts and backpacks out on rocks a few feet off the trail and ate our PB&J sandwiches. Karen was reading the park brochure while eating. She turned to me and said, "It says here to be careful where you put your hands and feet: watch for cacti, rattlesnakes, scorpions and centipedes." There was a couple of seconds delay, and then we both jumped up and brushed ourselves off. Carefully lifting our backpacks, we made sure there weren't any uninvited stowaways clinging to them. We finished our sandwiches while we hiked back.

October is a pleasant time to visit the park; the temperatures are cool and the colors are changing. On our hike back to the car, Karen kept pointing out the grasshoppers with red wings and the electric blue dragonflies. They fascinated her. I never saw either of them. If she sees them again in Carlsbad Caverns tomorrow, I'll have her checked out – or maybe checked in.

After leaving the park, we drove north to Carlsbad, New Mexico where we're spending the night. Tomorrow we'll visit Carlsbad Caverns National Park. Guadalupe and Carlsbad are close to each other; the distance between their visitor centers is about 40 miles.

I didn't spend much time checking out the accommodations in Carlsbad before I booked our hotel. I'm hoping we don't have a mouse-on-head, or scorpion-on-head, incident. The welcome card in our room said, "Dear Hotel Guest, Checkout time is 11:00am. The soap, shampoo and shower cap are complimentary. Please feel free to take them. We will charge your credit card if you take any other items from the room: hand towel $9.99, bath towel $19.99, washcloth $5.00, bed pillow $25.00, decorative pillow $15.00. If you stain the towels, bedding, or carpet the cleaning charge is $12.99 per stain." That was a nice welcome. *Don't steal or stain or we'll charge you.* We felt welcomed and warned at the same time. Too bad we're only staying one night.

Your friend,
Matt

~.~.~.~.~.~.~

From: **Karen Smith**
Subject: **#31 – Carlsbad Caverns National Park**
Date: **October 28, 2010**

Dear Bob and Sue,

I'm 50 years old, and I've never been in a cave, so I had zero expectations of Carlsbad Caverns. At 9am this morning we were in the visitor center taking care of business before our ranger-led tour at 10am. We wandered over to the adopt-a-bat desk. We considered adopting a bat, but then Matt started asking the volunteer questions: "Can we adopt a baby bat or do you only have older bats available? What's the waiting period before we can take our bat home with us?" When the volunteer started slowly backing away, I took that as a warning sign that she thought we were unfit to parent a bat, so we decided against it and moved on.

A couple of weeks ago, I bought tickets online for the Kings Palace Tour, a 90-minute tour through "four highly decorated chambers." We picked up our tickets and took the elevator down. There are two ways to get down into the cavern, take the elevator or walk via the natural cave entrance. We took the elevator.

After the 60-second elevator ride down into the cave, the elevator opened into an area with a lunchroom, souvenir stand, and restrooms. It was dim down there. The temperature is 56 degrees year round, and very humid. We hung out and talked with the other visitors on our tour while we waited for our ranger to show up.

The Kings Palace tour was unlike anything I've ever seen. Cave experts use terms like stalactites, stalagmites, speleothems, columns, soda straws and helictites for the formations we saw. But I would describe it as a frosty fairyland, a fantasy world that shimmers and sparkles and glitters and glows, a place where gnomes might live. (Matt hates it when I talk like that, so I do it whenever I can.) It was like being in a science fiction movie with the best special effects you could ever imagine. Each chamber we walked through was more elaborate than the one before; I couldn't take it all in.

At one point during the tour, I opened my purse, took out my mints and put one in my mouth. One of the many rules we were told was that food and beverages are forbidden on cave trails because the smells attract animals into the cave. But something as small as a breath mint isn't considered food, right? Matt saw me do this, leaned over, and whispered, "Right now there's a skunk or raccoon up there that smells your Altoid, and is on his way down."

When our tour was over, we walked through the Big Room, which is the only self-guided tour available. The Big Room Route is a one-mile stroll around the perimeter of the largest room in the cave. It took us about an hour to walk the loop, looking at the highly decorated and famous features including the Bottomless Pit, Giant Dome, Rock of Ages, and Painted Grotto.

The park service emphasizes that touching cave

formations is prohibited. They are easily broken, and oil from skin can permanently discolor them. I kept seeing these peculiar, white cave formations close to the trail that were smooth and shiny. They appeared to be wet. I held off as long as possible, and then I touched one with the tip of my finger to see if it actually was wet. It wasn't. I know it was wrong to do that, and I felt bad. Matt, who has assumed the role of the park police on this trip, said he was going to turn me in unless I showed sincere remorse. Apparently I did because he let me off with a warning.

Although the park service is meticulous about protecting the caverns, it wasn't always that way. Our tour guide told us that they used to let visitors break off cave formations and take them home. Visitors could smoke in the cave until 1955, and for a fee, people could host events in the cave. In the lunchroom, they used to cook hamburgers and fry chicken for visitors, 800 feet below ground with no ventilation. There's a layer of grease still on the ceiling from that era.

We took the elevator back up and ate lunch in the visitor center restaurant. The food was surprisingly good. After we ate, we walked back down into the cave through the Natural Entrance. From the Natural Entrance to the Big Room, it's a steep, 1.3-mile descent, the equivalent of about 75 stories. The park service recommends that only people in good physical condition access the cavern this way. It was an incredible walk down; we saw the entrance to the Bat Cave, Devil's Spring, the Green Lake Overlook, and the Boneyard, a complex maze of partially dissolved limestone rock that looked like Swiss cheese. We also saw Iceberg Rock, a single 200,000-ton boulder that fell from the cave ceiling thousands of years ago.

Seeing the Natural Entrance to the cave really made me admire the first cave explorers from around the turn of the century. Those explorers went down into this unknown black hole with only candlelight to light their way and no paths, paved or otherwise, to walk on. They showed early visitors their discovery by lowering them 170 feet in a two-person bat guano bucket. (Bat guano means bat shit, in case your Spanish is a little rusty.) In 1926, the owners built a 216-step wooden staircase into the cave. A year later, in 1930, the caverns became a national park, and in that same year, the park service installed an elevator.

The rangers encouraged us to stay for the bat flight program at 5:30pm. The program is conducted at the Natural Entrance amphitheater. The bats live in a part of the cave that isn't accessible to the public. Each evening, two million Mexican free-tail bats fly out of the cave at sunset to look for bugs to eat. I guess it's a pretty cool thing to see. Carlsbad Cavern is their summer home, and in late October, the bats migrate to Mexico for the winter, returning to the cavern in April or May. Although the bats were still here last night, the rangers said they would be leaving "any day now." One day, they simply disappear. The crowd gathers for the bat flight program, waiting and waiting, but no bats come out of the cave. We finished our tours by 2:30pm, and were unsure about sticking around for another three hours, hoping the bats would still be there. I asked the rangers what the odds were the bats would show tonight, but they were unable to give me a guess. We had a long drive ahead of us, so rather than taking our chances that the bats hadn't already flown the cave, we left for Pecos. That's where we're spending the night on our way down to Big Bend National Park.

Carlsbad Caverns is definitely a place that everyone should see before they die. It's not just a national park: it's a national treasure. I would love to come back, see the bat flight, and do some of the difficult tours. Of the park's 117 known caves, there are two others, Spider Cave and Slaughter Canyon Cave, which are open to the general public by way of ranger-led tours. I'd also like to see the Hall of the White Giant, where you crawl on your belly, squeeze through narrow passageways and climb slippery, vertical rock. I don't think I'll be able to get Matt to do it with me. He didn't seem to like the cave as much as I did. When you guys come here, please take me with you. I promise not to touch anything.

Your friend,
Karen

~.~.~.~.~.~.~.~

From: **Matt Smith**
Subject: **#31 – Carlsbad Caverns National Park**
Date: **October 28, 2010**

Dear Bob and Sue,

Karen loved Carlsbad Caverns. She would have given it a rating higher than "a magical place" if she had one. I thought it was like touring a dimly lit basement. If I never go in another cave as long as I live, I'd be okay with that. Karen was upset with me because I didn't think the cave was the greatest place I'd ever seen. I told her, "I don't like caves. It's not a choice. I was born this way."

She said, "Please don't write anything bad about Carlsbad Caverns to Bob and Sue."

"You mean, that I thought it was like touring a dimly lit basement?"

"Exactly, please don't say that in your email."

I said, "I'll think about it, but I can't promise." (There are so few things left that I have power over, I'm not giving up creative control of my own emails.)

This morning we arrived at the park with enough time to take care of business and look around the visitor center before our 10am King's Palace Tour in the cave.

Our ranger guide was a young man in his 20s named James. He was very enthusiastic and said he felt privileged to give tours at Carlsbad Caverns. Both his father and grandfather had worked at the park; his father also had been a ranger and gave tours of the cave. It's inspiring when we see a park ranger like James with that level of commitment and excitement toward his job.

James was a great guide, even though he followed the park service standard for giving tours: imagine everyone in your audience is seven years old, don't tell them the answer to a question – make them guess no matter how long it takes – and force them to repeat strange words and phrases. We all had to say alunite, speleothems, and calcite crust, even though it was obvious most of us already graduated from the third grade. But I was a good sport, and did whatever James asked. It's intimidating being 800 feet below the ground, and a mile into a maze of trails, and the 20-something-year-old in the ranger uniform is the only one who knows the way out. I'll repeat stalagmite and stalactite as many times as he wants if it improves my chances of seeing daylight again.

When the tour ended, Karen wanted to do the self-guided tour of the Big Room section of the cave. She realized that once we got into the elevator to exit, she wouldn't be back. But she was pushing her luck; it was close to lunchtime. I knew there would be no peaceful lunch without first touring the Big Room, so I agreed to the extra tour. I patiently followed Karen, shining my flashlight on the walls every few minutes in fake interest.

The park service tries its best to minimize visitor impact on the cave. Even the smallest contact with the formations can do irreparable damage. They've placed "cave watch" phones throughout the caves, so visitors can report vandalism or bad behavior. The sign on the phone boxes read, "Dial 3030."

I almost had to "3030" Karen. She was fascinated by a particular cave formation close to the path. She examined it from all angles with a goofy look on her face; I knew she wanted to touch it. I said, "If you touch it, I'll have to '3030' you." There was no one else around. She held her finger two inches from the shiny, wet rock for about a minute, like a little kid saying, "I'm not touching it. I'm not touching it." Then she touched it. Maybe it wasn't the thrill she'd expected, or maybe she felt bad about breaking the "do not touch" rule, but I could tell she immediately regretted it. I let her off with a warning.

Finally, she turned to me and said in a sad voice, "We should go eat lunch."

We were the only two visitors in the elevator on the way up to the visitor center. The woman operating the elevator gave a speech perfectly timed to the length of the ride. She told us more about the cave, the elevator, and the gift store. At the end, she told a joke and pinched my arm. After we exited the elevator, Karen said to me, "That woman was so nice. She's the kind of person you need in a job like that, someone who will make conversation with the visitors."

I said, "It was a script." Karen gave me a scornful look for being cynical.

We ate lunch at a picnic table on the patio outside the cafeteria. It was a beautiful day, just the right temperature and sunny; a perfect day to spend in a hole. After lunch, we walked to the Natural Entrance of the cave. It was an easy half-mile walk. I enjoyed being outside and feeling the sun on my face.

There's a man-made amphitheater with room for a few hundred spectators outside the Natural Entrance where visitors sit to watch the bats fly out each night. A trail from there leads into the cave and eventually to the Big Room where we were before lunch. Karen stood at the lower railing of the amphitheater, staring into the cave like she was watching a party that she wanted to join but couldn't.

It took all my strength to say, "It's still early. Maybe we should hike down the path into the cave for a little way." A few minutes later, we were walking back into the cave. We hiked all the way to the Big Room. Karen didn't touch anything this time, but she still had a goofy look on her face as she stared at the cave formations. An hour of this was all I could take. I'd been more than a good husband; I had voluntarily walked back into the cave to make Karen happy when I already satisfied my companion-for-life duty by being pleasant during our cave session this morning. It was time to get out of the hole.

We took the same elevator as before up to the visitor center. Again, we were the only visitors in the elevator, and the same woman was operating the lift. She spoke the same script. I thought for a moment she was a robot; I wanted to poke her to find out, but that would surely have been a '3030' offense. Each word, pause, wink and pinch of my arm was the same as our first ride up. After we'd exited the elevator, I said to Karen, "That woman was so nice." Karen gave me a scornful look, again.

Back in the visitor center, a ranger encouraged us to stay for the bat flight program at 5:30pm; but it was only 2:30pm. She said last night the bats flew out early, at 5:15pm. We wanted to know when the bats leave for the season, but she couldn't give us a definitive answer.

Karen asked, "So, you're not 100 percent sure the bats are still here? You can't give me a bat guarantee?"

The ranger replied, "A bat guarantee? No ma'am." The ranger caught my eye and gave me a look as if to say, "I think she may have spent too much time in the cave. You might want to walk her around outside in the fresh air and sunshine." I gave a reassuring nod back.

The timing of the bat migration is largely a mystery; no one knows why the bats leave when they do or where they go. Night after night, from May to October, bats stream out of the cave at dusk to search for insects to eat – moths, dragonflies, and wasps. Two million half-blind bug catchers scour the west Texas Panhandle. Then one night, they don't return. A ranger told us, "One day they're just gone. The crowd gathers for the bat flight program and… no bats. Some years the colony trickles down over a few nights, but it always happens in a very short timeframe." All they know is the bats migrate south. The ranger added, "We don't know where they go, but they return every May."

I find it hard to believe that the park service can't solve this mystery. Somewhere south of here, there's a cave where two million bats suddenly move in, someone must notice. They're Mexican bats, have they asked anyone in Mexico? I can imagine a Mexican National Park ranger telling a group of visitors, "We don't know what day the bats will show up, one day in October they're just here. Some years the colony trickles in over a few days, but it always happens over a very short timeframe."

An attentive third-grader asks, "Where do the bats come from?"

"Well, that's a very good question. We don't know exactly where they come from, somewhere up north."

Of course, if I imagine this conversation taking place in a U.S. National Park the ranger would reply, "Well, that's a very good question. Where do you think they come from?" The third-grader would respond, "If I knew where the bats came from, I wouldn't have asked the question."

Someone out there knows where the bats go. The park service needs to find that person, and ask them to notify Carlsbad Caverns. It's a simple phone call once a year to say, "The bats are here now; you can stop the bat flight programs."

Unable to get a bat guarantee, we left the park and drove to Pecos, Texas where we're spending the night. (We're on our way to Big Bend National Park.) I think we made the right decision not to wait for the bat flight program. The drive to Pecos took longer than we thought, and we lost an hour due to changing time zones.

I have a feeling we haven't seen the last of Carlsbad Caverns. Karen told me that she wants to go back and tour Spider Cave and Slaughter Canyon. Who comes up with these names? Spider Cave? If I didn't want to go into a regular cave, what makes her think I would want to go into a cave with spiders? I told her, "Yeah, that's sounds great. Maybe we could tour Put Your Scrotum in a Vise Cave while we're at it."

Your friend,
Matt

~.~.~.~.~.~.~

From: **Matt Smith**
Subject: **#32 – Big Bend National Park**
Date: **October 29, 2010**

Dear Bob and Sue,

We left Pecos early this morning to drive to Big Bend National Park. There wasn't much to see on the drive. The towns kept getting smaller the farther south we went. Many of them looked deserted with buildings falling down. The towns improved about an hour north of the park when we got to Marathon, Texas. Karen said it was a "cute little town." That's just below "darling" on her rating scale, but still a decent rating.

Marathon has a few art galleries, a nice town center and what appeared to be some interesting places to eat. It was too early for lunch, so we stopped only long enough to fill up the tank.

Big Bend National Park is mostly desert with the Rio Grande as its southern border. Sitting in the middle of the park is an area of mountains – the Chisos Mountains. That's where we're staying for the next couple of nights, at the Chisos Mountain Lodge. The only road to the lodge was closed until

5pm while a paving crew resurfaced it, so we spent the day in the other areas of the park until they finished.

We took care of our business at the Panther Junction Visitor Center – where I expected to see a panther but didn't – then drove to the Boquillas Canyon Trail parking lot in the southeast corner of the park. The Rio Grande cuts through Boquillas Canyon, and there is a short trail leading to the east from the parking lot on the U.S. side of the river. The park newsletter warns against buying anything from Mexican Nationals, and against crossing the border (Rio Grande) in any direction. Before 9/11, the border was open, but, "As a result of a 2002 US Customs and Border decision, there are NO authorized border crossings anywhere in the park."

Along the short hike from the parking lot to the riverbank, souvenirs sat displayed on rocks. Handwritten cardboard signs with prices for the souvenirs leaned against collection jars. These were items made by Mexican Nationals. They cross the river in small boats, place their items next to the trail for U.S. tourists to buy, and then go back across the river to Mexico and wait for customers. As soon as Karen stopped to look at a display of beaded wire scorpions, we heard someone yelling from the other side of the river. It was a guy sitting on the bank watching his merchandise. We think he was shouting his encouragement for us to buy something, but we didn't.

Farther down the trail, we came to the sandy bank of the Rio Grande where a man was standing on the U.S. side next to a tip jar singing "La Cucaracha." His voice rang off the canyon walls. We kept moving along the trail without slowing down.

There was a man and a woman hiking ahead of us on the trail. It didn't take us long to pass them. This is what we do; the goal of every hike is to pass the people in front of us. Karen doesn't like passing people because she has to increase her speed when she's already going faster than she would like. She says to me, "It's not a race." But she's wrong; it *is* a race.

When we passed the couple, we saw they were older

than us, maybe 65ish. Every inch of them was covered with clothing, except their faces. It was a hot day, but they were wearing gloves. They even wore reflective straps pulled tight around the cuffs of their pants. I'm guessing to keep out dust or bugs, but I'm not sure why. They looked like a HAZMAT team. A few hundred yards later, the trail ended, so we turned around and headed back toward the car. Just then, I saw a head floating in the river. It was the man we just passed on the trail. He'd gone to the edge of the river, taken off all his clothes except his briefs and was swimming across the river. Only his head was above the water. His wife, still in her HAZMAT suit was standing on the shore filming him.

The river's current was swift. I was concerned he wouldn't make it across, and even more concerned that I'd have to jump in and save him. He climbed out on the Mexican side of the river, and jumped up and down waving his arms for the camera. I'm not sure how he planned on getting back. I couldn't see a safe place where he could make it back across. We didn't want to interfere with (or witness) any more of this odd behavior, so we continued hiking toward our car. He must not have read the park warnings about it being illegal to swim across to Mexico, or the health hazards of swimming in the river. The park newsletter advises against swimming in the Rio Grande because, "Water-borne micro-organisms and other waste material can occur in the river and cause serious illness." It's a sewer.

At the car, we ate our PB&J sandwiches, but there were still hours to kill before the road to the lodge opened, so we drove several miles down a gravel road to the Grapevine Hill trailhead, and hiked to Balanced Rock. It was an uneventful hike, but we enjoyed hiking in the desert and getting the exercise. After an hour of hiking, we reached the balanced rock. Karen posed for a picture standing in front of the rock with her arms up, making the picture look as if she was holding the rock above her head. This is what we quit our jobs to do: take silly pictures of ourselves in the middle of nowhere. Well, it's better than working.

The road to the lodge opened, and by dinnertime, we were checked in to our room. The Chisos Mountain region is different from the rest of the park; it's higher in elevation at 5,000 feet and is cooler by about five to ten degrees. Tomorrow we plan on hiking in the mountains.

Your friend,
Matt

~.~.~.~.~.~.~

From: **Matt Smith**
Subject: **Big Bend day two**
Date: **October 30, 2010**

Dear Bob and Sue,

This morning we hiked the Lost Mine Trail in the Chisos Mountains, a 4.6-mile round trip. There was not a cloud in the sky; temperatures were mild and we could see for miles into Mexico from the top of the trail. We were half hoping we'd see a mountain lion on our hike this morning, and half hoping we wouldn't. They live in this section of the park. I've read stories of visitors seeing them walk through the parking lot of the Chisos Basin Visitor Center. We didn't see a mountain lion today. But, it's likely a mountain lion saw us.

After the hike, we ate lunch at the trailhead parking lot: PB&J sandwiches and animal crackers – again. When we arrived in El Paso earlier this week, I bought a 48-ounce bag of animal crackers for $2.99. While putting them in the car, the bag burst open and all the animals spilled onto the seat of the car. We've been driving around with an open mound of animal crackers in the back. All week I've been eating off the mound, but it doesn't look to be getting smaller. Karen is concerned to see me eat something that has touched the seat of a rental car because that's not like me. Normally I wouldn't, but it's a big pile; a 48-ounce bag is a lot of animal crackers. The ones on the top haven't touched the seat. I'll have to decide when I get to the bottom of the pile if I'll eat the ones that have come in contact with the seat where someone's butt rested. Probably not.

In the afternoon, we hiked The Window trail, which was a 5.6 mile round trip according to my GPS. The trail begins at the Chisos Mountain Lodge parking lot. It follows a dry wash that only runs after heavy rains. The end of the trail (the window) is a 200-foot drop that becomes a pour-off (waterfall) when the stream is running. At dusk, the window frames the sun setting over the desert below.

In my list of items to carry in my backpack, I need to add a leash for Karen – the shoulder harness type that parents use for hyperactive toddlers. Karen likes to walk to the edge of cliffs, ledges, and drop-offs, and lean over to get a view of what's below. I'm worried that one time she's going to disappear over the edge. That would be bad; the AAA membership is in her name.

After the hike, Karen and I sat at a picnic table in the shade next to the visitor center. We connected to the lodge's wireless; read our email, and got on the Internet so we could check the status of Hurricane Tomas. If the current forecast holds true, we will meet Tomas in two weeks at Virgin Islands National Park.

Five deer snuck up behind us while we were sitting there. We kept hearing people yelling from the deck of the restaurant, "Look behind you." When we turned around we could see that one of the deer was clearly smaller than the others. Karen has a soft spot for runts. I have nothing against runts, but I told her not to get too attached; mountain lions target the small ones. She didn't want to believe this. Later four deer came by. I don't know if they were the same group as before, but Karen was concerned there wasn't a little one with them. She kept looking around the parking lot for number five.

We ate dinner at the lodge, and then went back to our room and ate a bag of candy corn that I bought at a gas station yesterday. We don't know what's in candy corn, but neither of us could stop eating it. It must have an ingredient that's addictive. Twenty years from now, an investigative reporter is going to find a secret candy corn company memo that proves they've known this the whole time. It'll be on *60 Minutes*.

Your friend,
Matt

~.~.~.~.~.~.~

From: **Karen Smith**
Subject: **Happy Halloween**
Date: **October 31, 2010**

Dear Bob and Sue,

To celebrate Halloween, Matt and I dressed up like unemployed, middle-aged, don't-know-what-to-do-with-the-rest-of-our-lives hikers. The ranger at the visitor center said our costumes were spot on.

We spent today on the west side of Big Bend National Park. Our first activity was hiking the Upper Burro Mesa Pouroff trail; it was a 3.6 mile round trip. The first half-mile of the trail was across open desert, and then it descended through a narrow, rocky gorge to the upper lip of a waterfall. (It wasn't a waterfall when we were there. It's a waterfall only after a heavy rain.) Centuries of floodwaters carved a sandy pothole cave at the end of the hike where a narrow slot in the cave wall forms the top of the 100-foot pouroff. It was an amazing hike.

For our second hike of the day, we took the ranger's suggestion and hiked the Chimneys Trail, which was a few miles south of our first hike. From the trailhead of the Chimneys Trail, you can see across the desert floor to the turnaround point for this hike; a row of rock outcroppings called the Chimneys. Unless a hike itself is outstanding, like The Narrows or a slot canyon, I like it when there's a reward at the end – something to look forward to, like a waterfall. It keeps me going when Matt is on his death march. The hike *to* the Chimneys was not particularly interesting, but the ranger told us that Indians once lived there and left petroglyphs.

Once we reached the Chimneys, smaller trails fanned out between and around the formations. We found the petroglyphs carved on the flat stone surfaces along the base of one of the pinnacles. This hike ended up being a five mile round trip; on our way back we were baking like potatoes in the afternoon desert sun. The trail was all ours; we saw no one else the entire time.

Blasting the car's air conditioning, we drove to the Castolon Historic District in the southwest part of the park, a farming and ranching area from the early 1900's to the 1960's. We went to the visitor center and The La Harmonia Company Store. The store has been in operation for more than 90 years, now catering to tourists instead of farmers and ranchers. In addition to the store, Castolon includes the oldest known adobe structure in Big Bend National Park (the Alvino House), another store building (the Old Castolon), and numerous adobe ruins that were once homes for the Mexican-American and Anglo families that lived in the area.

We drove the short distance from the visitor center to Santa Elena Canyon. Along the way, we pulled off the road and hiked one mile to Dorgan House, which is a spectacular adobe ruin, formerly the home of Albert Dorgan. It was a working ranch house in the early part of the 20th century, but abandoned when the park service took the area over in 1944. The chimney is still largely intact and is made entirely of petrified wood found in the area. That alone was worth the one-mile hike.

At Santa Elena Canyon, we walked down to the edge of

the Rio Grande, one of the most famous scenic features of Big Bend. There, the Rio Grande cuts a 1,500-foot vertical chasm out of limestone. Looking west, the left wall of the canyon is in Mexico, and the right is in Texas. They say floating through the canyon is a spectacular adventure, but once Matt got a close-up view of the brown water, the chance of us ever doing that evaporated.

Our last stop of the day was Terlingua, Texas just outside the park. Terlingua has a few hotels, several restaurants and a couple of float-trip outfitters. It's another former mining town that was deserted after its mining operations ceased. During the late 1960s and early 1970s, tourism overflow from the park brought new life to the town. Terlingua became famous for its annual chili cook-off, and in 1967 was deemed the "Chili Capital of the World." The cook-off is always held on the first Saturday in November, so we'll miss it by six days.

A park ranger we met in Glacier Bay, who once was a ranger at Big Bend, recommended that we stop at Long Draw Pizza for dinner. But when we got there at 5pm, they weren't open yet. We found a restaurant down the road in the El Dorado Hotel, and ate nachos at the bar while we waited for Long Draw to open. The El Dorado was clearly a family-run place. There were two young girls sitting at a table behind us doing their homework. They spoke Spanish to their mom, who was tending bar. The mom said her daughters were asking her what my name was and where I came from. I turned around and chatted with the girls for a bit. They told me they couldn't wait to go trick-or-treating. They were adorable.

For Matt and me, an unexpected and wonderful bonus of our parks trip has been the opportunity to visit the small towns near the parks, check out the local restaurants and pubs, and meet the people who live there.

We headed back to the pizza place, which didn't look very promising from the outside; it's a weathered trailer in a gravel parking lot. However, there were quite a few people inside, which is usually a good sign for a restaurant. We sat at the bar, talking to the owner, Nancy, while she made our pizza. We've eaten countless pizzas on our parks trip, and Long Draw Pizza was one of the best.

I mentioned to Matt that I'm not sure we've eaten a vegetable in five months, unless we consider tomato sauce on pizza a vegetable. He pointed out that beer is plant-based, so it counts as a vegetable, and assured me that we're getting all the nutrients we need.

Nancy encouraged us to stay for their Halloween party. She was expecting the place to "get crazy" later on, but since we can't stay up past 9pm we declined. We finished our pizza and were out of there by 7pm. Tonight we have to pack and get ready for our flight home tomorrow from El Paso. Hope you're having a fun Halloween. Bob, maybe by next year we'll have that park ranger uniform for you to wear.

Your friend,
Karen

~.~.~.~.~.~.~.~

From: **Matt Smith**
Subject: **#33 – Virgin Islands National Park**
Date: **November 9, 2010**

Dear Bob and Sue,

We're pressing our luck trying to save a few dollars by visiting the Virgin Islands during hurricane season. Today, heavy thunderstorms, remnants of hurricane Tomas, caused our flight from Miami to St. Thomas to be diverted to Puerto Rico. Our plane sat on the tarmac in San Juan for a couple of hours before the weather improved enough to continue.

Yesterday we began a four-park trip to the Virgin Islands and Florida. The first park we're visiting is Virgin Islands National Park, on the island of St. John. There's no large airport on St. John, so we flew to St. Thomas, and took a shuttle bus and ferry the rest of the way.

We were already late getting into St. Thomas, and the shuttle bus ride from the airport to the ferry terminal took an hour because of slow traffic. The trip was turning into a grind. So, I was relieved when the guy sitting next to me on the shuttle bus talked on his cell phone the entire time. Karen was on one side of me, and cell phone guy was on the other. I was trapped.

He was explaining to the person on the other end of the phone how he and his family just ran the New York Marathon, and were spending the week on St. John as their reward. In case you're wondering, the last hour and a half of the marathon was torture for him; it was all he could do to keep putting one foot in front of the other. Now he's dealing with blisters on both heels and losing his toenails because the race was so hard on his feet. That's nice.

It was a long day and a half of travel, so we very much appreciated the Painkillers they served us on the ferry. A Painkiller is a local drink made with rum, fruit juice, and coconut.

The ferry took us directly to Caneel Bay Resort, where we're staying the next three nights. As we pulled up to the dock, the resort staff was lined up to greet us. Since the resort is spread out on 170 acres, a staff member drove us to our building in a golf cart. He gave us our keys and left. When we stepped inside, we noticed a small problem with our room: everything was wet. Not damp – wet. The welcome card from the hotel, the tile floor, the bed sheets, the pillows and the towels were all wet. The ceiling dripped. We walked to the front desk at the main building and told them that our room flooded; we couldn't imagine what else could have happened. The front desk clerk said, "We'll send someone to your room to mop the water off the floor." I said, "No it's not just the floor, everything in the room is wet." He said, "Sir, all the rooms are like that; it's very humid here, and it's been raining for days."

We ate dinner at the outdoor grill. The food and service were excellent, but the noise coming from the surrounding jungle was so loud we could barely hear each other speak. Karen described it as an, "Eeeeee! Eeeeee! Eeeeee!" shriek. She asked our waiter what the noise was. He said, "Creeckeets."

Karen said, "Creeckeets? Is that a type of monkey?"

I interrupted, "He said *crickets.* Those aren't monkeys. Where do you think we are?"

The waiter looked confused, "No monkey, is creeckeets."

After dinner, we walked back to our room in the darkness using the small flashlights that were sitting on our nightstand when we arrived. Karen was shining hers in the trees looking for monkeys.

Your friend,
Matt

~.~.~.~.~.~.~

From: **Matt Smith**
Subject: **Virgin Islands day two**
Date: **November 10, 2010**

Dear Bob and Sue,

Before going to bed last night, I put all my stuff in the dresser to keep it from getting wet. Condensation was dripping from the ceiling, and I was concerned that I'd wake up and not have any dry clothes, or worse, that my phone and my camera would be wet. We cranked the air conditioner to suck the humidity out of the room. I shivered all night. At four in the morning, the sheets on my side of the bed were finally dry enough for me to fall asleep.

Walking to breakfast we saw deer on the property lawn,

but no donkeys. We read there are wild donkeys on the island. Yesterday the resort manager told us that donkeys occasionally wander onto the property, but this week they're in a corral on the other side of the island. How wild could they be if they're in a corral?

We ate breakfast at the hotel's open-air restaurant. Like last night, the food and service were exceptional. We had to move several feet away from the roofline because it began to rain on us. As we ate, the rain got heavier. There are two paths to take when the weather is miserable: we can hunker down in our room and try not to kill each other until the weather improves, or we can go out in it and act as if we're having fun. Today we hiked in the rain.

I stuffed extra shirts for Karen and me in my dry-bag along with everything else I wanted on the hike: phone, camera, wallet, etc. The dry-bag went into my backpack a la The Narrows hike. The plan was to hike from Caneel Bay Resort through the park to the visitor center, a mile and a half through dense vegetation. (It was a jungle.) The visitor center is on the edge of the small waterside town of Cruz Bay. We wore flip-flops despite the hotel staff's recommendation against it. Two Caneel Bay umbrellas from the front desk completed our outfits.

On the hike, the rain never let up. The trail to the visitor center was a flowing stream. We hiked in flip-flops through ankle-deep water. The umbrellas kept some of the rain off of us when they weren't turned inside out because of the wind. It was one of the most enjoyable hikes of our parks trip. The temperature was warm, and the rain was invigorating. We were out doing it and having fun. It was much better than sitting in our hotel room trying to decide which personality traits we dislike the most about each other.

We were the only visitors in the visitor center. After stamping my passport, I double bagged it in sandwich bags before putting it back in the dry-bag. It's not likely we will ever be at this visitor center again, and I didn't want my passport stamp to get wet.

The ranger at the visitor center didn't say much. Usually I'm the quiet one in a conversation, but when I find someone less talkative than me, I turn into question guy. Coming from Chicago ten years ago, he's been a park ranger here ever since. He's concerned that the park "might not make it." He told us that one of the conditions the Rockefellers attached to their donation of this land to the federal government was that if it ever fails to be a national park the ownership would revert to the Rockefeller family. (In 1956, they donated a little more than half the island of St. John to the federal government, so it could be made into a national park.) With low visitors numbers and federal budget cuts, he's concerned the park might fail. We don't know if this is possible, but he seemed genuinely worried about it.

When the rain lightened, I set my camera on a tiny tripod in a puddle and took our picture in front of the park sign. Then, we walked two blocks to the center of town, but there wasn't much going on in Cruz Bay. At an open-air bar, we sat and ate a snack then walked around the small town.

Last night Karen found the recipe for Painkillers in a magazine; it calls for orange juice, pineapple juice, rum, and Coco Lopez. Karen took to-go cups of orange juice and pineapple juice from the breakfast buffet this morning in anticipation of making her own Painkillers this afternoon. Normally Karen doesn't do carry-out from buffets but when she saw the bill for our room package she figured everything was fair game. (She may have also brought the toaster back to our room.)

With the bottle of complimentary rum in our room, and the juice from the breakfast buffet, the only missing ingredient was Coco Lopez. Before hiking back to the resort, we went to a convenience store to look for Coco Lopez. Jackpot! We bought a bag of blue corn chips, two coconut long boys, and a can of Coco Lopez. (A coconut long boy is a chewy candy made from what appears to be low-grade motor oil and shredded coconut. I ate one and put the other in my backpack.)

The hike back to the resort was the same as before: rain,

wind, inside-out umbrellas, and ankle-deep water. It was enjoyable, just as before, except we both got blisters from hiking in flip-flops. In the afternoon, we drank Painkillers until we could no longer feel the blisters.

Tonight we wanted to walk along the road into town for dinner, but the hotel staff strongly recommended against it; there are no streetlights, sidewalks, or shoulders to walk on, just a narrow road with jungle on both sides. We took their advice and hired a cab. The cabs here are pickup trucks with bench seats in the bed and a canopy over the top. The drivers go very fast on pitch-black, curvy roads. It was a good thing we drank Painkillers before we climbed in the back of the cab; they kept us relaxed during the wild ride. Otherwise, we would have quickly jumped out and into the jungle. Fortunately, it was not a long ride into town.

Dinner in Cruz Bay was casual: burgers and beers. Hanging out in a locals' restaurant is more our style than an expensive dinner at the resort. After dinner, we strolled through town several times then caught a cab back to Caneel Bay. It was still early when we returned, so we walked back and forth along the short beach in front of the resort until we'd stretched our legs enough for one day. Tomorrow, if the weather improves, we're going to the beach.

Your friend,
Matt

~.~.~.~.~.~.~

From: **Matt Smith**
Subject: **We have a new best friend**
Date: **November 11, 2010**

Dear Bob and Sue,

Karen woke up with diaper rash. I didn't get any more

details than that. I had my own problems: the zipper on my shorts had rusted in the down position.

At breakfast, we did our best to eat our weight in food. I'm pretty sure I ate a pound of bacon alone; I was thirsty all day. We took as much orange and pineapple juice from the buffet as we could carry. Karen had a bagel hanging out of each pocket. We were no longer trying to be discreet. Karen said, "If they don't like it they know where to find us, in the room with the dripping ceiling."

By mid-morning, the weather cleared. We found ourselves at the beach lying on lounge chairs. There are several beaches on the Caneel Bay property. The one we landed on was perfect; it was secluded with clean, smooth sand and calm waves. We pulled our lounge chairs under the trees at the edge of the beach and enjoyed just being there.

Inflatable rafts were stacked in a pile. I grabbed a couple and dragged them to our spot. We alternated from lounging on our chairs to floating on the rafts. I floated belly down on my raft with my face in the water, lazy man snorkeling. When I got tired of paddling, I let the waves carry my raft onto the beach. I wouldn't move until the raft came to a complete stop on the sand. Then, I'd lie on my lounge chair for 20 minutes and repeat the cycle. This went on all day.

Normally I wear sunscreen, but today it seemed like too much effort. Deciding to go native, I declared it a sunscreen holiday. I thought the hair on my back and stomach would be at least an SPF 15. Nope, I got fried. But not to worry, we had something to kill the pain. Every hour or so, I would trek back to our room, make Painkillers, and bring them to the beach. Each time the ceiling dripped into one of the cups, I would make that one Karen's drink.

On one of my Painkiller runs, I saw a large iguana on the lawn. I set the drinks in the grass and took its picture. I didn't know if it was a biter, so I kept my distance. But, I must have gotten too close regardless because he flared his neck thing, so I backed off. It was time to move on to the beach anyway; bugs were jumping into Karen's Painkiller.

I could have saved time and long walks by ordering from the drink cart guy, but it was cheaper for me to make the drinks myself. I didn't realize how much cheaper, until in a moment of weakness, I ordered two Painkillers from him. While I watched him make the drinks, I was thinking that I could be doing this myself for free in our room. The only difference: he charged me $20!

Back at the beach I nudged Karen out of her sun/rum coma. She took one sip of her new drink, turned to me and said, "I've decided that we're going to dedicate our lives to the coconut." There was a pause. "No wait, the coconut is going to dedicate its life to us." It's at times like these I've found it best just to listen and let the wisdom flow without interruption. She continued, "The coconut represents everything that is good in the world; the way it smells, the way it tastes, you can rub it on your body, you can eat it, you can drink it, it relaxes you, it represents the vacation lifestyle." I looked at her in awe. She was silent for a while looking out over the ocean. Then she asked with surprising urgency, "Is it a fruit or a nut?"

Later there was some discussion about how we could enforce the declaration that the coconut would dedicate its life to us. We agreed we needed to work out some of the finer details, but otherwise it was a sound plan.

Bob and Sue, I hate to break this to you in an email, but we have a new best friend, and his name is Coco Lopez.

Your friend,
Matt

~.~.~.~.~.~.~

From: **Matt Smith**
Subject: **#34 – Biscayne National Park**
Date: **November 12, 2010**

Dear Bob and Sue,

This morning we said good-bye to St. John and Caneel Bay. Our flight from St. Thomas landed in Miami at 11:20am. With half a day left, we headed to Biscayne National Park.

From the Miami airport, we drove 30 miles south to Homestead, Florida and then east to the coast. Biscayne National Park is just south of Key Biscayne and just north of Key Largo. It's about 25 miles north-to-south and 15 miles east-to-west in size, but most of that is water. The park includes a narrow swath of mangrove trees on the coast; the keys in the bay are the only other land areas in the park. There's very little to do in the park that doesn't require a boat. We were planning to take a boat tour to the keys, but by the time we got our rental car and drove to the park it was too late for a boat tour today. We made reservations for an afternoon boat tour to Boca Chita Key tomorrow; we'll visit Everglades National Park in the morning.

Today was a day to get organized, do laundry, and to dry out. It felt good to be where the air is less humid. I bet no one has ever said that about Homestead, Florida before.

Karen and I got take-out pizza from the coal-fired pizza place down the street from our hotel. We've heard of wood-fired pizza, but not coal-fired pizza. Karen asked me to ask the manager of the pizza place if we were in any danger of getting black lung disease from eating coal-fired pizza. I answered, "No, but you can. Just make sure I'm not standing next to you when you ask him so he doesn't think we're together."

We sat in bed at our Hampton Inn and watched TV while we ate. Karen dropped a whole piece of pizza, business side down, on the white comforter. We're going to get a stain charge for that.

After eating her pizza, Karen turned to me and with a deep sigh said, "I've changed my mind. I don't think it's a good idea for the coconut to dedicate its life to us. The coconut lifestyle will make us fat and lazy." I wasn't prepared for this. I said, "We don't have to make this decision now.

Let's hold off and think about it for a while."

There was still plenty of time before going to bed, so I did what I always do when I get to a new hotel. I took everything out of my pockets, backpack and suitcase so I could clean out and organize my stuff. I said to Karen, "There's only enough room on the bed for one of us to do this at a time, so I'm going first." She didn't even look up from her iPad.

It was a good thing I cleaned and organized. I found the second Coconut Longboy; it melted in my backpack. Karen was right. There *is* a dark side to the coconut lifestyle. My flashlight, travel sized roll of duct tape, Spork, and reading glasses were all stuck together with a coconut goo ball at the center. It took all my Wet-wipes to clean the stickiness off everything. I told Karen, "I think sticky is my least favorite condition. I also don't like being damp." She looked up and said, "This is why we travel, to know ourselves better." Before turning in for the night, I went across the street to the drugstore for more Wet-wipes.

Tomorrow is a big day; we're visiting two national parks.

Your friend,
Matt

~.~.~.~.~.~.~

From: **Matt Smith**
Subject: **#35 – Everglades National Park**
Date: **November 13, 2010**

Dear Bob and Sue,

I'd wear cologne made of Deep Woods Off if it existed. It's one of the few non-food smells I like, although it makes me lightheaded. Spraying it on my body has the same effect as drinking two Coors Lights. Karen wanted to go into the Everglades wearing her non-toxic bug spray made from lemon eucalyptus oil. Please! Once the mosquitoes found the white meat on the back of her thighs she was begging for my Off.

This morning we drove to the Ernest F. Coe Visitor Center on the eastern edge of Everglades National Park to take care of our parks business and to do some hiking. Next week on our way back from Key West, we plan on spending more time in the park. The park is so large and diverse that today we only had a chance to see a small area of it. From the visitor center, we drove to the Long Pine Key trailhead and hiked for about an hour. Then we went to the Royal Palm Visitor Center and hiked the Anhinga and Gumbo Limbo trails.

We saw lots of alligators on the Anhinga Trail and took some fantastic pictures. Seeing the wildlife made me wish that I'd bought a better camera for our parks trip. The Gumbo Limbo trail wound through the trees away from the swamp. We didn't see any wildlife, but saw plenty of gumbo-limbo trees. I tried to find out why they are called gumbo-limbo trees, but with no luck. I found a reference that the first use of the name dates back to the early 19th century. I'd like to believe there was a contest to come up with the dumbest name for the tree and gumbo and limbo tied, so they settled on gumbo-limbo. It's a prolific tree though: any twig taken from the tree and stuck into the ground will grow. Fence posts made from gumbo-limbo wood have been known to sprout leaves and even turn into fully-fledged trees.

The entire time we were on the Anhinga and Gumbo Limbo hikes we heard a loud noise like an engine. We thought there must be construction going on close by, but we didn't see any signs of it on our hikes. In the parking lot, we found the source of the noise: a tour bus parked with its engine and air conditioner running. There was no one in the bus; the air conditioner ran so when the tour group finished looking at the alligators they would have a cool bus to come back to. Standing next to the bus, it sounded like an airplane taking off. The noise and the exhaust didn't exactly fit with the wilderness feel the park service is trying to create.

It was an easy drive from where we were in the Everglades to the Biscayne National Park Visitor Center. We drove right past the Homestead Miami Speedway. I hadn't thought to look at the NASCAR calendar when planning our trip to these two parks (or ever). Luck was with us, though, NASCAR is not in Homestead until next weekend. It would've been a huge pain – maybe impossible – to get through traffic if the race was this weekend.

Our afternoon boat tour departed from the pier in front of the Biscayne Visitor Center. It was a pontoon type, scuba diving boat with a Jimmy Buffet wannabe captain. The weather was good; the ocean was calm, and it was a very relaxing afternoon. At Boca Chita Key, we docked in the protected harbor. Large yachts occupied every slip except the one reserved for the park service. We had about an hour and a half to poke around the small key, which was enough time to see every inch of it two or three times.

While exploring the key, we had a noise pollution flashback from this morning. There was very loud, very bad, Julio Iglesias music coming from one of the large boats docked in the harbor. We could see the owner sitting on the back deck of his boat, with his shirt off, having a drink. Perhaps he thought he was doing us a favor by playing this music loud enough so we could all hear, or maybe he was deaf and didn't know his stereo was on.

Across the harbor, we climbed to the top of the ornamental lighthouse – we could hear Julio much better from the observation platform – then strolled through the campgrounds. Being a Saturday, it was packed with visitors. A man slept on an air mattress in the middle of the campground with his mouth open. Karen said he must have passed out because no one would be able to sleep through the loud music. Birds were picking through his stuff. If he left any food out it was surely gone by now.

The boat ride back to the visitor center was as uneventful as the ride out. That's not a complaint; uneventful is a good thing when crossing a large body of water in a pontoon boat. Tomorrow we will drive to Key West, and on Monday catch a tour boat to Dry Tortugas National Park.

Your friend,
Matt

~.~.~.~.~.~.~

From: **Matt Smith**
Subject: **Key West**
Date: **November 14, 2010**

Dear Bob and Sue,

Today alone, I've seen more man boobs than anyone should see in a lifetime. No man over the age of 40 should wear a tank top, especially a loose-fitting tank top, ever, not even in Key West.

Karen and I drove from Homestead to Key West today. The weather was perfect, so we sat outside at a pizza restaurant and watched the world walk by. The t-shirts on the passersby fascinated me. I said to Karen, "I need a t-shirt that expresses my personality."

"And what would that look like?"

"It's black, of course, and on the front, there's a wolf with eagle wings howling at the moon. The wolf is wearing sunglasses, even though it's midnight, and has a gold chain around his neck. There's a bullet hanging on the gold chain, and in the background the word 'Destiny' is printed in Japanese letters."

Looking around the restaurant, she could see that I borrowed those ideas from the t-shirts on customers sitting around us. She said, "You better keep your voice down or someone's going to beat you up."

"No one gets beat up these days. They get shot."

"Yeah, well the bullet would probably miss you and hit me."

"You're right. Let's change the subject to ponytails. I always thought that, because I'm going bald, a ponytail..."

Karen cut me off, "*Going* bald?"

"Nice. Anyway, I always thought that, because I'm going bald, a ponytail was no longer an option for me. But after seeing the guys down here, I think I might grow one."

"You'd have to dye it blonde to fit in."

"I could do that."

After lunch, we walked through the main tourist district of Key West. A huge crowd gathered at the west end of town; they were watching a hydroplane race. Every few minutes, the boats would scream past the crowd lining the waterfront. Helicopters followed overhead covering the race. It was a party atmosphere, and I began to get caught up in the island vibe. I stopped at a t-shirt kiosk and looked at tank tops. I particularly liked the one with a parrot dressed like a pirate printed on front. I was checking for my size when I noticed Karen staring at me in disbelief. I snapped out of it.

We walked back to our hotel, which was three miles from the main part of town. On our way, we found the pier where we need to be tomorrow morning to catch our boat to Dry Tortugas National Park. It's always good to be prepared.

When we reached our hotel, there was a large, black chicken in the drive by the front entrance - the area where cars pull in to unload and valet. Shadowing the chicken were six tennis-ball-sized chicks. The mother darted between passing cars. With a delayed response, the chicks followed, one was always far behind the others. I could see concern on Karen's face. "They're going to get run over," she said. I tried to explain that wild chickens avoiding cars was part of the natural process, and *we should not interfere*. What I was trying to avoid was sleeping with a room full of chickens tonight, which began to look like a real possibility. She settled for talking with the valet, and getting his personal guarantee that nothing bad would happen to the chickens. For his sake, I hope there are still six little ones tomorrow morning.

Your friend,
Matt

~.~.~.~.~.~.~

From: **Karen Smith**
Subject: **#36 – Dry Tortugas National Park**
Date: **November 15, 2010**

Dear Bob and Sue,

It's a beautiful Monday in Margaritaville.

This morning I woke Matt up by singing *Come Monday*, one of my favorite Jimmy Buffet songs. Matt cut me off saying, "No singing," like he always does. I know he's not saying it because I'm a bad singer; he just doesn't like spontaneous outbursts of joy. He's also banned my "bad dancing." Now I do it just to annoy him.

Today was our boat tour to Fort Jefferson in Dry Tortugas National Park. Seventy miles west of Key West, Dry Tortugas is a cluster of seven islands, composed of little else but coral reefs and sand. These islands sit on the edge of the main shipping channel between the Gulf of Mexico, the western Caribbean, and the Atlantic Ocean. Last night when I told Matt that the park is named Dry Tortugas because it is shaped like a tortuga – a deep-fried burrito – he seemed even more excited to see the park. You can imagine his disappointment this morning when he learned it's called Dry Tortugas because of the turtles that live there, and because there is no fresh water on the islands (Tortuga is the Spanish word for turtle, not deep-fried burrito.)

We boarded the Yankee Freedom II at 7:30am for an 8:00am departure. The boat ride to Fort Jefferson took just over two hours. As we approached the island, we could see the walls of Fort Jefferson rising up 50 feet; it was a spectacular sight. Surprisingly, the fort takes up almost the entire island, and a surrounding moat protects it from both invaders and the pounding surf. We disembarked, took our picture in front of the park sign, and found the gift store. (Not original to the fort.) After taking care of business, we took a short, guided tour of the fort. It's an impressive site.

The U.S. government built Fort Jefferson to protect the lucrative shipping channel; it's one of the largest remaining 19th century American masonry coastal forts. (We didn't know before today that "masonry coastal forts" was a category of thing.) Construction began in 1847 on Garden Key Island, and by 1860, the government had spent over $250,000, yet the fort was only half complete. It remained in Union control during the Civil War, even though Florida joined the Confederacy. Work continued during the Civil War, but stopped after the war ended. The fort was never completed due to several factors: the difficulty and cost of shipping workers and supplies, the weather, and concerns that additional bricks and cannon would cause further settling and more structural problems.

The fort also served as a military prison during the Civil War and up until 1874. We walked through the cell of its most famous prisoner, Dr. Samuel Mudd, the physician who set the broken leg of John Wilkes Booth. Dr. Mudd was convicted of conspiracy in the murder of President Lincoln. He was given a life sentence and sent to Dry Tortugas. Our tour guide told us that the phrase "your name is mud" came from Sam Mudd; that's how reviled he was.

But he got his chance at redemption. When an epidemic of yellow fever spread through the fort and the prison's physician died from the disease, Dr. Mudd single-handedly cared for the ill prisoners. Because of his heroic actions, President Andrew Johnson pardoned him, and he was released from Fort Jefferson in 1869.

When we walked around the outer moat wall, we could see where large sections of the fort's wall had collapsed into the moat. If nothing were done to save it, over time the entire fort would fall into the water. The park service has initiated a very expensive, multiphase preservation project to stabilize Fort Jefferson by repairing the damage caused by the salt, heat, destructive weather and water. To preserve the historic appearance of the walls, workers are using concrete made of local sand and coral – as in the original construction – and historic bricks that were salvaged during demolition.

We boarded the boat for lunch, and then spent the rest of the afternoon sitting on the small beach, enjoying the sun and the turquoise water. Some of the other passengers snorkeled. Earlier the captain told us that the boat would leave for Key West at 3:00pm sharp, and that he wasn't allowed to alert us by blowing the ship's horn because he was in a national park. Apparently, in the Everglades you can let a big-ass tour bus sit empty in a parking lot and run its engine, which can be heard a half a mile away, and in Biscayne, you can play bad music as loud as you want, but in Dry Tortugas you can't alert visitors that the ship is leaving by sounding its horn.

After we got back to the hotel, we walked the three miles to the main tourist area for dinner. We had a couple of "cheeseburgers in paradise" and some Margaritaville margaritas. Walking back home along the main drag, we stopped in front of a pet store window to watch four adorable puppies play with one another. They each had chomped down on a leg of a small, stuffed rabbit and were locked in a tug of war. I couldn't look away. We stood there watching them for a half an hour as crowds of partiers, drinks in hand, jostled by us. I guess that makes us officially old. Finally, Matt broke my trance by pulling me along the sidewalk toward our hotel. It's been a long day and we'll sleep well tonight.

Your friend,
Karen

~.~.~.~.~.~.~

From: **Karen Smith**
Subject: **Everglades again**
Date: **November 16, 2010**

Dear Bob and Sue,

Today we left Key West and headed to Naples where we're staying with Matt's parents for a few days. On our way across Highway 41, we stopped at Shark Valley in the north section of Everglades National Park.

Shark Valley has a visitor center, a few short trails and a narrated tram tour that follows a 15-mile paved path through the park. We planned to do the two-hour tram ride, but once Matt got a look at the tourists crowding onto the tram, he suddenly decided it would be fun to ride bikes on the path in 90-degree heat instead. I wasn't crazy about the idea because it was very humid and it didn't look like there would be any shade on the trail (there wasn't). As Matt started filling out the bike rental paperwork, the guy behind the desk looked me up and down and then shook his head, "Riding bikes on the path is hard work. You really should consider taking the tram."

Excuse me? I looked at him in amazement. This guy has never laid eyes on me before, yet he somehow knew Matt's foolproof way to get me to do something I don't want to do. Tell me that I can't do it. (Or, bribe me with a beer.) It took me years to figure out how to get Matt to do something he doesn't want to do, like hanging Christmas lights or cleaning out the garage. It's simple. I attempt to do it myself. He watches me for about five minutes and then he says I'm doing it wrong and takes over. It works every time.

So of course we rented bikes! I even took the one with the wobbly handlebars. We started out on the loop riding counter-clockwise in the opposite direction of the tram. It didn't take long to forget about the heat and humidity and the insulting bike rental man. I was too busy being amazed by how beautiful the Everglades were. Shark Valley is in the heart of the "True Everglades," or river of grass, that stretches 100 miles from Lake Okeechobee to the Gulf of Mexico. About half way around the loop, we stopped and climbed the 65-foot observation tower, which provides an outstanding view of this sawgrass prairie.

We rode by dozens of alligators lying next to the trail; most of them appeared to be asleep. Matt freaked out every time I rode within two feet of the edge of the path, yelling that an alligator was going to reach up and grab me. His concern was touching. He said, "If you lose a leg in there, I'm the one who has to go in after it and peddle it back to the visitor center to put it on ice." (It was unclear in this scenario how *I* would get back with only one leg and a bleeding stump. Maybe on the tram, although I didn't have a ticket.)

Besides alligators, we saw lots of birds, and even though we're not terribly interested in birds, these were spectacular: tall, long legs, beautiful feathers – prehistoric looking.

After we returned our bikes to the bike rental guy, I jogged back to the car. I wanted to finish strong, just to show him who he was dealing with. However, my butt was numb, the muscles in my thighs were seizing up, and my purse kept slapping crazily against my hip. I'm pretty sure I looked like someone who should have taken the tram.

We drove to Naples and arrived in time to go out for dinner with Matt's parents. Before we could leave their house, we waited while his mom got out pots and pans and spoons, and loudly *pretended* to cook dinner as their little dog sat at her feet and watched. The dog won't eat her dinner until she sees that everyone else is eating dinner. On nights they go out, Matt's mom has to fake-cook dinner so the dog will eat.

Matt said to her, "You don't need to pretend that you're making dinner. The dog will eat when she gets hungry enough."

His mom looked concerned. "Oh I couldn't let her go hungry." The dog looked up from her food and started to bark. I think she was asking for dessert.

Matt left the room and reappeared clutching a bottle of

Boodles gin he found in their liquor cabinet. I hope there's enough to last two more days.

Your friend,
Karen

~.~.~.~.~.~.~

From: **Matt Smith**
Subject: **Travel day – to American Samoa**
Date: **December 2, 2010**

Dear Bob and Sue,

Tonight Karen and I are in American Samoa, the only part of the United States south of the Equator. Among the many reasons I've been looking forward to being here is to see if it's true that toilets south of the Equator swirl in the opposite direction of toilets north of the Equator. I meant to test this theory on the plane from Honolulu. I was going to flush the airplane's toilet just as we were crossing over the Equator, but I fell asleep and missed my chance. That makes me wonder; which direction do toilets swirl that are right on the Equator? Is it a swirl-less, chaotic swoosh? Anyway, as I stood over the toilet tonight in our hotel room, watching the water drain from the bowl, I realized I hadn't a clue which direction our toilets swirl at home. For a moment, I felt like I was starring in my own version of *Dumb and Dumber*. It's a good thing that's not the only reason we made this long trip.

We left Issaquah at 5:40am this morning, and arrived at our hotel in Pago Pago (the largest town in American Samoa) at 11:00pm local time. To get here, we took a non-stop flight from Seattle to Honolulu, and after a four-hour layover, took a non-stop flight to American Samoa. All our travel went as planned, but it was a long day. With the three-hour time difference between here and Seattle, it ended up being about a

20-hour trip.

The flight choices to American Samoa are very limited. There's a Hawaiian Airlines flight to and from Honolulu every Thursday and Sunday. That's it, two flights in, two flights out each week. We're taking the Sunday flight back to Honolulu at the end of this week.

The Pago Pago International Airport was crowded when we arrived. It seemed as if the entire island came to greet the plane. The airport's main concourse is not very large and is open to the outdoors. A single, large flat screen TV hung on the wall in front of rows of chairs and benches. The locals were watching ESPN's *Sports Center* and waiting for their family and friends to exit the plane. Just below the TV was the rental car window.

I felt self-conscious enough wearing my Seattle-appropriate winter clothes in the South Pacific; but added to that, I had to walk to the front of the crowd, stick my head in the car rental window, and holler to get the attendant's attention. He told me to stay right where I was, and he would bring me the keys and show me where the car was parked. I turned around to see, what I imagined at the time was the entire island, looking at me. They were actually looking at the TV a couple of feet above my head, but it felt like they were looking at me. Karen was hiding in the back of the crowd. I waved for her to come stand next to me for no other reason than I wanted her to feel the same embarrassment I was feeling. She just looked away and slowly walked in circles around our bags with her arms folded. I was on my own.

We've rented a car so we can drive around the island and see as much as possible while we're here. Driving from the airport to our hotel, I wasn't completely sure where I was going. I didn't even know which side of the road to drive on. I felt unprepared; I hate that feeling. We waited a few minutes until another car drove by to make sure. (They drive on the right side of the road.)

The streets were dark, and the inside of the windshield quickly fogged because of the humidity. I knew if I found the main road along the water and headed east I'd be fine. It goes right past our hotel. I circled the airport a couple of times, making the same wrong turn on each pass, but eventually I found the main road and started heading in the direction of Pago Pago Harbor. Sadie's by the Sea, one of the few hotels on the island, will be our home until Sunday when we fly back to Hawaii to visit the two national parks there.

Too tired to tell you more, must sleep now.

Your friend,
Matt

~.~.~.~.~.~.~

From: **Matt Smith**
Subject: **#37 – National Park of American Samoa**
Date: **December 3, 2010**

Dear Bob and Sue,

This morning I was happy to see CNN on the flat screen TV in Sadie's restaurant. It was like a window to our world back home. We ate breakfast outside on the patio; it was sunny and in the 70s. The forecast today was for scattered showers and 80 degrees. We asked the woman who brought us coffee if the weather was always like this.

She said, "Well, it's hotter in the summer (January), you know like 82, and in the winter (July) it's cooler, the highs might be 78."

"So somewhere between 78 and 82 degrees year-round?" I asked.

"Yeah, that's about right. But, December is when we get the most rain."

We knew this was their rainy season, but December was the best time for us to come, given our other park trips. If we get wet, well, we've been wet before. I hope Karen's diaper rash doesn't come back.

We're spending all our time here on the island of Tutuila, the largest of the six islands that make up American Samoa. Tutuila is about five miles at its widest point and about 20 miles long. The island is mostly mountainous. A majority of the 55,000 residents live at lower elevations close to the water, but there are villages in the mountains. Two thirds of jobs in American Samoa are related to either government or the tuna packing plant. There's not much industry here and very few tourists.

This morning it took a couple of tries to find the park visitor center. We first went to the address for the original visitor center, which was a mile down the road from our hotel. But the entire building, which looked like it once housed several businesses as well as the visitor center, was closed. The 2009 tsunami damaged it severely. On September 29, 2009, an 8.1-magnitude earthquake 120 miles offshore caused a tsunami that slammed into the island and killed 31 people. There were places where the water from the tsunami went a mile inland. Some of the buildings along the water, including the one the visitor center was in, have not been repaired. They might never be repaired.

The new visitor center is in a small strip of offices about seven miles southwest of our hotel. Just inside the entrance of this makeshift visitor center was a wall partition with a folding table in front of it. The partition had a few maps taped to it, and on the table sat a sign-in register and the passport stamp. Karen and I stamped our passports and poked our heads around the partition to see if there was a ranger available. A young woman ranger came out and greeted us. She was very helpful with suggestions about hikes and other tips for seeing the island. She's been a ranger at this park for two years, and has been a ranger at seven other national parks, most recently Yellowstone. We swapped park stories about Yellowstone, and told her about how we were visiting all the parks, and that we were planning on snowmobiling in Yellowstone in a couple of months.

It was a good thing we found her; she gave us important information about the island and the park that we probably would have learned the hard way if we hadn't talked with her. She told us that if we wanted to go to the island of Ta'ū (the southern half of Ta'ū is part of the national park) we would have to take a private boat from Tutuila. She said those boats are not Coast Guard approved, many don't have life jackets, and we would have to, "Appraise the situation ourselves" to decide if we wanted to take the risk of riding in them. She also told us to be prepared in case the boat doesn't come back for us at the agreed upon time. I whispered to myself, "Doesn't come back for us?"

When we told her we had a rental car she said, "Then you should drive to some of the villages. The people are very friendly and welcoming to visitors. There's very little crime on the island but watch out for the roaming dogs. They can be aggressive toward people they don't know and – they're biters." I did *not* like the sound of that.

From the visitor center, we drove into the mountains. We were anxious to see the park and go for a short hike. We also wanted to find the park sign so we could take our picture in front of it. On the north side of the island, we found a pullout along the road with national park interpretive signs. The signs indicated that there was a hike from there to Craggy Point, a cliff overlooking the ocean, less than a mile away. At the far end of the trail it detoured to a clearing with views of Pola Island, a dramatic rock outcropping separated from Tutuila by less than 100-yards of ocean. Also along the trail, we could see the Village of Vatia. The village was below us on the water in a protected bay. We decided to drive to the village and take a look around.

On the way to Vatia, I spotted an official national parks sign. Graffiti was scratched onto its surface, but the sign was still legible. I thought it might be the only park sign we would find, so we stopped the car and took our picture. The sign read, "Paka O Amerika Samoa." We're a long way from the rest of Amerika, and it feels like it.

A few miles down the mountain and we were in the village. The setting was beautiful, but the homes looked run down. There were few people about, only a handful of small children playing outside. Every house seemed to have a dog sleeping in the yard. All the dogs on this island look like they're related; they probably are. A couple of them barked at us and chased our car. They had vicious barks, not "Come throw my ball for me" barks. I wasn't going to get out and stroll through the village with barkers and biters everywhere.

It was just before noon, and the sky was darkening, rain was coming. We canceled our plans to hike and drove around the island, seeing it from the car. A sign next to one of the few strip malls on the island pointed to Shane-J Filipino Fast Food. At Shane-J's we sat under an awning out of the rain. At a small table with a red and white-checkered, plastic tablecloth, we ate peppered beef and BBQ pork sticks over rice for lunch. The woman who served us kept calling Karen *mommy*. "What you have mommy? You have Pepsi too, mommy?"

I said to Karen, "She thinks you're my mom."

"She doesn't think I'm your mom. It's a universal sign of respect, like when someone refers to the Queen as *mum*."

"Are you saying she thinks you're the Queen?"

"No, I'm saying you're an idiot."

After our lunch, we went back to Sadie's and napped for a couple of hours. In the early evening, the rain stopped and it was pleasant outside. We sat outside at Sadie's bar until dusk and drank a glass of wine. Sitting there I heard a crunch like an apple being eaten, but it sounded as if it was coming from above us. It was. There was a bat in the tree above the patio eating some kind of fruit. I could hear it chewing. The fruit bats here are the size of dogs; they're called flying foxes. They can grow to have wingspans of 36 inches or more. That's a big bat. I'd like to see two million bats that size fly out of a cave.

Today we were a bit jet lagged; hopefully tomorrow we will have our energy back and the weather will be clear. We're planning on going for a long hike in the park.

Your friend,
Matt

~.~.~.~.~.~.~

From: **Matt Smith**
Subject: **American Samoa continued**
Date: **December 4, 2010**

Dear Bob and Sue,

A kitten pawed a wine cork at our feet as we ate breakfast on the patio this morning. Karen put her hand down to get the kitten's attention with no luck, so she tossed a piece of bagel in its direction. She said, "I'd like to take this one home with us. I'll just put it in my suitcase; no one would ever know." If I had a nickel for every time I heard that...

The rain cleared out overnight. While sitting at breakfast, it looked as if it would be a good day for a hike. Mount Alava Trail follows the ridgeline of the mountains to the north above Pago Pago Harbor. It marks the south boundary of the national park. That would be our hike for the day. At Fagasā Pass, we parked our rental car by the trailhead. Clouds were forming and we felt a few raindrops. We weren't going to turn back because of rain; we only had a couple of days to see the island, and we were hiking today no matter what. The trail cut a path through the jungle, and the thick trees shaded us for the first couple of miles. As we got closer to the peak, the clouds cleared and there were open areas on the trail where we were in the direct sunlight. We sweated like soaker hoses.

In one of the clearings, we saw a strange tree just a few feet from the trail. It had what looked like an unopened flower bud the size of a football hanging down about ten feet off the ground. Bright green shoots grew out of the stalk about a foot above the flower bud. Later we learned this was a banana tree; the green shoots were new bananas. The banana tree flower initially shoots up, but its weight eventually causes the flower stalk to bend toward the ground. By the time the bananas grow out of the flower stalk, it's upside down, and the bananas grow toward the sun.

There was an old communications tower at the trail's peak. From the base of the tower, there was a panoramic view of Pago Pago Harbor on one side and the north shore of the island on the other, all 1,500 feet below. There we were, standing in the jungle on the top of a mountain ridge in the South Pacific with incredible views of the ocean, islands, villages, and the unusual vegetation around us. This is one of the great things about our parks trip: it's taken us to places we would never have thought to go otherwise.

It felt good to have already hiked seven miles while the day was still young. Back at the car, we noticed another park sign. This one was in better shape than the one from yesterday, so we took our picture in front of it. Now we have a couple to choose from when we make the photo album of our trip.

There aren't many dining choices on the island, so we went back to Sadie's for lunch after the hike. The same waiter who served us breakfast was our server for lunch. He was a nice kid; he looked to be about 20 years old.

Karen asked him, "Do you like living here?"

He said, "Oh yeah, I wouldn't want to live anywhere else."

"Have you ever been to the mainland of the United States?"

"No, I don't want to go there."

"Why not?"

"It scares me. I heard that there are a lot of shootings there. I'm afraid I'll get shot. There is very little crime here.

No one has a gun."

Karen said, "It's not as bad as you think. Or at least, it's not something that should keep you from visiting."

He said, "I've also heard that everyone smokes, even little kids."

"That's also an exaggeration. People smoke but not little kids. I've never seen little kids smoking."

"Well, that's what people here believe."

American Samoa may be far from the rest of the United States, but they seem very proud to be Americans. There is an Army Reserve Unit and an Army Recruiting office on the island. Even some of the graffiti on the concrete barriers along the road has a patriotic theme; one read, "Happy 110 Years American Samoa." An American flag was painted next to those words.

While we ate lunch, we could see the hotel staff preparing tables for a large party. We asked our waiter about the event. He said, "The Army Reserve Unit is putting on their Christmas party here tonight."

I asked the waiter, "Are many of the residents on the island in the military?"

He said, "Some people who live here are in the reserve unit, but when young people go into the military they usually don't come back until they're finished with their service or retire. There are a lot of people on the island who are retired from the military."

He explained, "There aren't many jobs on the island so after high school they go into the military as a career, and when they retire they come back and live very well on their military pension. Yeah, the people you see driving new cars on the island are mostly retired military. They come back, build a nice house for their entire family, buy a new car and live pretty well for little money."

It turned out to be a perfect afternoon to drive and see the island. From our hotel, we drove on Highway 001 toward the east end of the island. The road was near the ocean the entire way and in pretty good shape. We averaged about 30 miles per hour on the long, twisting road. On the other side of Pago Pago Harbor from our hotel is a tuna packing plant. There used to be two major companies with tuna packing plants on the island, but one of them closed and left many people out of work. The remaining plant is responsible for creating about a third of the jobs on the island.

Beyond the tuna plant, we drove through village after village. Many times we saw signs for villages but saw no more than two or three houses close together. Each village has a chief and a fale tele or "big house." A big house is an open-air pavilion, usually with a thatched roof, where villagers hold community and family gatherings; the chief also holds his council meetings there.

Every big house was unique. Some were elaborate and well cared for with paved parking areas in front; others were small and looked like a strong wind would knock them over. Most of the big houses we saw today were empty – except for a dog or two napping in the shade of the roof.

The farther east we went on the island the fewer homes we saw. The views were iconic South Pacific: white sand beaches, palm trees, and a blue on blue horizon. Now and then we saw groups of kids, in a wide range of ages, all playing together in the shallow water. What a great place for a kid to grow up.

The one place my research assistant said we absolutely must visit on the island was Tisa's Barefoot Bar. It's located at Alega Beach on the east end of Tutuila Island. (Everyone calls it Tisa's.) Tisa has a home on the beach, and built a hut next to it, so she can serve food and drinks to the few tourists and visitors who make it to her end of the island. It took us a couple of passes, but we finally found it.

Tisa's is as authentic as a beach bar could be. She built it – at least partially – with stuff that washed up on her beach. Karen and I sat on the deck outside overlooking the ocean and drank a beer. We didn't want to leave. The only other customers were two women from Washington D.C. who work for the federal government and were here on business. They came to Tisa's on their day off while waiting for the Sunday flight back to Honolulu.

Two hours at Tisa's and we were thoroughly relaxed. We drove back to our hotel, cleaned up and went to Sadie's sister hotel down the street for dinner, the Sadie Thompson Inn. We were lucky to have good weather today. We're still feeling jet lagged from Thursday, so we're going to bed early. Tomorrow we start our trek back to Hawaii.

Your friend,
Matt

~.~.~.~.~.~.~

From: **Matt Smith**
Subject: **Travel day – to Hilo**
Date: **December 6, 2010**

Dear Bob and Sue,

By the time we made it to the patio for breakfast yesterday, the Sunday NFL games were on TV. With the time difference, the games come on earlier than on the mainland. Football is popular in America Samoa; there are more college and NFL football players from America Samoa (per capita) than from anywhere else in the United States.

The Army Reserve Unit's Christmas party from the night before went late; I could hear the music past 1:00am. The staff had already cleaned the patio area, but some of the trash ended up in the harbor. The wind must have blown a trashcan into the water during the night. After breakfast, I sat on the hotel's small beach looking at the harbor. I had no motivation to pack. Instead, I watched the debris slowly wash onto the beach.

I'd choose a piece of trash in the harbor and root for it to make it to shore. It would wash up and stay for a moment, but the next wave would take it back out. Finally, it would land high enough on the beach to stay for good. Then I'd choose another piece and root for it. I gave up on the Styrofoam cup after its many weak efforts, and instead rooted for the plastic Sprite bottle. "If the coconut can make it, so can you," I encouraged the Sprite bottle – not out loud of course.

Karen came out to the beach and said, "It's getting late. You should come in and start getting ready to leave."

I replied, "As soon as the Sprite bottle makes it ashore I'll take a shower and pack."

Our flight to Honolulu was scheduled to leave at 11:20pm. That gave us all day to fill with odds and ends. We checked out of the hotel and looked at each other with the same "What do *you* want to do for the next ten hours?" expression. One thing was for sure; we needed to do laundry. Everything I owned smelled like the island, and not in a pleasant tropical fruit/coconut way. A mile from the hotel was a Laundromat. It was about noon when we realized we'd joined an American Samoa Sunday-after-church tradition: laundry day. Just after we loaded our washing machine, a hoard of families arrived, each with what looked like at least a week's worth of laundry. Everyone was pleasant with us, but we got more than a few strange looks. I think we used someone's regular machine, setting their Sunday plans back an hour.

With our laundry done, there were only seven or eight hours left to kill. I don't kill time well. We decided to drive the entire length of the island from west to east. Starting from the middle of the island, we drove first to the far west end. It was interesting to see the entire island. There seemed to be more churches than the population could support. Many were elaborately decorated for Christmas. One had 21 plastic Santas on its facade (I took a picture of it and counted them.)

After our drive, there were still hours to spare, so we went back to Tisa's. She wasn't surprised to see us again, even though we said our goodbyes the day before. We're not the first people to kill time at Tisa's waiting for the 11:20pm

Sunday flight.

She said, "Let me fix you dinner." The smells coming from her kitchen made it impossible to refuse her offer. Her son-in-law fixed us huge steaks with grilled bananas on the side, which he cut from a bunch hanging by the bar. He told us that he spent eight years cultivating this type of banana, called King's Bananas. His original plants came from the Manuʻa Islands just east of Tutuila; they're the only kind of banana that grow right side up. His story fascinated me and I believed it completely, but Karen wasn't so sure, she said she found a Chiquita sticker on her plate. Either way, they were fantastic.

Tisa sat and talked with us for a couple of hours, telling us about the American Samoa culture, both the good and bad. After our early dinner, she encouraged us to walk along the beach in front of her house/bar/restaurant. She told us that the beaches are the property of the villages, and visitors should ask permission before using them. The water was very clear, and not more than knee deep for a long distance from shore. Brightly colored fish swam around our legs. It was like snorkeling with our heads above the water.

After more goodbyes, we were off to the airport for a very early check-in. We returned our rental car at 7:30pm. I thought this was ridiculously early until I saw the check-in line; it was at least 100 people deep. I could tell as soon as we got in line that something wasn't right. A Hawaiian Airlines agent came on the public address system and said, in a tone that sounded like she was making a routine announcement, that our flight was being delayed until 5:00am. She added, "So everyone should just come back about 3:30 am." Did I mention I don't kill time well?

We got our rental car back – no charge – thank you Avis, and Hawaiian Airlines paid for an extra night at Sadie's. We drove back to our hotel and napped in our clothes until 2:00am. From that point forward, everything went smoothly. At least I think it did; I was delirious for most of it. When we got to Honolulu, we caught a quick flight to Hilo, where we're staying for two nights.

Tomorrow we're visiting Hawaii Volcanoes National Park, and maybe a nut factory.

Your friend,
Matt

~.~.~.~.~.~.~.~

From: **Karen Smith**
Subject: **#38 – Hawaii Volcanoes National Park**
Date: **December 7, 2010**

Dear Bob and Sue,

This morning when I reached into the bottom of my suitcase and pulled out a pair of shorts, there was a melted Peppermint Patty stuck to the butt. It's really sweet of Matt to hide these in my suitcase and surprise me, but I wish he would double bag them. Now I have a brown stain (surprise!) on the backside of my shorts in the worst possible place for a brown stain to be.

I've been looking forward to this day for a long time. The images I've seen of Hawaii Volcanoes National Park are spectacular – fiery molten lava sputtering, oozing, and flowing from Kilauea. In addition to Kilauea, one of the world's most active volcanoes, the park has another volcano, Mauna Loa, the world's most massive.

Here are some fun facts I read about Kilauea. The word Kilauea means "spewing" or "much spreading" in Hawaiian. It has erupted 35 times since 1952, not including the current episode. The volume of erupted material is large enough to pave a road around the world three times. Millions of tourists visit Kilauea each year, making it the most visited attraction in Hawaii and the most visited volcano in the world. The USGS considers Kilauea the most dangerous volcano in the U.S.

After all this hype and anticipation, when we got to the

park, the volcano was just sitting there doing nothing. At the Kilauea Visitor Center, a message on the wall said that no lava was flowing today. We had assumed lava was always flowing. Thinking this must be a mistake, we asked a park ranger if this were true. She said, "No lava flowing anywhere in the park." There's a hotline to call to find out where lava is flowing, so I called it just to make sure. I called every two hours for the rest of the day just in case it started flowing again. No luck. As Matt put it, "We got a dud day."

We hiked along the crater rim trail and the Kilauea Iki trail, four miles round trip. Not what you'd call a pretty hike. It was mostly grey scorched rock with very little vegetation. As we got to the middle of the crater, we heard a voice talking very loudly and couldn't figure out where it was coming from. I thought it might be Pele, the volcano goddess who lives there. Then we passed a woman, a mere mortal, sitting on a rock by the trail talking on her cell phone. She was conducting a conference call right beside the trail. Nice. Matt goes into a tailspin every time he sees someone talking on a cell phone in a national park wilderness area. We stopped while he took pictures of her. He also took a short video clip if you'd like to see the call in action.

Images and stories of Pele are prominent throughout the park. Apparently she lives in the craters of the Kilauea Volcano, and sends ribbons of fiery lava down the mountainside. Today must have been her day off. Legend has it that Pele puts a curse on anyone who steals from her home. Each year, guilty people from all over the world mail thousands of lava rocks back to the park, claiming to have had terrible things happen to them since taking the rocks from Pele's home. If every park has a god or goddess watching over it, then it's a good thing I didn't take the penis driftwood from Olympic National Park.

After lunch, we drove the Chain of Craters Road. It descends 3,700 feet in 20 miles and ends at the coast where a 2003 lava flow crossed the road. We parked along the road and hiked to the Pu'u Loa Petroglyphs, one of the best and largest petroglyph fields on the Big Island. It was 1.4-miles round trip. This particular field has over 15,000 petroglyphs, which have been scratched or pecked into the hard pahoehoe lava surface.

When we were almost back to our car, we saw grandparents with two little girls just starting out on the hike. They were only 100 feet from the parking lot when we heard one of the girls whining, "I want to go back to the caaaaaaar." We could tell this wasn't the first time she said it. The grandfather told her, "We *are* going back to the car, just as soon as we see the pictures on the rocks." Matt and I are very familiar with the "I want to go back to the car" whine, which is usually followed by the "I can't walk anymore" wail. That's the point when our kids would go limp, making us carry or drag their dead weight back to the car. It's amazing how a 40-pound kid can make herself seem twice as heavy when she doesn't want to do something.

On our way back to Hilo, we stopped at the Mauna Loa Nut Factory, hoping to get free macadamia nut samples. They told us that we'd have to take the tour to sample the nuts, which sounded like too much effort for a nut. We wandered around the nut store until Matt started doing his imitation of Harlan Pepper (Christopher Guest's character from *Best In Show*) naming nuts: "*Pea*-nut, *hazel* nut, *cashew* nut, *macadamia* nut, *pine* nut, *wal*-nut, *pistachio* nut, *red pistachio* nut..." He does the accent and everything.

All day long, we looked forward to having dinner at Ken's House of Pancakes. On their reader board, they advertise coconut pancakes and coconut syrup. Even though the coconut is no longer dedicating its life to us, and we realized we weren't in a healthy relationship with Coco Lopez, we couldn't resist.

Tomorrow we're heading to Maui to visit the other Hawaiian national park – Haleakala.

Your friend,
Karen

~.~.~.~.~.~.~.~

From: **Matt Smith**
Subject: **#39 – Haleakala National Park**
Date: **December 8, 2010**

Dear Bob and Sue,

Karen and I visited Haleakala National Park before. We came to Maui eight years ago to celebrate our 20th wedding anniversary, and got up early on the morning of the big day to drive to the park. Not realizing before the trip that it would be cold at the top of the mountain, we hadn't packed any warm clothes, so we stopped at Wal-Mart to buy sweatshirts on our way to the park. While there, we ate breakfast at McDonald's. As we were eating, Karen took my hand and said, "Twenty years ago, I couldn't have imagined that you would take me to a McDonald's *inside* a Wal-Mart for our 20th wedding anniversary. Thank you for making all my dreams come true."

What I remember about the park from before is the long drive up the mountain, the drop in temperature when we got to the visitor center, and the Silverswords. A Silversword is a plant that grows at high elevations in Hawaii. It can live up to 50 years and blooms only once, and then it dies. We didn't hike in the crater on that visit and later we regretted it. Today we hiked in the crater.

The road to the park is a twisting climb through open range. I had to watch my speed; several times there were cattle in the road just around a hairpin turn. Whenever we stop for cattle in the road, Karen rolls down her window and talks to them. Mostly she asks them questions, "What are you doing in the road?" "Are you supposed to be in the road?" "Does your mother know you're in the road?" They have yet to answer her. She never tires of seeing them; she considers them a wildlife sighting, which is odd because she considers deer in the road a nuisance.

Once we reached the park, we saw several signs depicting a silhouette of a large bird with chicks following behind. The signs were cautioning us to watch for nenes, a goose native to Hawaii. They're sort of the park mascot; the park passport stamp has a nene on it. We didn't see any but we were watching for them.

At the Haleakala Visitor Center, we asked a ranger for hiking suggestions. She gave us a trail map that looked like it was a copy of a copy of a copy. Someone needs to find the original. We decided to take the Sliding Sands Trail to a point three miles out, for a total of a six-mile round-trip hike.

Karen asked the ranger, "How long should it take us to do that hike?"

The ranger said, "Three to four hours."

"That seems long. Six miles usually takes us about two hours." I recognized Karen's tone. It's the one she uses when telling the person who is answering her that they have *not* given the correct response, and they get one more try.

The ranger replied to Karen slowly, as if talking to a ten year old, "You need to remember that it will take *two to three times longer* to hike back up than it will to hike down."

This had the same effect as saying to her, "Biking the Shark Valley loop is hard, you better take the tram." Karen decided right then we would do the six-mile hike in two hours, or die trying.

The trail started at the visitor center and dropped steadily for 1,400 feet on its way to the Ka Lu 'u o ka 'Ō 'ō cinder cone. (By the way, it took me 20 minutes to figure out how to type the correct symbols for this name.)

The park service doesn't call the crater a crater anymore; they called it an "erosion zone." The landscape in the erosion zone looks like a different planet. It's what I imagine Mars would look like up close, but with Silverswords here and there. The three miles down took us an hour. From the visitor center, the cinder cone hadn't looked very far away, but the distance was deceptive. The constantly changing clouds, the view of the ocean, the colors of the cinders, it was all very dramatic and beautiful. Regardless, Karen was intent on making it back to the visitor center in an hour.

At our turnaround point, there was a couple with a young boy who was in the midst of a meltdown. He had enough of the Sliding Sands Trail and was letting everyone within a half a mile know about it. We shuddered as we walked by and heard their attempts to calm him down. The mom and dad were shivering and protecting their faces from the cold wind as they tried to interest the boy in, well, we're not sure in what; there's nothing that could interest a three-year old in this vast, empty landscape. We're also not sure how they got him back to the car. Every time they picked him up he arched his back and kicked. Note to self: don't take small kids on a long hike in an extinct volcanic crater – I mean erosion zone.

Maui may be a tropical island, but at 9,000 feet, it's cold. The temperature was *maybe* 50 degrees, and the wind was steady at 30 miles per hour. We froze our asses off. I don't remember being colder on any other hike on our parks trip. While hiking back up, we knew the faster we went, the sooner we would be warm and out of the wind, but our lungs were burning. Still, there was no stopping or slowing down; Karen was the one who had us on a death march this time. When we got to the parking lot we'd been gone for two hours and ten minutes. It was time to hit the beach.

It wasn't a long visit to the park, but we took care of business. The next couple of days we'll spend at sea level and then fly home on Saturday.

Your friend,
Matt

~.~.~.~.~.~.~

From: **Karen Smith**
Subject: **#40 – Saguaro National Park**
Date: **January 19, 2011**

Dear Bob and Sue,

I was embarrassed after I picked up the newsletter at the Saguaro National Park visitor center and realized we've been pronouncing the name of the park incorrectly. There it was, in huge font for us to sound out – Sah-WAH-Row. Matt and I have been calling it Swa-HA-Row. We forgot the rule that "gua" is pronounced like "wa," with heavy breathing. And to think we each completed four years of high school Spanish. We probably should have spent more time studying and less time at *fiestas con cerveza*.

A saguaro is what most people probably picture in their minds when they think of a cactus: tall, green, with "arms" on the side that sweep up. Taco Time's Ned is a saguaro. Every direction you look in the park there are thousands of them, some as tall as 50 feet. I think they look like armies of soldiers protecting the park, but actually it's the other way around: the park is protecting them. (Harming a saguaro in any way is illegal by state law in Arizona, and when houses or highways are built, special permits must be obtained to move a saguaro.) Every ten years, they survey the number of saguaros in the park. In 2010, it was estimated that there were 1,896,030 saguaros, up from 1,624,821 saguaros in 2000.

Saguaro National Park has two units on opposite sides (east and west) of Tucson. We started on the east side, which is called the Rincon Mountain District. They've built an extensive, well-marked network of hiking trails. As we were hiking, an animal the size of a coyote streaked across our path then stopped. It was the biggest jackrabbit we've ever seen, straight out of Alice in Wonderland; its ears were at least a foot long. Later we saw a family of javelinas crossing the road, big ones with their little ones. Many people who live here think javelinas are a nuisance, but to me, they seem very sweet. As we drove out of the park, we saw a dead javelina on the side of the road. I'd like to think it was a grandparent javelina who died peacefully of old age, but Matt said that it was probably run over by someone whose wife complains when he swerves for animals in the road.

On our second day, we headed farther out of town to the west unit of the park, called the Tucson Mountain District. We climbed Wasson Peak, the highest mountain in the district at 4,687 ft. It was a great eight-mile round-trip hike with amazing views of the desert to the north. We thought we might see a gila monster, but the only animal we ran into on the trail was an off-leash German Shepherd.

I found some helpful information about gila monsters on a welcome-to-Tucson website. A gila monster is one of only two venomous lizards in the world. Most of a gila monster's teeth come equipped with two small grooves that conduct the venom deeper into their victim's wound. The venom is a nerve toxin. The toxin is not injected, as it is with a snakebite, but instead flows freely into the wound as the *lizard continues to gnaw and chew on its victim*. While the bite-delivered toxin can overpower the gila monster's enemies and prey, it's rarely fatal to humans, even though it's as potent as the venom of the western diamondback rattlesnake. It is, however, quite painful and has other negative and undesirable effects.

Gila monsters lock themselves tightly onto whatever (or whomever) they bite, and when bone is included in the bite, they can hang on for an extremely long time and be difficult to remove. If it does remain firmly attached to a body part, there are several ways to remove it safely from the victim. You can try to detach the lizard by prying its mouth open with a stick or pen or any other similar object. Or, use a lighter or matches to put heat directly under its jaw. If there is a suitable body of water present (or a bucket or tub of water), you can immerse the lizard until it releases. Finally, if none of these methods work, you can try my personal favorite, which the website warns to use "ONLY AS A VERY LAST RESORT." You can grab the animal VERY FIRMLY by the tail and with a swift, powerful motion, pull it off. This is NOT advisable as there will almost surely be extensive damage to the victim.

I was very concerned after reading these facts about gila monsters because even though Matt is well prepared for an emergency, he doesn't have a lighter or matches or a bucket or tub of water in his backpack. If the situation arises, I'm pretty sure he would use the grab-and-yank method to remove a gila monster from my body.

After making it safely down Wasson Peak, with all body parts intact, we went to the Signal Hill picnic area where we ate our lunch and looked at the petroglyphs that the Hohokam Indians pecked into stone. The interpretive sign said these drawings could have been made as far back as AD 300. However, I think the "Do it!" petroglyph may have been a little more recent.

We've had a great time here in the Tucson area. Besides exploring the national park, we also hiked in Sabino Canyon, which is part of Coronado National Forest. We love being out hiking in the sun every day rather than hibernating in the Seattle rain. We can feel our Vitamin D levels increasing already. It's also inspiring to see so many older people here who are active, physically fit and enjoying life. And the Mexican food and margaritas are *muy bueno*.

Tomorrow we're driving to Palm Springs to visit Joshua Tree National Park.

Su Amiga,
Karen

~.~.~.~.~.~.~

From: **Matt Smith**
Subject: **#41 – Joshua Tree National Park**
Date: **January 24, 2011**

Dear Bob and Sue,

Karen told me twice today that I was being rude. My personal best is three times in one day, so I'm staying up late just in case I get one more opportunity to match the record.

We visited Joshua Tree National Park today. Our first hike was to the top of Ryan Mountain, a three-mile round trip. This is the highest point in the park at 5,458 feet. The hike to the peak was fairly steep; we were breathing hard on the way up. The trail wound in and out of the sun. It was windy but not as windy as yesterday. I was hot and cold at the same time for much of the hike. Karen seemed to be fine. At the peak, there's a 360-degree view of the park and the surrounding beautiful and desolate desert.

The top of Ryan Mountain is not a large area. In the center, there's a pile of rocks about ten feet tall; it's the highest place on the mountain. From the top of the rock pile, you can see in all directions. Sitting at the base of the rocks was a guy talking on a cell phone. It was clear from his conversation that he was on a conference call, which was good because that's what we were hoping for – to come to a national park in the middle of the desert, take a hike to the top of a mountain, basically get as far away from people as we possibly can, so we can look at the amazing vistas and listen to this idiot's conference call.

I went up to him to get his attention, and to ask him to knock it off. Karen doesn't like it when I confront people's rude behavior. She says it's rude. I stood two feet away looking straight at him; he turned his back to me and kept talking loudly. So, I took a few pictures of him to make him even more uncomfortable, and we hiked down the mountain.

That was not the first or even the tenth time we've experienced people in the middle of a national park talking loudly on their cell phones. When we spent the night at Crater Lake Lodge, I woke up startled at 6:30am thinking someone was in our room. We were on the second floor and slept with the window open. A man was talking loudly on his cell phone right below our window. He went on and on, "Yesterday we went for a hike and saw a squirrel... then we saw another squirrel... no, we don't know if it was the same squirrel as the first squirrel... then we saw a third squirrel..." I leaned out the window, looked at him and quietly said, "Dude." He looked at me like I was chipped paint on the side of the building, and just kept talking. Why do people do that? It's like giving everyone else the middle finger. Why is there cell service in the middle of the wilderness in the first place?

After Ryan Mountain, we drove to a picnic area and sat in the sun at a table eating our PB&J. The wind died down, and it was very nice. The area where we were eating had several picnic tables scattered amongst large boulders. The tables were arranged so each had its own semi-private area. A family with two small kids pulled into the parking lot, and with great effort and drama, unloaded their kids, cooler, toys, diaper bag, etc. After they arranged their picnic area just the way they wanted, they walked over to *our* picnic area, so their kids could climb on the rocks right next to us. Now, I know you're probably thinking I'm a bit anti-social after the cell phone rant, but come on, they had rocks to climb on in their own picnic area. Why were they over here? I wanted to offer to trade them spots; obviously they wanted to be in our picnic area rather than theirs. Karen said, "No, that would be rude."

I took some deep breaths, and acted like I didn't see the dad turn his back on his two-year old as she almost fell head first off a four-foot rock just a few feet from me. I wasn't going to offer parenting advice; that would be rude. I remained silent and polite.

I placed a scrap of bread on the ground next to me. It took a chipmunk about two seconds to find it. (You're not supposed to feed animals in a national park, but I couldn't resist.) This brought squeals of joy (or terror, I couldn't tell which) from the small children, and an angry, "Don't!" from Karen. (Remember, Karen's not a fan of squirrel-like animals.) I did it again. More chipmunks, more squealing, more "Don'ts!" This upset everyone just enough that the parents, with kids in tow, went back to their picnic area for lunch. For a moment it looked as if Karen was going with them.

With lunch finished, we drove to the Lost Horse Mine trailhead and hiked the four-mile loop. I really enjoyed this hike. It was moderately flat and went back into a secluded area of the park where we felt we were the only ones for miles around. As the loop started to bend back toward the trailhead, the trail flattened out along a dry wash. We kept seeing shallow holes in the sand that looked freshly dug; they were about a foot in diameter. Later we asked a ranger about them, and she told us that desert tortoises probably dug those holes. We didn't see any tortoises on the hike. We've found that it's rare to see wildlife in the desert except at dawn and dusk.

On the last mile of the hike, we walked past all shapes and sizes of Joshua trees. They thrive in the Mojave Desert and are fast growers for desert plants. Thousands of individual fibers make up their trunks, which don't have growth rings, so it's very difficult to determine their age. Plant experts believe Joshua Trees are able to survive in harsh desert conditions for hundreds of years. They look like a strange cross between a pine tree, a cactus and a palm tree; something you would expect to see in a Dr. Seuss book. Karen loves Joshua trees.

Tomorrow we're hiking Indian Canyons in the Agua Caliente Indian Reservation just outside Palm Desert, and then we'll fly home the next day.

Your friend,
Matt

~.~.~.~.~.~.~

From: **Matt Smith**
Subject: **#42 – Yellowstone National Park**
Date: **February 6, 2011**

Dear Bob and Sue,

It started looking like winter when we reached Bozeman. By the time we turned south onto Highway 89 in Livingston, we felt as if we were entering a deep freeze: ice-covered roads, very few cars, and rest stops with unplowed parking lots. We're on a two-park trip to see Yellowstone and Grand Teton National Parks. Yesterday we drove from Issaquah to Butte, Montana, and got an early start today.

At Gardiner, we entered Yellowstone National Park through the famous Roosevelt Arch. The park service plows the road from Gardiner to Mammoth Hot Springs, and a couple of miles beyond. They also plow the road into the Lamar Valley east of Mammoth. Those are the only roads in the park that are open from mid-October to mid-May. Otherwise, travel through the park is limited to snow coach or snowmobile.

We reached Mammoth Hot Springs Hotel by mid-day, too early to check in, but we tried anyway. The woman at the front desk said she could do the paperwork, and give us our keys later. She told us the rooms on higher floors tended to be warmer, sometimes too warm, and asked if we would prefer one of the rooms on the first floor, which tend to be *cooler*. We chose the cool room; I can't sleep if the room is too warm.

With time to kill, we went to the visitor center to take care of business. There were few visitors there, so we pestered the ranger with questions about what it's like to visit the park in winter. He was very patient with us.

At the passport stamp station, a young girl, who looked to be about six or seven years old, was abusing the passport stamp. She held it like an ice pick and stabbed the desk, killing imaginary bugs. I shuddered at the sight. Her mother – I'm guessing the adult standing next to her was her mother – stood without expression while the child burned off energy.

Every time the stamp slammed into the desk I pictured in my mind the stamp image being mashed beyond recognition. Clearly the mom/adult wasn't going to intervene even though it was obvious I wanted to use the stamp. I said to the girl (in my kind, soft voice), "Do you mind if I borrow this for a moment?" It wasn't a question as much as a notice: I was taking control of the stamp. I placed my hand over the stamp handle; for a moment, we both had a firm grip on it. She resisted for a couple of seconds then let go. I gave her mom/guardian a smile sending her a silent message, "That's right. There's a new sheriff in town."

I tested the stamp on a scrap of paper to make sure it was readable and the date was correct, which it was, and then turned to Karen, who was watching from across the room and said, "Sweetie, do you want to stamp your passport?" I was holding the stamp in the air as far away from the child as the chain it was attached to would let me. The child undoubtedly expected me to hand the stamp back to her, but there was no way I was giving it up.

The girl looked at her mom/babysitter, then back at me, then back at her mom/older sister. She had three choices: wait me out (unlikely given her short attention span), throw a fit (likely), or move on. Soon, the swath of bear fur laid out on the table nearby was too much temptation. She moved on.

Karen came over, staring at me with cocked head and wide eyes and murmured, "So, you're now wrestling the stamp away from small children are you?" I handed her the stamp and closed my passport. The child was already bored with the bear fur and was now molesting a stuffed prairie dog that had a "DO NOT TOUCH!" sign attached to its leg. I looked at Karen and whispered, "That's right. There's a new sheriff in town."

Back outside, steam rose from thermals a few blocks south of the visitor center; it looked like the aftermath of a forest fire. A handful of elk stood a few yards away from the smoldering landscape. Across the road, a lone buffalo pushed snow away from the ground with his head, looking for something to eat. We were anxious to get into the park, but it was getting dark, so we went back to the hotel and checked into our room. It was an early night; we watched the first quarter of the Super Bowl in the main hall of the hotel – eating peanut butter and jelly sandwiches for dinner – and then read in our room. Tomorrow we will explore the park.

> Your friend,
> Matt

~.~.~.~.~.~.~

From: **Matt Smith**
Subject: **Yellowstone day two**
Date: **February 7, 2011**

Dear Bob and Sue,

We froze our asses off last night. This morning when we woke up, the thermometer on my combination whistle / thermometer / compass / magnifying glass read 45 degrees. This must be what the woman at the front desk yesterday meant by *cool*.

I opened the door to the hallway thinking that maybe the heat was out in the entire hotel. A wall of warm air greeted me. It felt so good I wanted to curl up against the wall and sleep out there. As I stood there in my pajamas, a security guard walked by. "Anything wrong?" he asked.

"No," I replied. He smiled and kept going. It wouldn't have mattered if all the guests in the hotel were standing in the hall outside our room; it felt too good to close the door. Karen pulled the covers away from her face just long enough to say, "Leave it open!" Then, she disappeared again. For ten minutes, we laid under the blankets with the door open waiting for our room to warm up enough for us to get dressed. People have given us grief about not camping out on our parks trip. Karen and I decided that last night counts as sleeping outside.

At 7:00am, hotel guests packed the lobby waiting for their tours to depart. Some were going on snowshoeing, cross-country skiing, or wildlife photography tours. Others were taking snow coaches to Old Faithful Snow Lodge where they would spend the night. Another group was getting ready to begin a three-day snowmobile trek through the park. Karen and I were waiting for a bus to take us to the warming-hut about a mile away where we would be outfitted for our all-day snowmobile tour to Old Faithful.

Snowmobiling in Yellowstone has been a controversial issue for many years. We were hesitant about doing it because we'd read complaints about the exhaust pollution, the noise pollution, and how the snowmobiles are a threat to wildlife. But, a ranger told us that conditions have improved; the snowmobiles used today in the park are quieter and put out less pollution than in the past. The park service enforces rules requiring that concessionaires use "best available technology" snowmobiles in the park. As far as the threat to wildlife, park rules require snowmobiles to stay on designated paths. Snowmobiles are not allowed to approach wildlife, and the total number of snowmobiles allowed in the park is limited to 318 per day. Finally, the only way to snowmobile in the park is with a guide; even experienced riders must be in a guided group. These rules seem to have resulted in a compromise between the pro- and anti- snowmobile advocates.

At the warming hut, they fitted us for our snowmobiling gear. We didn't need to bring our own cold-weather clothing. The tour company provided everything: full body suit, boots, gloves, and helmet. The body suit went over our regular clothes. Once suited, Karen looked like an astronaut, only in black. Through the windshield of her helmet, I could see the concern in her eyes as she tried to figure out how all this gear would come off when she needed to pee in the wilderness.

Karen and I each drove our own snowmobile. It was

more expensive for both of us to ride single, but we think it was worth the cost for the experience. There were ten people and seven snowmobiles in our group: our guide, Cody, three other couples riding double, a single woman, and Karen and I. The snowmobiles were sleek and looked new. Each had a milk carton on back to put anything that absolutely had to make the trip with you. I put my backpack in the carton and secured it with a bungee cord.

It was 20 degrees, overcast, and snowing lightly while we stood in front of our snowmobiles for our orientation talk. We learned how to operate the machines, and most importantly, how to adjust the heat, especially the handgrip warmers. Operating the machines was surprisingly simple; they're idiot proof – I should know. Cody said we were lucky today because it was warm. They do this tour even when the temperature is zero degrees; they cancel when it gets much below that. We climbed onto our rides, started them, and followed Cody single-file into the park.

Karen and I couldn't talk to each other while riding, but I knew what she was thinking as we pulled away from the warming hut, that we were entering a *magical place*. It was magical. The path we took was the main park road (Highway 89) south from Mammoth Hot Springs, the same road we've driven many times in summer. This time, though, instead of riding on pavement, we were on top of five feet of snow. Since snowmobiles and snow coaches use this path daily, the park service grooms it, smoothing out the deep grooves and washboard ruts.

We weren't a half a mile into our ride when Cody stopped. We all parked behind him while he pointed out the mule deer carcass a few feet from the trail. He said wolves made the kill yesterday. As I rode by, I could see only the ribs and half the hide remained.

We continued south along the trail. The conditions changed constantly – from gently snowing, to calm and sunny, to sideways blowing snow. There was one stretch of the trail that Cody called "the flats." It was a few miles long with no trees. It's always windy there. Every 100 feet or so, fluorescent orange poles marked the trail. When we rode through the flats, it was a whiteout. The snow was blowing so hard that all I could see were the markers; I couldn't even see the snowmobile in front of me. Without the markers, there's no doubt we each would have veered off in a different direction and lost one another. It was a blast.

We were cold, but even with the wind it wasn't unbearable. The heated handgrips kept our hands from ever being uncomfortable, and the rest of our gear blocked the wind and snow. I wouldn't want to do this tour at zero degrees though.

Not far past the flats, we saw two large buffalo on the trail ahead of us. (I know buffalo is a misnomer and their correct name is bison, but I'm going to call them buffalo. I didn't collect *bison* nickels as a kid, I don't eat *bison* wings while watching the Super Bowl, and *Bison* Bill wasn't a famous cowboy performer.)

The park's website says in bold print, **"It is illegal to willfully remain near or approach wildlife, including birds, within ANY distance that disturbs or displaces the animal."** That meant when we came upon buffalo on our trail, we had to stop and wait. The first time this happened, it was unclear to me what we were waiting for. Buffalo, I thought, could stand blocking the trail all day if they wanted to. Surely we weren't supposed to sit there forever. But, the buffalo know the drill; they are accustomed to seeing humans all year round. They don't move quickly, unless you piss them off, but they do move. Each time we stopped for buffalo on the trail, they eventually moved away so we could pass. Sometimes they would amble into the trees and disappear; sometimes they would walk in the direction we were heading and move off to the side of the road, and sometimes they came at us.

That's what they did on our first encounter; they came at us. We've seen buffalo on roads before, but always in the summer. Looking out a car window at a massive animal three feet away is a bit unnerving, but even so, I like my chances inside a 3,000-pound steel enclosed vehicle if a buffalo decides he's having a bad day and wants to let off some steam in my direction. Today, however, we were sitting in the open, the only thing between us and the buffalo was a thermal snow suit and a plastic visor, and mine was missing a couple of the snaps holding it to the helmet.

We stopped about 100 yards short of the buffalo and turned our engines off. Cody told us to stay on our snowmobiles, relax and don't make too many movements if the buffalo came close. He didn't want us to agitate them – nor did we. But, he also wanted us prepared to start our snowmobiles, and move away quickly if we needed to. As they began to walk toward us, it was hard to relax. Cody had been through this routine countless times, but we hadn't. They kept coming, moving deliberately. I took one of my gloves off and carefully searched the pockets of my suit for my digital camera. I got it out and filmed the buffalo as they walked past us. At one point, they were about five feet away. They looked forlorn; the fur on their big heads was encrusted with ice like frost on a bag of French fries that had been in the freezer too long. But, they are well adapted to these conditions. Besides, in Yellowstone, there are plenty of places animals can go in the winter to warm themselves. They live amongst the highest concentration of thermal features on the planet. If they want, they can find a steam vent and get facials any time of the day.

The buffalo walked past us peacefully. As soon as they were beyond the last snowmobile in our group, we started our engines and continued. At Gibbon Falls, we stopped and walked to the overlook to view the falls. The depth of the snow created odd proportions. The small roof over the information sign had three feet of snow piled on top. The snow was deeper than the roof was wide. It was, as Karen would say, very Who-ville.

Farther south, we stopped to look at bald eagles and elk along the Firehole River. I joke about Karen calling her favorite places *magical* or *fairy-tale*, but Yellowstone in the winter is otherworldly. Steam coming up from the thermals, buffalo and elk wandering by, snow falling – there can't be another place like it. It's something everyone should see at least once. As beautiful as it was, it was getting close to lunchtime, so we saddled up and made a beeline to Old Faithful.

The visitor center at Old Faithful is open in the winter even though the road to it is not plowed for car traffic. Visitors arrive by snowmobile or snow coach. The Old Faithful Snow Lodge, across the parking lot from the visitor center, is open for guests in the winter. The area was packed with people: guests staying at the lodge, visitors on snow coach day trips and snowmobile tour groups like us. We ate at the snack bar and then went to look inside the new visitor center. It opened in August 2010.

I like it when visitor centers have animal pelts on display. Karen thinks they're disgusting. I keep telling her that I'm going to start a pelt collection, but so far I only have two rabbit pelts – a grey one and a white one. Karen uses the white one as part of her Christmas decorations every year – she thinks it looks like snow when she puts her ceramic ski chalet on it. I imagine having an extensive pelt collection, with both a weasel and an ermine to demonstrate how some animals' fur changes with the seasons, and when people come to our house, I would give interpretive talks. I've floated this idea with Karen and she said, "You're not making our friends pet dead animals when they're over for dinner."

In the visitor center there was a wolf, mountain lion, and black bear pelt on display. I searched every inch of the mountain lion trying to find the bullet hole. I can never find the bullet hole on the display pelts. How did these animals die? Old age? Road killed? How did the park service get these pelts? I have a lot of pelt questions.

There was still 45 minutes before our snowmobile caravan was due to leave. Karen said her snowmobile boots were too uncomfortable to hike in, so she stayed in the visitor center while I walked the boardwalks and trails around Old Faithful. Just as I reached the boardwalk in front of Old

Faithful, it went off. How convenient.

By 1:30pm, our group was together and ready to retrace our path back home. A few miles into our return trip, Cody asked if we wanted to stop and see the mudpots. We were making good time, and the group was up for it, so we took the short detour. It was a popular side trip; we were one of probably ten snowmobile tours there. As we were dismounting, Cody said, "Make sure you take your backpacks with you, or cover them up. I've seen crows unzip backpacks before." I laughed at his remark. I thought, "A crow isn't going to get into a backpack in a matter of just a few minutes, especially not with this many people around." Regardless, I took my backpack with me. We walked the boardwalks and saw all the bubbling mud. Mudpots are interesting, but at the same time, I felt stupid looking at them. I mean it's mud that bubbles.

Karen and I walked back to our snowmobiles and waited while the rest of our group returned and used the restroom. There were several lines of snowmobiles parked closely next to one another – we were between two other groups. A man in one of the other groups got off his snowmobile, placed his helmet on his seat, and grabbed a granola bar out of his backpack. He then set his backpack on the seat of his snowmobile, and started walking toward the mudpots. Just then, a crow – a large one – landed on the guy's snowmobile, grabbed the zipper loop of the backpack in his beak, and jerked it. The crow did this several more times, looking around nervously after each jerk. This happened ten feet in front of me. In less than a minute, the crow unzipped the backpack. He stuck his head inside, pulled out an empty granola bar wrapper, and flung it. He poked his head inside a few more times, and then flew away – empty beaked. I sat corrected; now *I've* seen a crow unzip a backpack.

Having seen the mudpots and crow tricks, we pulled out of the snow-packed parking lot and back onto the main trail. We were making good time. There were stretches where I think Cody was trying to see how fast he could get us to go.

My speedometer read 40 miles per hour a couple of times. At that speed, I felt only partially in control of my snowmobile. I was planning on going faster when we reached the flats, but when we got there it was a whiteout again. This time I could barely see the fluorescent trail markers. I was going 25 miles an hour, which is damn fast on a snowmobile, especially when you can't see where you're going, and using all my concentration to see the next marker. The snowmobile in front of me could have been 30 feet or half a mile away, I don't know. I couldn't see it. It seemed like we were on the flats for an hour; it was probably ten minutes.

Past the flats, our visibility improved dramatically. It was still snowing, but the wind was gone. Cody, at the front of our group, stopped and stood up on his snowmobile. He then continued slowly for a short distance while standing up, barely reaching his hand controls. He did this a couple of times, and then stopped and got off. He walked back to where we all stopped. It was silent. There were a couple of inches of new snow on the ground that fell within the last hour or so. Cody pointed to the trail and showed us fresh wolf tracks. He thought he'd seen wolves on the trail in front of us; that's what he'd been looking at. Although we'd never seen wolf prints before, it was obvious these tracks were made recently. We could see paw details in the tracks, and with the snow coming down so hard, those details would have been covered quickly.

We continued on, but at a slow speed. I could see the tracks on the trail next to us. The farther we traveled, the clearer the tracks became. Then the tracks left the trail and went up a hillside. Up front, Cody was pointing to the hill. As I looked up, I saw a bushy tail disappear over the crest of the hill. Karen got a better look than I did.

Cody had us moving slowly after the wolf sighting, hoping we might see them again. The trail meandered around a rock outcropping, and we circled the area a couple of times. We were close to where we'd seen the deer kill this morning, so Cody thought that maybe they would stay in this area. We didn't see them again, but we felt lucky to have gotten the glimpse we did.

The remaining ride back to the warming hut was short. When I shut off my engine, the trip meter read 107 miles. That's a long ride on a snowmobile. We were tired and walking bowlegged, but exhilarated by the day. This has been one of the highlights of our parks trip so far. It's something we'll definitely do again.

Your friend,
Matt

~.~.~.~.~.~.~

From: **Matt Smith**
Subject: **Yellowstone day three**
Date: **February 8, 2011**

Dear Bob and Sue,

When we woke up this morning, it was 55 degrees in our room, a big improvement. Yesterday after our snowmobile tour, I asked the woman at the front desk if she would please have the heat in our room checked. They found that someone (me) fiddled with the radiator in our room preventing it from heating properly. Last night I stayed clear of the radiator controls, and we had a better sleep.

We hurried across the parking lot to the restaurant for breakfast; it was -5°F. It was sunny today, but I'm glad we snowmobiled yesterday. I'll take 20°F and snowing over -5°F and sunny if I'm going to ride in the open at 40 miles an hour.

A year ago, Karen went snowshoeing in Whistler with friends. Ever since then, she's wanted to snowshoe again. Last fall, I bought snowshoes for both of us, and today we tried them out for the first time in the Lamar Valley, one of my favorite places in Yellowstone. It's a wide, undisturbed valley – except for the road that runs through it and it's home to a herd of buffalo. In the summer, the road through the valley can be crowded with visitors, although it's rarely as congested as the other main roads in the park. We were looking forward to spending time there today without the summer crowds.

I was expecting the buffalo to have vacated the valley for a warmer place in the park, somewhere closer to the thermals. But, when we drove through the valley this morning, there seemed to be as many buffalo there as in the summer. There were certainly fewer people. We saw only a handful of cars all day.

By the time we pulled off the road and parked, the temperature warmed to 0°F. In our ski and snowboard outfits, we strapped on our new snowshoes and crunched across the parking lot to the start of the trail. We snowshoed next to a set of cross-country ski tracks leading away from the main road. The tracks followed the outline of a service road that was eight feet below the snow.

The snow was powdery and light. I kept sinking up to my knees; my snowshoes didn't have enough surface area to support my weight. Every time a leg would disappear, it took tremendous effort to bring it back to the surface. That was the hardest part of the hike. Karen floated on top of the snow with ease, looking back at me with expressions of frustration like she wanted to say, "Quit messing around."

It was sunny with no wind and 0°F, but we weren't the least bit cold. It felt good. Snowshoeing is hard work, especially in deep, fine snow where every step is a struggle. It kicked my butt; I was sweating through my snowboard jacket.

The ski tracks went about a mile into the backcountry. After that, we were on our own. We could no longer see the Valley Road and the only tracks in the snow – other than ours – were animal tracks. We don't know what most of them were. Some were clearly the trodden paths of elk or buffalo, but others were tiny poke holes in the snow, like someone hovered above and jabbed a stick every couple of feet into the snow. We're guessing a fox or coyote made them; rabbit tracks would have been closer together. We didn't see any wolf tracks. After yesterday's encounter, we knew what those look like.

We came upon a group of elk. They were lying in an area of packed-down snow; the edge of their circle was just high enough to block the wind. They looked so much larger than when we've seen them through our car window or even from the snowmobile. Being on foot next to the big animals puts their size – and strength – in better perspective. We felt small.

About three miles into our hike, we came over the crest of a hill; in front of us and to our left was a stand of trees. Halfway past the trees, I glanced over and saw an enormous head; I about peed myself. It was a buffalo, a big one. He was motionless, like a museum exhibit, but looking right at us. Karen said, "Don't make eye contact" – too late. His big black eyes were shiny like glass. It was just him and us in the middle of the wilderness.

We stopped. At first, we were not sure if it was a good idea to walk past him, but we were already about as close to him as we were going to get so we kept going. His big head followed us. Not only do the animals look bigger when you're alone with them in the wilderness, but you realize how vulnerable you are. On snowshoes, we weren't going anywhere quickly if he decided to pay us a visit. Our only option was to keep a respectful distance and go about our business.

After another mile, we turned around and started back, although we wanted to keep going. Common sense won; we didn't have food or water with us, and we were getting farther from the car. It wouldn't have been a good idea to go deeper into the unknown, even on a beautiful day like today.

On our trek back to the car, we found our buffalo friend right where we left him, as if he was waiting for us. I was relieved he wasn't standing in our tracks. Trying to detour around him without getting lost in the woods would have been tricky.

When we started our parks trip, Karen and I had a list of

things we wanted to do. We thought we'd do them and check them off the list for good, but our list never gets shorter. Just like snowmobiling yesterday, snowshoeing in Yellowstone is something we can't wait to do again.

Your friend,
Matt

~.~.~.~.~.~.~

From: **Matt Smith**
Subject: **Travel day – to J-Hole**
Date: **February 9, 2011**

Dear Bob and Sue,

It was 20 degrees below zero this morning, colder than our snowmobiling day by 40 degrees. When we were ready to leave for Jackson Hole, Wyoming we were surprised that our car started without hesitation. In summer, the drive to Jackson Hole from Mammoth Hot Springs is 150 miles, about three hours. In winter, it's twice the distance and time because the roads through Yellowstone are closed. We had to drive north and west to Bozeman before driving south and around the park, approaching J-Hole from the west. (Karen and I have renamed Jackson Hole *J-Hole*.)

We took our time on the slick roads and stopped at a deli in West Yellowstone for lunch. The drive was uneventful until the last hour. Driving over the mountain pass west of town, it was snowing heavily. The traffic was heavy and bad drivers made it worse. Snowboarders were walking along the edge of the highway, and the prospect of skidding off the road into them was nerve wracking.

We're staying at the Hampton Inn in town. We walked to dinner and being that it was numbingly cold, we didn't mess around looking at menus in windows. We ducked into the first place we came to with open seats – a cowboy bar. We should've braved the cold and spent more time looking through the window before coming in. There's nothing wrong with cowboy bars; cowboy authentic is fine, but this was cowboy kitsch. The bar stools were full size horse saddles. You look like an idiot if you sit on them side saddle, and you look like a bigger idiot if you straddle them.

I said to Karen, "I don't want to sit on a saddle bar stool. My butt is still sore from riding 107 miles on a snowmobile."

Karen asked, "If your butt wasn't sore, would you want to sit on a saddle bar stool?"

After one beer, sitting bow-legged on an over-sized saddle, we plunged back into the cold. A couple of blocks later we found a place that was more *us*. The restaurant was packed, but there was plenty of room at the bar. Sitting at the bar is a crapshoot because you can't always control who sits next to you. I usually try to grab the end spot, that way Karen is on one side of me and no one is on the other. Tonight was different; we threw caution to the wind and sat right in the middle of the bar, empty seats on either side.

A woman in her twenties came up to the bar and sat a few stools away. She was texting intensely on her phone. Within a few minutes, three friends joined her: her boyfriend and another couple. They crowded against me; Karen was on my other side.

I angled toward Karen while we talked quietly, ate nachos, and drank our beer. We were having a pleasant dinner while our four bar mates got off to a quick start. The first thing they ordered was a round of shots to celebrate the end of a long day of work.

They were having a good time without us, but even for me, an introvert, ignoring them seemed rude. I centered myself toward the bar, looked at the kid sitting next to me, and said hello.

His name was Chad. I don't remember the others' names. Remembering one name is my daily limit. Details of Chad's life filtered through our start and stop conversation. He was being pulled in two directions, the party with his friends and a conversation with Karen and I.

At first, he talked to us as if we were his parents, respectful and guarded. We sensed his discomfort. But after a while, he realized we didn't care if he was doing shots with his friends and using the f-word in every other sentence.

Finally, he asked why we were in town. We told him that we'd quit our jobs almost a year ago, and were visiting all the national parks. "Grand Teton National Park will be our 43rd park in nine months," I said. Chad thought that was very cool. We talked about the national parks he'd been to. He shared with us his fond memories of visiting them as a kid. The more we talked about the parks the more impressed he was. Then he paused, stared at us for a moment with his mouth open slightly, and said, "You guys are killin' it." We think, given the context, this was a compliment. I'm not sure what we're killing, but Chad's advice was to keep killing it. (Whatever "it" is, it must be hard to kill.)

Karen and I exchanged more stories with Chad, talking over the racket coming from his end of the bar. When we were ready to leave, I quietly asked the bartender to put the Chad foursome's drinks on our bill. We paid and wished them well as we bundled up for the cold walk home. We were almost out the door when the bartender told Chad we picked up their tab. From across the restaurant, we heard, "Matt and Karen. Dude!" We went back and got hugs and high fives from our new friends. We banked a lot of karma for a small sum. Nothing kills it like a stranger picking up your bar tab.

Tomorrow it's more snowshoeing – in Grand Teton National Park.

Your friend,
Matt

~.~.~.~.~.~.~

From: **Matt Smith**
Subject: **#43 – Grand Teton National Park**
Date: **February 11, 2011**

Dear Bob and Sue,

We had every intention of spending the day in Grand Teton National Park yesterday, but the most we could do was get to the visitor center, stamp our passports, and take our picture in front of the park sign. I woke up at 2:00am yesterday morning with a severe headache, which didn't let up all day. I think it may have been altitude sickness. It felt exactly like what I experienced in the middle of the night at the Wuksachi Lodge in Sequoia National Park. (J-Hole is at an elevation of 6,200; Wuksachi Lodge is at 7,200 feet.) On the Sequoia trip, as soon as we drove to lower elevation I felt better.

Karen and I are still calling this an official park visit since we made it into the park and the visitor center. We'll have to go back and visit the park properly before we wrap up our parks trip. Right now we're on our way back home to Issaquah.

Your friend,
Matt

~.~.~.~.~.~.~

From: **Karen Smith**
Subject: **#44 – Wind Cave National Park**
Date: **April 24, 2011**

Dear Bob and Sue,

For a sparsely populated area, South Dakota has quite a few national park sites; they're all in the southwestern part of the state. There are two national parks (Wind Cave and Badlands), a national memorial (Mount Rushmore), a national monument (Jewel Cave), and a national historic site (Minuteman Missile). They also have a Corn Palace, which isn't a National Park Service site, but sounds like someplace I'd like to see.

After spending the weekend in Denver, we started out early on our five-hour drive to Wind Cave National Park. We wanted to get there in time to reserve a spot for an afternoon cave tour before they sold out. The park service doesn't take advanced reservations for these tours, and we didn't know how many people might choose to spend Easter in a cave.

Twelve miles from the park, we passed through the charming, historic town of Hot Springs. As Matt drove, I read to him from a brochure I picked up at a gas station. The town was originally called Minnekahta, an Indian word meaning *hot water*. Like the town of Hot Springs in Arkansas (coincidentally home to a national park), this town became popular for its mineral springs, palatial hotels and sanitariums. After the railroad built a train depot in 1891, thousands of visitors came to Hot Springs to reap the health benefits of medicinal spa treatments. They had names like "medicated baths, needle baths, silver, vapor, and Turkish baths."

Matt made a gagging sound. He hates baths. He always says, "Why do people want to sit in a tub of their own filth? Take a shower for God's sake." And, bathing in hot springs with strangers? There isn't a bottle of hand sanitizer in the world large enough to kill that many germs. (Bathing in Purell? Now that's something he might do.) I continued reading aloud from the brochure, "In Hot Springs, at the turn of the century, you could rent a bathing suit for an additional charge of 25 cents." Matt grabbed the brochure and flung it into the back of the car.

There were few people at the visitor center when we arrived, so we signed up for the next tour, which left 30 minutes later. We took care of business and put our backpacks in the car; we weren't allowed to bring anything with us on the tour. There were a dozen other people taking the tour, including a couple of kids and a crying two-year-old who made enough noise for ten people. It's hard for me to think of anything Matt would like less than being stuck underground with an unruly toddler, maybe a mineral water group bath. But we caught some good luck also; park ranger Don was our tour guide. Don has worked at Wind Cave for over four decades. He's a legend: the Michael Jordan of cave tour guides.

During the summer months, park rangers lead many different cave tours, but this time of the year they only offer one, the Natural Entrance Cave Tour. It's available several times each day. This 75-minute tour goes through the middle level of the cave where you see one of Wind Cave's wonders, a rare cave formation called boxwork. Approximately 95 percent of the world's discovered boxwork formations are found in Wind Cave.

There are no self-guided tours in Wind Cave; the park service can't have people wandering aimlessly through the fifth longest and most complex cave in the world. It has 136.55 miles of explored passageways, and they are discovering an average of four miles of new cave every year.

Our tour began at the walk-in entrance near the cave's only known natural entrance. Once we entered through the wind-lock doors, we immediately descended 300 stairs. For most of the 75 minutes, we walked single-file through long, narrow passageways. At times, it felt as if we were shuffling in a chain gang; when the person in front of us stopped to take a picture, we all stopped and waited.

The boxwork was interesting. Thin blades of calcite projected from the walls and ceilings, forming a honeycomb pattern, but the cave was not as fascinating as Carlsbad Caverns. The cave formations – stalactites and stalagmites – that make Carlsbad Caverns so amazing are rare in Wind Cave. Surprisingly, Matt liked Wind Cave better than Carlsbad Caverns. He said the tight winding passageways reminded him of the slot canyons we hiked in Utah. That's one of the great things about the parks – each visitor comes away with his or her own impression. For some, Wind Cave may be their favorite park of all.

When we came to the areas of the cave where the path was wide enough for all of us to stand together in a group, Don would share with us interesting facts about the history and the geology of the cave. He needed to speak loudly and repeatedly over the crying, squirming two-year-old and some adults who were talking amongst themselves. Many were doing things he told us *not* to do, like stepping off the path or touching the walls. One entire family leaned against the wall of the cave to have their picture taken. Don was very patient, but I felt bad for him. He's obviously passionate about Wind Cave, and it must be discouraging when visitors don't share his enthusiasm and respect for the cave.

My favorite story that Don told us was about Alvin McDonald, one of the earliest and youngest cave explorers. In 1889, at the age of 16, Alvin moved from Iowa to South Dakota with his dad, who'd been hired to oversee a mining claim. Alvin fell in love with Wind Cave, and systematically explored eight to ten miles of passageways by candlelight, using rolled out string to guide him back out. He kept a detailed journal in which he described the cave, his explorations, and the naming of the rooms and passageways. In his own words, he was "the chief guide" at Wind Cave, and for three years, he shared his passion with visitors. Tragically, in 1893, Alvin died of typhoid fever at the age of 20.

Some think that Alvin's spirit is still down in the dark, cool recesses of Wind Cave. Occasionally, survey teams find pieces of his string. As recently as August 2009, when explorers "discovered" a room in Wind Cave that they believed no one had ever seen before, they found his signature carved onto the ceiling. The signature was dated July 1893, making it the latest known signature left by Alvin McDonald in Wind Cave. Maybe there are other Alvin McDonald signatures left to be discovered.

When the tour was over, we took an elevator up to the

visitor center, and then drove north through the park. The Black Hills region is beautiful. The park has rolling hills of mixed-grass prairie and ponderosa pine forests. Making our way toward Rapid City, we drove through Custer State Park, one of the most impressive state parks we've ever seen. On the Wildlife Loop Road, we pulled off and watched the herd of buffalo roam. Custer State Park has one of the largest, if not *the* largest, herd of buffalo in the U.S. We never get tired of watching them.

In Rapid City, we ate dinner at one of the only restaurants in the city that was open on Easter, and then called it an early evening. Tomorrow we're visiting Badlands National Park.

Your friend,
Karen

~.~.~.~.~.~.~.~

From: **Matt Smith**
Subject: **#45 – Badlands National Park**
Date: **April 25, 2011**

Dear Bob and Sue,

While drinking our coffee this morning, I got on the Badlands National Park website. I wanted to see what was in store for us today. I stumbled upon a story about the black-footed ferrets that live in the park.

I said to Karen, "It says here that the last captive black-footed ferret died in 1979, and at the time, scientists believed the species to then be extinct."

Karen replied, "Good."

"No, not good. Why would you think that's good? Anyway, I'm not finished. The article goes on to say, 'In 1981, the scientific community received astonishing news. Black-footed ferrets were discovered alive and well in the wilds of Wyoming.'"

"And you care because?"

"Because it's an uplifting story about how a species once thought to be extinct is making a comeback. The park website says, 'With high hopes and little fanfare, 36 black-footed ferrets were released in the park in 1994.'"

Karen asked, "What *is* a ferret? A big weasel?"

After a quick check of Wikipedia, I replied, "You are correct. It's a member of the weasel family."

I continued to tell Karen about how the park is planning a Ferret Festival this fall including a puppet show – I'm assuming they're ferret puppets – scientific lectures, a live ferret exhibit and "a ceremonial release of several captive ferrets back to the wild." We may have to come back for that.

Karen said, "Does it concern you that the park is pushing their weasels so hard? Is that their main attraction?"

I replied, "They're not *pushing their weasels*, this is just something I found on their website. They have other attractions, like buffalo, and grass, and eroded hillsides."

"I can't wait."

Karen's excitement level increased after the coffee did its job. It took about an hour to get from our hotel to the park border. We drove east from Rapid City along I-90 and turned south at the town of Wall, South Dakota on highway 240, and followed it into the park.

Badlands National Park looks larger than it is because it's surrounded by the Buffalo Gap National Grassland. The park was established in 1978, and despite being so desolate, it draws a million visitors each year.

The Badlands have a strange beauty that you must see in person to appreciate. The constantly changing light, the odd formations, the multicolored bands of exposed rock; we've seen this before in Death Valley, Petrified Forest and Bryce Canyon national parks to name a few. These areas aren't places where you'd want to settle – build a little house and start a new life – but they are beautiful to look at, especially at dawn and dusk.

Once inside the park, we drove the Badlands Scenic Loop road southeast to the Ben Reifel Visitor Center. The first few miles of the drive cut through the rollercoaster hills of the badlands. I was awe-struck by the scenery; we stopped several times to take pictures, but it was like a cruel trick. After each shot, I would look at the photo on my camera, but I never captured the magnificence of the scene. You'll have to trust us when we say it is worth the trip to see the badlands.

For the past 500,000 years, water has eroded the hillsides in the park revealing layers of rock and sediment that are up to 75 million years old. Besides being interesting to look at, these exposed surfaces are rich with fossils. Paleontologists have used this area as an outdoor laboratory for over a century.

In 2010, a seven-year-old girl – a Junior Ranger no doubt – spotted a fossil sticking out of the ground and alerted a ranger. After several days of careful excavation, paleontologists removed the fossil from the surrounding rock. Later they identified it as a 30-million-year-old saber-tooth cat skull.

April is a tad early for the vacation crowd; we were fortunate to have the park almost to ourselves. We also lucked out with the weather. It's the beginning of the rainy season here, and large puffy clouds with dark bottoms floated overhead for most of the day, but it never rained on us.

Not far from the visitor center is Castle Trail. It was our hike for the day. The hike was perfect for Karen – five miles out to a flush toilet and five miles back to the car. It was an uneventful hike, the kind we like. We enjoyed being in the middle of nowhere with sweeping views of the wilderness.

Karen was concerned about getting sunburned, even through the clouds. Halfway through our return hike, I looked back to see her hiking with her jacket over her head – vampire style. "I don't want the sun to make my skin look any older than it already looks," she said.

"I'd rather you look old than walk around with a jacket over your head. You look like a crime boss on the way to prison."

"Why do you care? There's no one out here to see me."

"I can see you. It's just weird."

She pulled the jacket off her head, but I'm sure she put it back on as soon as I turned around to start hiking again.

On our way back to Rapid City we drove through a long stretch of the national grassland south of the park. I had wanted to see what a national grassland looked like. It was a large expanse of prairie grass; nice, but we should have taken the route back through the park along Sage Creek Rim Road instead. A ranger at the visitor center told us that's where the buffalo were roaming today. Why did I choose grass over bison? No worries, I have a feeling we will be back here again to see them someday.

It was too early to go to dinner when we got back to our hotel, but we went anyway. It was happy hour, and the beers were surprisingly cheap. So cheap we thought the price was a typo; we quickly ordered, excited that we might be getting away with something. By 7:00pm we were back in our room with hours to kill before bedtime.

Between Karen and me, we had a full load of laundry to do, so with an armful of dirty clothes, I went looking for the hotel's washing machine. An hour and a half later, as Karen was digging her clean clothes out of the warm pile on the bed, she looked at me and asked, "Where's my underwear?"

I thought it might be a trick question; the happy hour beers hadn't worn off yet. "I don't know where your underwear is. I'm assuming you have a pair on."

"No, I mean where is the underwear I gave you to wash? I gave you three pairs."

"They should be in the pile," I said.

"Well, they're not. Are you sure you didn't drop them on the way back from the laundry room?"

I replied, "I think I would have known if I dropped something on the way back. Please."

Karen went to the door and looked in the hallway. "There's one right there!" She ran out and grabbed the red pair before anyone walked by. The door locked behind her. I was expecting a knock right away, but several minutes passed before I heard it.

I opened the door to find Karen, grasping several pairs of underwear in her hands and giving me a look as if she expected an explanation. She said, "I found one in the hallway, one in the stairwell, and one neatly folded on the table in the laundry room." She stood looking at me waiting for my response.

I had nothing to say.

"Well, I can't wear the pair I found in the laundry room until it gets washed again. I can only imagine how long it was sitting on the dirty floor before someone picked it up."

It was nice to have mostly clean clothes again, but we should have stayed in the park longer. Next time – maybe when we're back for the Ferret Festival – we'll hang out in the park until it's dark enough for the ranger-narrated stargazing program. We can do happy hours and laundry at home.

Your friend,
Matt

~.~.~.~.~.~.~

From: **Matt Smith**
Subject: **#46 – Theodore Roosevelt National Park**
Date: **April 26, 2011**

Dear Bob and Sue,

For as few cars as we saw in Theodore Roosevelt National Park today, there were a surprisingly high number of road-killed prairie dogs. The natural order of things dictates that the smaller an animal is, the quicker it needs to move when cars approach. Buffalo can stand in the middle of the road all day if they want; squirrels need to get the hell out of the way, and fast. Prairie dogs haven't learned this lesson. As we pulled away from the p-dog town, one sat still in the middle of the road as our car went by. I expected him to move, but he didn't; we missed him by about a foot. He sat upright on his back legs, his front paws in Karen pose, and squinted his eyes when the breeze from our car hit him.

The park has two units, a north and a south; both are in western North Dakota. The south unit is about 30 miles west of the town of Dickinson. The park preserves a section of the North Dakota badlands, which are ideal for wildlife viewing, trail riding on horseback, and hiking.

Our drive today from Rapid City to the park took four and a half hours. We used the afternoon to get the lay of the land and make a plan for tomorrow. At the Medora Visitor Center, just south of the park, we asked the ranger for hiking suggestions. We also walked through Teddy Roosevelt's Maltese Cross Cabin, which sits adjacent to the visitor center.

The park is named after Roosevelt because he came to this area in the 1880's and 1890's to hunt buffalo and ranch. He sold his interest in the ranch a few years before he became president. His cabin, the one on display at the visitor center, was originally built a few miles south of Medora, but was moved many times to be displayed when TR became president. It's spent the last 50 years where it sits today.

From Medora, we went into the park and drove the 36-mile Scenic Loop Drive. It was raining off and on but was still a pleasant day. We saw very few other cars or visitors in the park.

Early in the loop we came to a large prairie dog town. Karen asked me, "Why are they called prairie dogs? They're not dogs; they're rodents."

"Because prairie rodent sounds stupid," I said.

I pulled the car to the side of the road and rolled down our windows to get a good look at the little fellas. Stretched in front of us were hundreds of acres of p-dog town, like a giant Whac-A-Mole game. P-dogs have a well-tuned early warning system to alert one another of approaching danger. The dogs closest to the threat bark, wag their tails nervously, and dance in circles to let the rest of the town know something isn't right. I even saw a couple of back flips. One acted so agitated I thought it was going to faint. That's a lot of energy to put out every time a car approaches. If I were a p-dog living next to the road, I'd consider moving farther into town. With some encouragement from me, Karen agreed to let them keep their "dog" moniker, although I explained to her that she didn't have any official say in the matter.

One of the main attractions in the park is the buffalo. In the mid 19th century, there were an estimated 60 million buffalo in America; 50 years later there were fewer than 100. Had the federal government not aggressively intervened there's little doubt that hunters would have killed every last one. Ironically, Roosevelt, known as the conservation president, came to North Dakota to hunt buffalo. He was part of the problem he was crusading to fix. What could be more American?

On the loop, we stopped at least a dozen times to look at buffalo by the road. The ranger told us they were starting to see newborns in the park. We saw several small buffalo, but weren't sure if they were newborns. The small ones had short horns, so we figured they must be yearlings rather than newborns; mother buffalo probably weren't giving birth to babies with horns, at least not more than once.

Near the end of the loop, we came across yet another group of buffalo. Lying in the tall grass, in the middle of the herd, was a newborn. Karen said it was her "dream come true." I stopped the car and rolled down the windows. We sat for a long time trying to get a picture of the baby. The angle was never good; the newborn was either facing away from us or had its head down in the grass. Finally, the newborn got up and stood next to its mother facing us. Karen shouted, "That's your money shot!" She startled the baby buffalo and me, but I was able to get at least one good picture of mother and baby before they moved away.

After leaving the park, we drove to Dickinson where we

checked into our hotel room. I asked my research assistant where we were having dinner tonight. This is one of Karen's most important duties on our parks trip: researching local eateries so we don't spend hours at the end of our long days looking for a decent place to eat. Tonight it was take-out Thai food. I wanted to go to IHOP, (Karen likes it when they make silver dollar-sized pancakes for her by special request) but there's only one IHOP in the state and it's in Fargo. We ate the Thai food in our hotel room, and I am pleased to report that Karen's record remains perfect for finding good food when we travel. Her job as a research assistant is safe – for now.

Your friend,
Matt

~.~.~.~.~.~.~

From: **Matt Smith**
Subject: **Teddy Roosevelt continued**
Date: **April 27, 2011**

Dear Bob and Sue,

Buffalo definitely have the right-of-way in the park – anywhere really. We had to stop our car many times to wait for them to cross the road. They may seem passive and slow-witted, but they are neither. A ranger told us that a few days ago, a visitor here at the park rolled down his car window and reached out to pet one. The buffalo climbed onto the hood of his car, crushing the windshield. He had to go to the hospital for stitches where the broken windshield had cut him.

We are only visiting the south unit of the park on this trip. A ranger told us there are more buffalo in the north unit, despite it being smaller than the south unit. The buffalo in the north become so overpopulated that the park service rounds up and culls the herd every year or so. The culled buffalo are then given to Indian tribes or sold to ranchers.

Several of the trails we wanted to hike today were impassible due to high streams, so we chose the Upper Talkington Trail, which cut across an open plain with no water crossings. By 9:30am we were hiking the eight-mile round-trip trail. It was a great hike, sunny, 60 degrees, with beautiful panoramic views of the park's badlands. We saw wild horses and antelope, but no buffalo or other hikers. The sign-in register at the trailhead showed that the last group to hike this trail was April 12th, over two weeks ago.

About three miles into our hike, the trail cut through a p-dog town. When we passed through the town, the dogs barked and did their odd danger dances. There was a story in the park newsletter about how ranchers wiped out p-dog towns in the olden days; they killed millions of them. Now, they're protected inside the park. They're an important part of the park's ecosystem, primarily because they're a food source for other animals. When the p-dog population decreases, it sets off a chain reaction in the ecosystem. For example, the near extinction of the black-footed ferret is due to the decrease in p-dogs – pretty much the only thing they eat. Biologists believe that a single black-footed ferret requires 100 acres of p-dog town to survive. That's a lot of p-dogs for one ferret to eat.

After the hike, we ate cold, leftover Thai food in our car (not recommended), and then headed out of the park. On the way out, we came across a herd of buffalo. We stopped our car in the middle of the road, and the herd slowly surrounded us as they passed by. Just as the last few were coming out of the tall grass, we noticed a baby buffalo in the group. It was the second newborn buffalo we saw in two days.

The drive from TRNP back to Rapid City, South Dakota is about 250 miles. I wanted to type the notes from the day on my laptop, so Karen was driving. As soon as she got on the highway – driving 75 miles per hour in the rain – Karen discovered a tick on the back of her neck. It's tick season in North Dakota. She managed to keep the car on the road –

barely – while I removed it. I assured her that it was most likely the only tick we picked up while on the hike, as I removed another tick from my arm without her seeing me. She drove twitching and squirming. She said she could feel them crawling all over her body. Karen's nickname for the rest of the afternoon was "Itchy." I stopped counting after I found the sixth tick; all were embedded on the back of her neck or in her hair. By then I'd lost credibility with Itchy when I tried to convince her that we finally got them all.

About an hour into the drive, I looked up from my laptop to see Itchy trying to pass a line of four cars and a U-Haul. We were on a two-lane highway and approaching a hill that we could not see over. She made it past the U-Haul and two of the cars and then, still in the left lane, slowed way down and said, "Uh oh, I wonder if that first car is an unmarked police car." I couldn't speak. I had to try not to pee my pants. I shouted, "It doesn't matter now, you're in the wrong lane!"

Itchy floored it and made it back into the right lane just before we got to the top of the hill. I looked over at her with wide eyes. All she said was, "Good thing that wasn't the police." Just when I got the nerve to start typing again she hit the brakes. I looked up and saw a car coming toward us in our lane. It swerved back, just missing us. "That one wasn't my fault," she said.

Five minutes later we came to a small town. Itchy saw a mailbox and decided it was the perfect time to pull off the road to mail her postcards. This took just long enough for the four cars and U-Haul to pass us.

Right now, I'm typing these notes as Itchy tries to peek around the string of slow cars. There is a hill coming up and it's still raining. She's going to try to pass them again. If you're reading this email then either we made it without crashing, or a state trooper found my laptop and decided that since writing this was the last thing I did before I died, it was important enough to send to you.

Your friend,

Matt

~.~.~.~.~.~.~

From: **Karen Smith**
Subject: **#47 – Congaree National Park**
Date: **June 19, 2011**

Dear Bob and Sue,

We're sitting at the bar at the Lexington Avenue Brewery in downtown Ashville, N.C. watching the guy next to us email naked pictures of himself from his iPhone. He must be running for Congress.

We drove here from South Carolina, where we've been for the last two days. We flew from Seattle to Charleston, and when we finally arrived at our hotel room at midnight, we got an extra-special welcome. When I walked into the room and threw my stuff on the bed, I thought I saw something scurry across the floor and under the dresser. I assumed it was a mouse, since we were in a historic hotel in the old part of the city. Matt knew he'd never get any sleep unless he moved the dresser, and showed me that nothing was there. So he moved the dresser, and nothing was there. He said it must have been a shadow. As soon as he walked back to his side of the bed, he saw the "shadow." It was a bug the size of a mouse; it's what I would call a cockroach on steroids, but what the people in South Carolina call a palmetto bug. It was too big to bludgeon, so Matt put the trashcan over it upside down, pushed it out into the hallway, and went to have a conversation with the front desk. They sent the hotel maintenance man who came in with a huge canister of bug spray and offered to fumigate our room. We declined; we decided it would be safer to sleep with giant bugs than to breathe DDT fumes all night.

We had a great time yesterday exploring Charleston, too good of a time. (After officially proclaiming this *The Summer of the Margarita,* we felt obliged to sample the margaritas at every bar we wandered into. They got progressively better as the evening wore on.) It was brutal getting up at 5:45 this morning to drive to Congaree National Park, just outside Columbia. We needed to be there by 8:45am for our canoe tour in the park. On weekends throughout the year, park rangers provide a limited number of free, guided canoe tours along Cedar Creek. They say it's the best way to see the park. Reservations for the canoe tours fill up very quickly, so you have to call months ahead of time to get a spot.

Ranger Bill was our guide. Helping him were two enthusiastic volunteers who kept Matt and I and the two other families from tipping our canoes over, or turning off down the wrong tributary never to be seen again. The youngest child on the tour was a small six-year-old boy, who may not grow any bigger after his grandmother sprayed his entire head and body with DEET.

The water level in the creek was unusually low, but to our relief it didn't smell bad and it didn't seem too swamp-like; there were not many bugs and the humidity was low. The water was so brown that it looked like the river flowing through Willy Wonka's chocolate factory. There were trees and bushes with low branches that hung over the creek. Bill warned us to steer our canoes clear of them; snakes like to hang from the branches, and could drop on us and into our canoes if we brushed against them.

The canoes were the size that seat two adults, so Matt and I were in a canoe together. The tour moved so slowly that only one of us needed to row. Matt told me that I was the "rudder," which meant whenever we needed to turn the canoe, I had to stick my oar in the water on the *opposite* side of the direction we wanted to turn. At first, when my ruddering skills were still a little rusty, things got a bit tense. I steered us into a few big logs, and ran us aground once, but as soon I got the hang of it, floating in the canoe was languid and peaceful. We (Matt) paddled past large bald cypress and water tupelo trees draped with Spanish moss. The tour was very interesting and quite beautiful, for a swamp. Ranger Bill said it's not a swamp; he said it is a *biologically diverse river floodplain ecosystem*. (Our GPS map, however, still labels the area as Congaree Swamp, even though *Swamp* was dropped from the name when it became a national park in 2003.)

The canoe trip lasted three hours, and ranger Bill and the volunteers said it had been a good wildlife-sighting day. We saw snakes hanging from trees, a baby yellow-belly turtle, a couple of white ibises, a blue heron and a kingfisher. We stopped and looked at what I thought Bill said was a barn owl. Matt later corrected me (while laughing), and told me that it was a *barred* owl, not a barn owl. He couldn't believe I could mix up the two when they look nothing alike. I didn't tell him that I didn't mix them up. I never knew there was such a thing as a barred owl. Anyway, how is he suddenly an owl expert? He doesn't even keep a life list of birds.

When the canoe trip was over, we dragged our canoes out of the water and said our goodbyes to ranger Bill and the volunteers. At the Harry Hampton Visitor Center (a beautiful new facility), we made sandwiches outside at the picnic tables. We finished our day in Congaree on solid ground, hiking the Weston Lake Loop, which was a great five-mile hike through an old-growth forest.

All throughout South Carolina, one thing that made a big impression on me (besides the bug) was how friendly and welcoming the people were. This morning after we told ranger Bill about all the parks we've been to, he asked us which park was our favorite. When we said we couldn't choose a favorite because there are so many incredible parks, he said very sincerely, "Well after you spend the day in Congaree, I know *it* will be your favorite park." Very, very sweet.

We're staying in Asheville tonight, and tomorrow we drive to Great Smoky Mountains National Park. That's all for now; we gotta go see what our congressman is up to.

Your friend,
Karen

~.~.~.~.~.~.~

From: **Matt Smith**
Subject: **#48 – Great Smoky Mountains National Park**
Date: **June 20, 2011**

Dear Bob and Sue,

Smoky Mountains National Park has been misspelled for so long that the misspelled version is now correct. There's no "e" in smoky like there is in Smokey Bear. Speaking of Smokey, as strange as it may sound, Karen and I try to spot Smokey Bear signs when we travel. I think I speak for both of us when I say that he's our favorite fictional, government agency mascot. The National Park Service needs a mascot like Smokey. But, I've never understood why he wears jeans – with the cuffs rolled up. He's a bear; he doesn't need jeans, and if he did, why wouldn't he wear a pair that fits? And, if he does need pants, shouldn't he wear a shirt also? They need to give him a proper uniform if they're going to make him wear clothes. He has a nice hat though. Smokey works for the National Forest Service, not the National Park Service, so we'll save the Smokey Bear discussion for another time.

The North Carolina-Tennessee border splits the park in half at a southwest to northeast diagonal. We entered from the North Carolina side, stopped at the Oconaluftee Visitor Center, and then drove the Newfound Gap Road through the park.

When I think of mountains, I think of ranges in the western United States: the Rockies, the Cascades, the Sierra Nevadas. I was surprised then at the elevation gains as we drove west through the park. At its highest point – the Newfound Gap – the elevation of the road was over 5,000 feet. It was there we took a detour onto Clingmans Dome Road.

A couple of miles south on the road, we parked to do

some hiking. We followed the Road Prong Trail into the forest for two to three miles, but were forced to turn around when the trail merged with a stream and became impassible. Back at the car, we still had time and energy, so we hiked a few miles of the Appalachian Trail; the AT runs parallel to Clingmans Dome Road.

It was a pleasant afternoon of hiking, a good break from riding in the car for so long. While hiking on the AT, we ran into a couple of twenty-something year-old guys who looked like they might be through-hikers. We stopped and talked with them. When I asked if they were enjoying their hike, they hemmed and hawed. "It's been raining a lot lately," one of them said. "We're just happy to be dry." Their response wasn't making me wish we were on "A Walk in the Woods" from Georgia to Maine. They looked hungry and desperate.

I was holding a half-eaten Snickers while we were talking with them. They both kept shifting their focus from my eyes to the Snickers in my hand. I'm pretty sure if they hadn't been worn out from days of hiking in the rain, they would have killed me for it, and made Karen carry their packs for them for the next 1,800 miles. It came back to me why you shouldn't talk to strangers in the wilderness.

I covered the remainder of the Snickers with my hand and placed it in my pocket as Karen and I politely ended our conversation and slowly backed away. Our bear attack avoidance training was kicking in. If they started to follow us, my plan was to throw the half-eaten Snickers and the bag of Cheez-Its from the side pocket of my backpack on the ground to buy us a few extra seconds while we ran, but it never came to that.

We arrived safely at our car, and were truly surprised that we hadn't heard dueling banjoes through the trees. We hiked enough for one day, so we drove down the other side of the divide to the town of Gatlinburg, Tennessee where we're spending the next couple of nights.

Driving out of the treed, calm, and utterly pleasant national park into the town of Gatlinburg is a shock you can't prepare for. Gatlinburg is... well... damn. Much like the Grand Canyon, my description won't do it justice. I can only describe small bits hoping you get a sense of it. It's a funnel cake, arcade, fudge-shop, souvenir shot glass encrusted strip mall. Across from our hotel, local schoolgirls, wearing way too much make-up, were performing a clogging routine to very loud Dolly Parton music. The restaurant next door had a talking, animatronic, hillbilly bear welcoming guests and passersby. We actually heard dueling banjoes. It concerned me that Karen didn't hate it. I kept waiting for her complaints, but they never came. She was in a daze by how over-the-top it was. My concern grew when she said, "Oh look, a rock shop!"

I would have liked to explore the town, but we needed to do laundry first. Our hotel didn't have washing machines, but their sister property across the parking lot did. We took our laundry to the other hotel, started our load and went into the lobby. We had time to kill, which turned out to be a bonus because it was happy hour at the lobby bar and they made a killer Margarita. It was meant to be.

After doing our laundry, we found a nice pizza place down the street and then called it an early night. Tomorrow we plan on hiking to the top of Mount Le Conte inside the park.

Your friend,
Matt

~.~.~.~.~.~.~

From: **Matt Smith**
Subject: **Smoky Mountains continued**
Date: **June 21, 2011**

Dear Bob and Sue,

It was a beautiful day for a hike in the park. We got an early start and drove half an hour south from Gatlinburg, on

Newfound Gap Road, to the parking area for the Alum Cave Trail. From there, we hiked to the top of Mount Le Conte, an 11-mile round trip. The hike was fairly easy until we got close to the top of the mountain. The elevation gain for the first four and a half miles was 1,200 feet, but the gain for the final mile was an additional 1,200 feet. It felt good to get the exercise.

Just below the summit, we ate lunch at a picnic table near the Le Conte Lodge, elevation 6,360 feet. The lodge sits a couple of hundred vertical feet below the peak of Mount Le Conte, and has spectacular views of the Smoky Mountains to the north and west. The lodge provides cabins and meals for overnight guests, but the only way to get there is to hike; there are no roads to the lodge. Pack animals carry all the supplies up the mountain that the lodge needs; they also carry trash and dirty laundry back down the mountain on their return trip.

In the past, the lodge used horses for this chore, but horses tore up the trail and weren't always sure-footed enough to make it up the mountain safely. In 1986, they switched from horses to llamas. Now, a llama train, about eight llamas at a time, brings supplies three times a week when the camp is open from late March to late November. Llamas can carry 30 percent of their body weight up the steep mountain trail, and have a lower impact on the trail than horses. Llamas are also more mountain savvy; they can navigate the steep trail more easily than horses. Once they make it to the lodge, the crew unloads the llamas' saddlebags, and rewards them with a lunch of pancakes. We didn't see the llamas today, but I found an interesting video about them on The Great Smoky Mountains Association's website.

By the time we got back to Gatlinburg, it was late afternoon, a perfect time to do laundry. The fact that it was happy hour again at the hotel across the street had nothing to do with our decision to do laundry a second day in a row.

At the bar, we met a young couple – they looked to be in their 20's – from Ann Arbor, Michigan. They reminded us of ourselves at that age. They told us that they drove here from Michigan, and were in Gatlinburg on vacation for a week. I asked if they were here to visit the national park. They said no. Their plan was to spend most of their time in Gatlinburg. Really? A week of Bubba Gump Shrimp Co. and Ripley's Believe It or Not? We didn't want to sound like their parents and tell them what they were missing, but we purposefully talked about how great our hike was today, and how beautiful the drive through the park is. Hopefully they will wander into the park this week and see for themselves.

After laundry/happy hour, we went to the Smoky Mountain Brewery for an early dinner. There were more people in the bar area than we expected there would be; it was trivia contest night. We were just in time to get the last two-seat table. I usually don't like audience participation activities, but we decided to play anyway. It was better than our other choice, which was to wander through town and fight the crowds for a table at Flapjack's Pancake Cabin or Hungry Bear BBQ.

We suck at trivia. The MC felt sorry for us and gave us credit for wrong answers. "The answer is—Amy Winehouse, but I will also accept Amy Whitehorse from the Seattle couple sitting here to my left." We didn't win, or even finish in the top three, but the MC told us that we were "very competitive for a team of two."

Tomorrow is a travel day; we're driving to Horse Cave, Kentucky where we're spending the night so we can visit Mammoth Cave National Park the next day.

Your friend,
Matt

~.~.~.~.~.~.~

From: **Matt Smith**
Subject: **#49 – Mammoth Cave National Park**
Date: **June 23, 2011**

Dear Bob and Sue,

On our way into the park yesterday, I saw an animal that looked like a huge house cat with no tail. It was 20 feet from the road. We pulled the car over and watched it for a few minutes before it walked into the forest. The ranger at the visitor center said it was probably a bobcat, and that very few visitors had ever reported seeing one in the park. I keep telling Karen that there's interesting stuff on the surface at these *cave* parks; it's not always about what's in the hole. I tried to convince her to skip the cave tour, so we could hike in the park instead; maybe we'd see another bobcat. My suggestion didn't slow her down as she marched to the ticket window to get our tickets for the Grand Avenue cave tour.

The Grand Avenue cave tour "is not recommended for visitors who have heart or respiratory illnesses, diabetes, or walking difficulties." The park's write-up of the tour says it's "physically strenuous." We chose this tour hoping the description would weed out the slow walkers. The tour covers four miles of underground passages and lasts four and a half hours.

About 65 people showed up for our tour. There was a short orientation talk at the visitor center, and then a park service bus took us, and our ranger guide Steve, to the cave entrance a few miles away. We all lined up at the entrance and walked two-by-two down a couple of hundred stairs into the cave. The family behind us was excited to get into the cave; they followed us as close as they could without stepping on our shoes. Had I hesitated for a split second, they would have plowed into us, causing a domino effect all the way to the bottom of the cave entrance. As soon as we started down the stairs, the young girl behind me began asking her dad questions. "Where are the bats? How big is this cave? How long is the tour?" She asked 17 questions before we made it to the bottom of the stairs. I was counting.

The cave was impressive if for no other reason than its size. That's why it was named Mammoth Cave, and not because they found mammoth fossils in the cave, which is what many people – like us – mistakenly think.

I expected that the cave would be a single massive room underground, but it wasn't. It's a maze of passages. Acid in the surface water above created the cave by dissolving the limestone below as it seeped through the ground. We also learned that the cave has many levels. Our tour started at the surface, but we traveled through the second and third levels of the labyrinth at different points in the tour. When we stopped along the way, ranger Steve would tell us what level we were on. He explained how there were cave passages above and below us. Still, it was difficult for me to picture exactly where we were. Once I can no longer see daylight, it's all the same to me. Karen was fascinated just the same. She kept asking me, "What level are we on?" I never knew, but I made up an answer each time anyhow.

On these cave tours, I spend most of my energy maneuvering amongst the group to avoid certain people: question girl, humming man, whining toddler, body-odor boy, close walkers. Why do people need to walk so close? If I can feel your breath on the back of my neck, you are too close; back it up. It's not easy changing places in line in a cave. I have to bide my time until we get to an open spot where the ranger gathers us together and gives a little talk. Then I can move sideways through the crowd to get a better position. The trick is to get Karen to sidle along with me. She's usually engrossed in whatever the ranger is talking about, such as a captivating story about how people used to explore the cave with a candle in a tin can as their only light source. Not only do I have to find a better place in the crowd, I need to nudge Karen along without her snapping at me. Cave tours stress me out.

For a long stretch, we were stuck in front of a young

woman who talked constantly about her frustrations with the changing menu at Taco Bell. "I can't believe they don't have the green sauce anymore! I loved the green sauce. It was awesome. I wonder if they will bring the green sauce back..." People, please!

Halfway through the tour we stopped for lunch in the cave's cafeteria. We sat with ranger Steve and told him about our goal to visit every national park. He was visibly impressed. He sat silently for a moment, and then looked around making sure none of our cave-mates could see him as he reached into his pocket and pulled something out. With a closed fist, he handed it to Karen; it was a wooden nickel. On one side was printed, "Mammoth Cave - Kentucky." On the other, "The longest cave in the world." There was an image of a bat stamped into the center.

Karen looked down at the wooden nickel. I looked down at the wooden nickel. I looked up at Steve. It was a sweet gesture on his part, but I thought, "Where's *my* wooden nickel Steve?" Karen could sense my disappointment. Later, when Steve wasn't around, she said, "We can share the wooden nickel."

The bus dropped us back at the visitor center. It parked at the curb next to a contraption we were required to walk across as we exited. It was a spongy mat with a wet, foamy substance on top; it sanitized our shoes. The park requires this of anyone who goes into Mammoth Cave to prevent the spread of White-Nose Syndrome. The disease is lethal and has caused millions of deaths in recent years – of bats, not people. There's a notice on the park's website that reads, "All participants on cave tours must walk on bio-security mats immediately following the conclusion of their tour. **No exceptions.** This extraordinary measure is due to the confirmation of White-Nose Syndrome in Kentucky."

WNS is becoming a problem all over the country. At Carlsbad Caverns National Park, all visitors must have their shoes, clothing, and equipment screened before entering the cave if they have been in another cave. WNS has been confirmed in Great Smoky Mountains NP, Cuyahoga Valley NP, and Acadia NP, just to name a few. The disease can kill an entire colony of bats. I don't like caves, but I have nothing against bats. As a matter of fact, I like bats; they're an important part of our ecosystem. They eat bugs. I hope this disease abates quickly. Who will eat the bugs if there are no bats?

Karen loved the cave, as I expected she would. I enjoyed it also. I wouldn't say I've become a cave fan, but I could see myself doing more cave tours in the future.

Your friend,
Matt

~.~.~.~.~.~.~

From: **Matt Smith**
Subject: **Back in Alaska!**
Date: **July 6, 2011**

Dear Bob and Sue,

We're back in Alaska, sitting in Anchorage and ready to go to Katmai National Park tomorrow. With the time and expense it takes to get here, we decided to go back and visit Denali; that's where we've been the last couple of days. This time, we stayed two nights at the Denali Backcountry Lodge at the end of the park road.

It rained most of the time we were there, but we hiked anyway; we don't get these days back you know. Last year we visited Denali in August, and there were almost no bugs; this year – a month and a half earlier – they were in full force. A ranger told us that mosquitos can take as much as a pint of blood a day out of a caribou at the height of mosquito season.

Last week I tried on mosquito headnets at REI; I was checking them out for this trip. I put one on and walked through the store to draw attention so when I found Karen in the women's clothes section I would inflict maximum embarrassment. When she saw me coming, she started to duck into a changing room, but I called her name out; she just froze, standing there with slumped shoulders. She knows that resisting will only result in a bigger scene. I said to her, "I'm getting one of these for Alaska. Do you want one?"

She said, "I don't care how bad the bugs are in Alaska. I wouldn't be caught dead in one of those things."

I bought her one anyway. Two minutes into our first hike in Denali she groveled for it. In Alaska, you can look stupid wearing a head net or you can look stupid wearing a hundred mosquito welts on your face – it's a simple choice.

But you also need bug spray. Before we left the lodge for our half-day hike, we put on a non-toxic insect repellent made from lemon eucalyptus oil; Karen is very concerned about putting chemicals on her body. The lemon eucalyptus oil seemed to excite the mosquitos rather than repel them. Then I sprayed the cuffs of my pants with an insect repellent made from 30% DEET. I was careful not to get it on my skin; DEET is pretty toxic. By the time we reached the turn-around point of our hike, I was spraying Jungle Juice – 100% DEET – on everything. I closed my eyes tight and sprayed it directly on my face. The 100% DEET and the head net kept the mosquitos from taking a pint of my blood. (The DEET melted the rubber coating on my binoculars and the brim of my hat, but it kept the bugs away.)

Your friend,
Matt

~.~.~.~.~.~.~

From: **Matt Smith**
Subject: **#50 – Katmai National Park**
Date: **July 8, 2011**

Dear Bob and Sue,

As our floatplane banked left and dropped toward the water, the first thing we saw was a mother bear and cub. The bears were walking along the edge of the lake, slowly moving away from the planes that were parked tail-first in front of Brooks Camp. By the time we landed and taxied to shore, they were at a safe enough distance that we could exit the plane. We were hoping to see bears in the park; what we saw far exceeded our expectations.

This was Katmai National Park, designated a national monument in 1918 and made a national park and preserve in 1980. The park preserves the site of the still-smoldering Novarupta Volcano eruption, which blew in 1912 with the force of over ten Mount St. Helenses. The Valley of Ten Thousand Smokes – the name of the eruption site – is a popular visitor attraction, but another significant part of the park's mandate is the preservation of its brown bear population. We came to see the bears.

Katmai is 200 miles southwest of Anchorage, Alaska at the base of the Alaska Peninsula. It's in the bush, meaning no roads lead to it (that is, no roads that connect to the rest of Alaska). King Salmon – a town of 500 – is a couple of miles west of the park border. Most visitors who come to see the bears and the Valley of Ten Thousand Smokes fly into King Salmon, and then take a floatplane from there to Brooks Camp. That's how we got here.

The park service doesn't let you jump off the plane and head off looking for bears, which was my first instinct. They required us to sit through a bear orientation at the visitor center – Karen called it bear school – before they gave us free access to the park. At the conclusion of bear school, we got pins that we were to wear at all times while in the park, so the rangers could see we'd been schooled. Karen lost hers.

Bear school taught us to be alert; bears could be anywhere at any time, especially now during the heavy salmon run. We weren't supposed to eat or drink anything other than water outside the lodge, the cabins, or the electric fences that enclosed the outdoor eating areas. (I could see through the window of bear school several campers eating lunch surrounded by an electric fence. It looked like yard time at a medium security prison.)

We were not to approach a bear. If we unexpectedly came upon one, we were to talk calmly, so it knows we're human, avoid eye contact, back away slowly at a diagonal, allow it a clear path to move away, and (this is my favorite) get behind a tree if possible. I laughed out loud when the ranger told us that one. Don't climb the tree – that's a bad idea for a bunch of reasons – just get behind it. That seemed silly to me. If a bear wants to attack you, the tree would slow it down by what, a quarter of a second? Maybe the idea is to hide from the bear. I'd like to see how that works. An enraged bear, intent on attacking, is in full pursuit when suddenly Karen and I (while backing away slowly at a diagonal) slip behind a tree. The bear stops abruptly, sniffs the air, looks around and then thinks, "Where the hell did they go? They were *right here* a second ago. I can't believe it, that's the third time this week."

There was one piece of advice they underscored. *Never run from a bear.* The ranger said running from a bear "activates a predatory response," which means they *will* chase you – not *might* chase you – *will* chase you. It's like a Labrador retriever with a tennis ball. If the ball sits motionless on the floor, the lab is not going to jump on it, but throw the tennis ball and the lab will go over, under, and/or through almost anything to get it. Same deal here, except *we* are the tennis balls, and the bear is 15 times larger and stronger than a lab. Oh yeah, the ranger also said if you run, the bear *will* catch you – not *might* catch you – *will* catch you. After the bear catches you, it's downhill from there, which brings us back to their original advice. *Never run from a bear.*

Someone asked what kind of bears are in the park. The ranger said they're "browns." Brown bears and grizzlies are now considered the same species; genetically they're the same animal, although there are other differences. Grizzlies live away from the coast (usually 100 miles or more); they are mostly vegetarian, and they are smaller. Where they live dictates their diet, and their diet determines their size. She added that Kodiak bears are also brown bears that have evolved into a different species because of their isolation on Kodiak Island, Alaska. I asked how large a brown bear could get. The ranger said, "We don't think there is a limit. As long as they keep eating, they keep getting bigger; their food intake is only limited by the food supply and competition from other bears."

Requiring visitors to sit through a bear orientation is a good idea. All things considered, the training seemed light. Mixing humans into a dense bear habitat creates the potential for dangerous encounters. Everyone needs to be on his or her best behavior, and know what best behavior entails. The ranger finished her talk on an upbeat note; no bear had ever killed a person in the Brooks Camp area of the park. There had been "contacts" – bites and scrapes – but no deaths. That was very reassuring; no one had ever died doing what we were about to do; just a few had been mauled.

Brooks Camp is on the west side of the park, on the shore of NakNek Lake. It's a few hundred yards from the river (Brooks River) that connects NakNek to Lake Brooks. Located at Brooks Camp are a national park visitor center, campgrounds and Brooks Lodge. The lodge has 16 rooms (some in single room cabins and some in multi-room cabins), a small gift store and a main building that serves meals. The campground has a maximum capacity of 60 people, and it's difficult to get a camping reservation there during the summer. There are also facilities where rangers live. Between lodge guests, campers, rangers, and day-trippers who come in on floatplanes, the total number of people in the Brooks Camp area during the day is around 200.

The cabin we stayed in had two sets of bunk beds, a private bath, and shower. As with most park lodges we've stayed at, we didn't expect to spend much time in our room; a clean, safe, warm, and dry room was all we needed, and that's what we got.

We were anxious to get out and look for bears. They come to Brooks River for the salmon that run from June through September. Early July is ideal for bear viewing because it's the heaviest salmon run. Salmon returning from their two-to-three year swim-about in the ocean enter Kvichak Bay west of the Alaska Peninsula and swim upstream through NakNek River (past the town of King Salmon) to NakNek Lake inside the park. Making it that far alone is a miracle, but the trip isn't over for the ones destined to spawn in Brooks Lake or points beyond. Those salmon have to make it up the two-mile Brooks River, which has a set of falls – Brooks Falls – at its halfway point. The falls are just one more obstacle these fish face on their long journey – a single jump of five to ten feet – but it may be the most dangerous. The falls slow the salmon down, which makes it easier for the bears to catch them.

The park service built three bear-viewing platforms along Brooks River: the first at the mouth of the river where it fans out into NakNek Lake, a second – the Riffles Platform –a mile upriver and a few hundred yards below the falls, and a third – the Falls Platform – adjacent to Brooks Falls. Each platform is about ten feet off the ground with gates to discourage bears from accessing them.

A short walk from the lodge brought us to the mouth of the river. The first viewing platform is on the other side; a floating footbridge lets humans cross the river while bears can swim under the bridge or walk around it on shore.

Karen and I crossed the river and went to the top of the first platform. It had a panoramic view with Brooks River on one side and the lake on the other, but there were no bears. After a few minutes and many mosquito bites, we decided to keep walking; our destination was the Falls Platform. The ranger on our platform was standing at the gate. When we approached the gate, he said, "I need you to stay here. There's a bear in the area." The rangers all have radios to report bear sightings and movements to one another. Our ranger heard a bear was heading toward us, and he was holding everyone on the platform until the bear passed.

We looked in the direction of the river and then toward the lake; we saw nothing. Everyone on the platform was searching, and hoping to be the first to spot it. I thought it was a false alarm, but we politely stayed on the platform. It was our only option since a ranger was blocking our exit. A few minutes later, I was looking in the direction of the trail to the Falls Platform – the trail we were about to walk down – and coming out of the trees no fewer than 100 feet away was the biggest bear I've ever seen, zoos included. I think I felt the ground shake as he walked past us – it could have been my imagination.

Once the bear walked a few hundred feet toward the lake, and was clearly moving away from us, the ranger opened the gate, stood aside, and gave us a smile. Before leaving the platform, I had a silent chat with myself that went something like, "Wait... Wait a second... A fur-covered Volkswagen just walked out of the woods on the trail we're now going to walk down. What if... what if we would have walked down that trail a few minutes earlier? What would we have done? What if that isn't the only bear in the woods?" I had no answers to my questions. I'd already forgotten everything they told us in bear school. Were we supposed to look at the bear but don't talk to it? Run at a diagonal then climb a tree? I hesitated at the gate and asked the ranger, "Is it okay for us to walk to the Falls Platform?" I was pointing to the trail that thunder paws just came from.

"Oh yeah, just watch for bears," he said.

"But, had we not stopped here first, we would have been walking right toward that one. And, that's okay?"

He was searching for my bear school pin when he asked, "You've been through bear orientation haven't you?"

"Yes we have, but, here's the part that worries me a little, I don't think a 20-minute bear talk is enough preparation for meeting a bear that size in the forest." (I wasn't really paying attention in bear school. I thought there would be cookies afterward; I spent most of the time looking for the treat table.)

The ranger said, "If you see a bear, keep your distance, move away slowly, talk to it, don't make eye contact, give it plenty of space, so it can walk past you. You'll be fine. It helps to get behind a tree."

I didn't laugh this time.

It was a half a mile hike through the forest from where we were to the Falls Platform. We walked briskly, like when I was a kid and had to retrieve my Frisbee from the neighbor's yard – the one with the German Shepherd – hoping the dog didn't see, hear, or smell me before I jumped back over the fence. At the end of the trail, there was a raised boardwalk with a heavy gate. Once through the gate, we felt safe again. The boardwalk led to both the Falls Platform and Riffles Platform. Falls Platform is the prime bear viewing spot. It's closest to where the bears congregate to fish for salmon. During salmon runs, usually there's a waiting list for the Falls Platform. There's only room for about 40 people at one time. We put our names on the list, and the attending ranger told us the wait might be as long as an hour. The park service limits each stay on the Falls Platform to an hour, but you can put your name back on the list as soon as your time is up. It's less of a hassle than it sounds. We waited on Riffles Platform with the other visitors.

The ultimate fishing spot for the bears is right at the falls. Salmon collect in the pools at the foot of the falls, gather their energy, and take flying leaps to get over the rapids. It usually takes several tries to make it. I doubt there's a salmon that made it to the spawning grounds of Lake Brooks that hasn't felt the breath of a bear on its dorsal fin, perhaps several times.

The bears here spend up to six months every winter

hibernating. They don't eat year-round. When not sleeping, they need to eat as much as possible to store huge amounts of fat, or they might not survive. Fishing is a matter of life or death. It is no surprise that the bears don't have a waiting list for who gets to fish at the primo locations. The biggest meanest bears get the best fishing spots, and they stay there as long as they want (or until another bear pushes them out).

We noticed that not all the bears were catching the same amount of fish; a small percentage of the bears caught a large percentage of the salmon. Looking down river from the falls, we saw a perfect map of the local bear hierarchy. The farther you get from the falls, the smaller, younger, and less experienced are the bears.

Down at the Riffles Platform it was the minor leagues. Younger bears – maybe three or four years old – were lunging at fish, burning huge amounts of calories splashing with wild fury, and ending up with nothing to show for their efforts. After a few minutes of flailing, they would sit on a boulder in the middle of the river, half resting and half confused at why the flashes of color in the water were so hard to catch. As entertaining as this was to watch, it was serious business; survival for these bears depends on getting the most calories for the least calories spent. Young bears may have playful energy, but they cannot afford to splash around all day and not have anything to eat. The faster they learn to fish, the better their chances of thriving, or surviving.

Soon enough, it was our turn on the Falls Platform. Every inch of the upper and lower deck railing was occupied when we got there, but within a few minutes, a spot opened at the far end closest to the falls. Karen and I scored a prime location, and no one tried to kill us – another advantage of being at the top of the food chain. My digital camera looked silly compared to the cameras the others were using. The platform looked like a paparazzi gathering; half the group looked like professional photographers, or at least very serious amateurs. When you see a picture in a magazine, web site, or travel brochure of a brown bear standing at the top of a waterfall with salmon jumping through the air, that picture was more likely than not taken from the Falls Platform.

For the most part, the behavior on the platform was civil. Even though it was crowded, people made room for one another so they could have a front row view. Every few minutes, the ranger would come through with her clipboard and tell people that their time was up. The couple next to us acted like they couldn't understand the ranger when it was their time to leave. Finally, the wife acknowledged the ranger and headed toward the exit. Her husband followed for a few steps, but then came back, and sat down at my feet between my legs and the end railing. He waved to his wife to go on. When the ranger got to the gate, she looked around, and seeing only the wife shrugged her shoulders and put her hands out, palms up, in a show of frustration as if to say, "Where's your husband?" The couple apparently didn't speak English. The wife said, "No. No." The ranger marched back to the platform, and found the husband hiding behind me. She came over to him, put her face close to his, and pointed her thumb toward the exit. He said, "No. No." She wasn't falling for the "I can't understand what you're saying" trick; she'd seen it all before. She booted him off the platform.

During the hour we were on the platform, I used as much memory on my camera's data card as all our previous parks trips combined. In one shot, I counted nine bears in the picture frame. Downstream, there were many others. All the bears at the falls were big; the biggest of the bigs, but one seemed to be the alpha bear. He sat in a pool below the falls with his entire body underwater except for his head. At first, this didn't look like the best way to catch fish, but soon it was clear that it was. The other bears were lucky to catch a fish an hour; the alpha bear caught six or seven while we were on the platform. Salmon would gather in the pool at his feet preparing to make their leap. When one would graze his leg, he would dive beneath the surface and come up with it in his mouth. A few yards downstream he ate his catch. In four to five minutes, he would eat a six-pound salmon and then return to his fishing hole. The other bears would try to sneak into the hole when the alpha bear was eating. They did so at considerable risk; the alpha bear had visible scars on his face and neck. A furless patch on his shoulder was still bleeding from a recent run-in with another bear. He was constantly defending his spot. As soon as the alpha bear gave the slightest indication he was ready to return to his fishing spot, the other bears hastily cleared away.

A short distance downstream from the falls was a small island in the river. Sitting on the island, crouched over, breathing heavily, and with his front lip hanging loose touching the ground was a very old bear. Karen called him the old man bear. He was huge; his frame was larger than the bears fishing at the falls, but that's all there was – bones and fur. He looked like he was wearing a brown bear fur coat three sizes too large. The park service has a database of every bear in the park. They know how old each bear is, who's related to whom, what part of the park they hang out in, etc. The ranger on the platform said the old man bear was 30 years old. That's very old for a brown bear. He couldn't fish anymore and he moved slowly; even so, the other bears gave him a wide berth as if they had encounters with him in the past that didn't end well. They didn't want to find out if there was any fight left in this slow moving bag of bones. Karen asked the ranger if they ever help bears in distress. The ranger said they don't intervene in the natural process, no matter how painful it is to watch. Even when a small cub is being attacked and killed by a larger bear, they're not allowed to interfere.

The old man bear didn't look as if he would make it one more winter, or even *to* next winter. The ranger said most bears in his condition go into hibernation and don't wake up the next spring. He sat on the island watching the alpha bear fish. When the alpha bear would catch a salmon, he'd walk close to the island and eat the fish right in front of the old man. He'd eat most of it, and then leave the last couple of bites in the river for the old man bear. There was no mistaking he did this on purpose. The alpha bear was feeding the old man. We saw this happen a few more times. He let only the old man bear eat his scraps; none of the other bears were allowed to come close.

When our time on the platform was up, we were ready to take a break from the mosquitos and head back to the lodge. But here's an important point to make: the bears weren't just in the river; the forest was also filled with bears, more so as we were leaving than when we arrived at the platform. As we walked to the end of the boardwalk, where the heavy gate separated us from the rest of the park, we kept seeing very large bears just under and near the boardwalk. It became frightfully obvious that just because the boardwalk extended a couple of hundred yards away from the river, the gate didn't indicate the beginning of a safe zone. The bears we just saw in the river walk through the same forest, and sometimes on the *same trails*, as the visitors. "It's a bear highway," Karen said. Exiting through that gate felt as if we were walking into a zoo, the inside part where the animals live.

Have you ever been to the MGM in Las Vegas where they have lions in a glass enclosure next to the casino? Imagine the glass gone, but the lions still there. Now imagine that every so often a lion strolls through the casino, between the craps tables and past the Wheel of Fortune; terrified guests back up diagonally and stand behind slot machines. That's what Katmai is; except with bears instead of lions, and wilderness instead of a casino.

If Karen was on edge walking back to the lodge, I was on the edge of the edge. The only thing that kept me from panicking was the fact that other people were walking on the trail with us: old people, families with young children, rangers... It really took a while for me to accept that the park service allows people and bears to be so close to one another.

Halfway back to the lodge, Karen stopped at the restrooms along the trail. I was facing toward her and away from the trail when she came out. She took one step out of the restroom and gave me a startled look – like she just realized she dropped her cell phone in the pit toilet. She gasped and said, "There's one!" I turned around and saw a hump of brown fur moving through the trees about 30 feet away. We both turned and ran. A few steps into our sprint we stopped as our brains remembered the number one lesson from bear school – *never run from a bear*. We stood and watched the bear silently amble through the forest. He no more wanted to chase us than we wanted him to. Once he moved to a safe distance, we continued on to the lodge.

Next to the dining area in the lodge's main building is a round fireplace with chairs circling it. Most of the day-trippers had left; campers and overnight lodge guests were all who remained. At the lodge's small bar we got a beer, sat by the fire, and started a conversation with the couple sitting next to us. By the second round of beers, it was time for me to find a restroom. I only share this detail with you because there is no restroom in the main building, so I had to go outside to a separate building a short distance away. I walked out the front doors of the lodge, turned right to head toward the restrooms, and guess what came out the bushes right in front of me? A bear. A big one. I didn't run, nor did I pee myself. Although, it was a close call considering I had to pee in the first place. The bear sauntered off without incident. I took care of business and re-joined my foursome around the fire.

The three of them were deep into a conversation. At a pause, I announced that I ran into a bear while going to the restroom. They looked at me briefly, and the husband said, "Yeah, they're all over," and went back to the conversation. That's Katmai. Running into a bear while going for a pee is no big deal.

After dinner, we decided to take a walk around the lodge area: the beach, visitor center, and campgrounds. The weather was good, and this being our only night in the park, we wanted to see as much as possible. Earlier in the week, we got plastic cups at the Denali Backcountry Lodge. They were grown-up sippy cups with plastic lids to keep from spilling. We had a bottle of wine with us in our room, and Karen said, "Let's put wine in our Denali cups and take them with us on our walk."

I replied, "That's not allowed in the park, only water."

She looked at me with contempt and said, "I don't think the bears are interested in Sauvignon Blanc."

Going against my better judgment, I went along with Karen's plan. We put on our jackets and backpacks, poured the wine into our sippy cups, and headed toward the visitor center. We hadn't walked 30 feet from our cabin when we heard, "Folks, what do you have in your cups?" A ranger – the authoritative looking one with the gun – headed straight toward us. She scared me more than the bears. We were so busted. She didn't even wait for our mumbled responses. She knew what we were trying to pull. She barked, "I need you to go back inside with your drinks. Thank you." With a, "Yes ma'am" we spun around and slinked back to our cabin. I was kind of hoping Karen would sass her, but she didn't.

This morning after breakfast in the lodge, we hiked to Brooks Lake. We were surprised not to see any bears. On our way back, we stopped for another hour on the Falls Platform. The same show was playing as yesterday, only this time there were bears on top of the falls trying to catch salmon as they leaped through the air. I read on the park's website that not all visitors to the park see bears. That was a surprise considering we saw, without exaggeration, at least 100 bears in our day and a half visit. It all has to do with timing; when the salmon run the bears will be at the river.

From the Falls Platform, we hiked back to the lodge for lunch. When we passed the ranger at the mouth of the river, there was a lot of chatter on her radio. I heard, "Where did you see her last?" and, "Where are they now?" Several rangers were walking quickly between the river and the lodge. We were walking toward the lodge when a slightly frantic voice from behind us said, "I need all you folks to stay where you're at." There were eight to ten of us on the trail. The ranger came over and said, "Let's all move up on this hill and stand together." (The hill was a small grassy area in front of the gift shop.) The ranger turned her back to us and walked a few yards down the trail. Just then, a large mother bear walked out of the tall grass along the trail; very close behind her were two young cubs, then a third popped out of the tall grass. Number three was half the size of the other two. An audible "ahhhh" came from the group when the little one scurried to catch up.

The mother and two larger cubs paid no attention to the ranger or us. They kept their heads down, walked along the trail, and cut through the trees toward the beach. The runt gave us a look like he'd rather check us out than follow his mother. The ranger gave the little one a stern arm gesture pointing toward the mother bear. Karen said, "Oh, he looks like a little monkey." He was cute for sure. I told Karen he doesn't have a good chance of surviving being so small and having two larger siblings. She said, "Don't say that! The mother will love him more because he's small." I'm not sure it works that way with bears, but there was no use explaining that to Karen.

Mother and cub family groups are extremely cautious near Brooks River because the large male bears will try to kill the cubs. This is why they spend more time around the lake and lodge than the river. A mother bear has three main jobs: keep other bears from killing her cubs, feed them, and teach them to fish. But here's her problem: she can't fish where it's easy because the bigger bears will run her off or kill her cubs, and fishing downstream is difficult, so she might spend all day fishing and end up catching nothing. It's a small wonder that any cubs make it to adulthood, even in a place with so many fish.

The white board in the lodge office said we were on the 5:00pm flight to King Salmon. That was not enough time for another trip to the falls, so we hung out around the lodge and walked along the beach. In the afternoon, the beach is a busy place: people standing around waiting for their flights, new visitors taking a first look around, even bears passing through.

Karen and I were standing on the beach with a handful of other visitors. We were about 100 yards from the visitor center. A quarter mile away was a bear slowly walking toward us along the water's edge. The beach is a passageway for bears. They come down from Brooks River and follow the beach around the bump out of land in front of Brooks Camp to get to their permanent habitat. The bear walking toward us was in no hurry. Every few yards he would wade into the water, turn over a rock, paw at something that looked like food, and then continue moving toward us.

The rule is you're not supposed to be within 50 yards of a bear; that's of course if you see the bear soon enough to give it space. It was obvious in this case that we should move away as the bear approached. I'm not exactly sure how far 50 yards is. I know it's half the length of a football field, but it's a guess really when a bear is walking toward you.

The bear finally got close enough that Karen and I started backing up toward the visitor center. There was a man and his teenage son between us and the bear. The father and I were both taking pictures of the bear when I said, "I think we should get back to the visitor center." As the father turned toward me, a lens fell out of his camera bag onto the beach. He bent down to pick it up while I watched the bear. I said to him, "You need to hurry. The bear is looking at us." The father grabbed the lens, and as he stood up everything else fell out of his camera bag and onto the beach – another camera, a couple of lenses, it was a lot of stuff. I said, "Just leave it!" But he frantically tried to gather his gear. Meanwhile, the bear kept looking at us from the lake. I became genuinely concerned for this guy. I instinctively ran a few steps toward him to help him pick up his stuff.

Now, here's a tip I learned that they don't teach you in bear school. A tip, I realize, most people don't need to be told, but I suggest the park service add it to their curriculum. The only thing worse than running *from* a bear is running *at* a bear. What our lake bear saw was not me running to help a fellow human. No, the bear saw *me* running at *him*. I looked up from our crouched position and saw a very large, and from all appearances angry, bear running full tilt toward us. I grabbed the guy, and we did the second dumbest thing we could do, we ran *away* from the bear. Karen was a few feet ahead of us this whole time.

I've always thought I could outrun Karen if I had to, but here's something else I learned today: when a bear is chasing us, Karen is quicker than me. She ran like, well, like an angry bear was chasing her. I had no chance of catching her.

We all ran toward the visitor center (because bears aren't allowed in the visitor center). I thought the bear might pull up after a few yards, but when I looked back he was still coming at us. I scrambled up the path that led away from the beach to see a wall of people desperately pushing their way into the front door of the visitor center. The visitor center was no longer an option for me. Glancing at the electric fence, I decided in an instant I couldn't make it there in time. All that came to mind at that moment was – shit! Just then I heard someone in the crowd say the bear veered off and was now running down the beach away from us. I don't know how close he got to us, but it was too close.

Later Karen said the bear was only chasing us for fun, and would have never attacked. Interesting. That must be why she ran like an escaped convict.

We're back in Anchorage now, safely inside the Courtyard by Marriott. There are no bears in the parking lot or in the bushes next to the front door. It feels – tame. But not for long. Tomorrow we head back into the bush, to Lake Clark National Park.

Your friend,
Matt

~.~.~.~.~.~.~

From: **Karen Smith**
Subject: **#51 – Lake Clark National Park**
Date: **July 9, 2011**

Dear Bob and Sue,

Lake Clark National Park is one of the most beautiful pristine wilderness areas on the planet, but we're here for one specific reason: to visit Dick Proenneke's cabin on Twin Lakes. Matt had been dying to see Dick's cabin ever since he saw the documentary about it years ago. He talks so much about "Dick's cabin" that I keep saying Dick Clark National Park by mistake. Today Matt's dream came true.

Dick Proenneke was a guy who built a cabin in the Alaskan wilderness, and lived there by himself for the better part of 30 years. Before that, he was a carpenter in the Navy during World War II, and later worked as a heavy machinery operator and repairman at a naval base in Alaska. While at the naval base, a retired navy captain (Spike Carrither) invited him to Twin Lakes. From that first visit, Dick was hooked on the place. In 1967, he selected a site for his own cabin, and spent the summer cutting down the trees he would use the following summer to build it. In late May of 1968, *at the age of 51*, Dick Proenneke entered the wilderness with 150 pounds of provisions, including the hand tools he would use to build his cabin.

While building his cabin, he filmed himself. He also filmed and photographed wildlife throughout his years at Twin Lakes and kept a journal. The first year of Dick's journal was edited into a book titled *One Man's Wilderness*. The book's success made Dick famous among wilderness enthusiasts. Dick died in 2003, and the footage he shot of building his cabin was made into a documentary titled *Alone in the Wilderness*, which is often aired on PBS television channels, especially during pledge drives. Every time it comes on, Matt watches it, eyes glued to the TV. All the details that went into building the cabin fascinate him, from trimming the logs so they fit tightly, to making the hinges for the front door out of bent tree stumps.

Matt has told me over and over again that we're going to sell all our possessions and build a cabin in the wilderness. I know he would love building it, but living in it? I'm not so sure. Dick didn't have electricity, running water, a telephone – any modern utilities at all. And the Alaska winters are brutal. Matt complains because I've programmed our thermostat to drop to 63 degrees at night. Besides, he has no idea what I would look like after a long winter with no hair dryer or straightener.

Dick built his cabin on federal land before it became part of the national park system. The park service let him continue to live in the cabin after the area was designated a national park in 1980. Dick left Twin Lakes for good in 1999, at the age of 82. The extreme weather and the hard physical work became too much for him. He donated his cabin to the park service, and since then they've maintained the cabin exactly how he left it, down to the smallest detail.

Twin Lakes is in the center of the park; a short stream connects the two lakes. Dick lived on the upper lake and built his cabin a few hundred yards away from Spike's. The lake sits at 2,000 feet elevation; the surrounding mountain peaks are 5,000 to 6,500 feet. In the summer when the lake is free of ice, the water is a turquoise blue. Many of the lakes in the park have that amazing blue color; there's one named Turquoise Lake ten miles north of Twin Lakes.

In size, the park is 2.4 million acres, about twice the size of Yellowstone. It's roughly 120 miles north to south, and 70 miles east to west in size; its northern tip is 100 miles straight west of Anchorage. There are no roads into the park and no services available. Visitors wanting to camp in the park have to be flown in with all their provisions. A park brochure warns visitors considering a trip into the backcountry that, "Lake Clark National Park is a wilderness park, exceptionally remote and isolated... Help, if any, may be days away." If you don't want to strike out on your own, several lodges skirt the perimeter of the park, and their guests can choose from many guided activities ranging from bear viewing, salmon fishing, backpacking trips, photography excursions, and of course, a day-trip to visit Dick's cabin.

Yesterday, we took a six-passenger plane from Merrill field in Anchorage to Port Alsworth on Lake Clark, just outside the southwest boundary of the park. For the first 50 to 60 miles we flew over nondescript lowlands southwest of Anchorage, but suddenly the mountains came into view. For a few minutes, it looked as if we were going to fly right into the mountainside rising in front of us. Matt sat in the front seat next to the pilot, so he could see everything, while I sat in the back seat for the opposite reason. My strategy backfired however, because I could still see clearly out the front of the plane, but I was too far back to tell what the pilot was doing. It wasn't reassuring to see him constantly looking down at his phone in his right hand. I'm not sure if he was using a navigation application, texting his girlfriend, or playing Tetris, but fortunately he cleared the ridge before I embarrassed Matt by yelling, "Pull up, pull up!"

Once we entered Lake Clark Pass, the landscape changed dramatically to a heavily forested valley framed by glacier-topped mountains. It took just a couple of minutes to realize that we left civilization and passed into the wilderness. The view from the plane was so beautiful I forgot about my fear of flying in small planes.

Port Alsworth is the park's field headquarters, but it's not much more than a remote clearing with an air strip, a couple of lodges, a few lakeside homes, a church and the park's visitor center. No roads lead into Port Alsworth.

We're staying at the Farm Lodge, which Glen Alsworth, Jr. manages. Glen's grandfather "Babe" Alsworth was the bush pilot who brought Dick Proenneke mail and supplies while he lived at Twin Lakes. Lake Clark Air – owned by Glen Alsworth, Sr. – provides air taxi service for visitors wanting to get into the backcountry of Lake Clark National Park and the locals who live in the surrounding remote villages. After our plane landed, we had time to go to the visitor center to take care of business, and then we hiked to Tanalian Falls. The Tanalian trail system is the only maintained trail system in the park. We just made it back to the lodge in time for dinner.

Glen, Jr. arranged for a guide – Robert – to go with us on our tour of Dick's cabin. Robert is in his 20s and from Wyoming. This is his second summer working at the lodge as a guide; he's also a pilot. He told us at dinner that he recently completed his pilot training, bought a plane, and has it parked at the airstrip in Port Alsworth. Small planes are a way of life in Alaska. It seems like everyone is a pilot and owns a plane.

From Port Alsworth this morning, a pilot flew the three of us to Twin Lakes. The flight took about 45 minutes in the small, four-seat floatplane. It was a beautiful flight over the park, a little rainy and bumpy, but the pilot said he'd flown in much worse. I spent most of the flight looking down at the terrain, scouting out areas where we could crash land and still survive. The glaciers looked deceptively soft. When our plane approached Twin Lakes, the pilot circled the area by Dick's cabin, checking the water and wind to make sure it was safe to land. We taxied to the beach less than a rock's throw from Dick's cabin.

The cabin and the surrounding area were pristine; it looked like a movie set. This is how Dick kept it when he lived there. Visitors who came to see Dick would comment on how particular he was about the appearance of his cabin, the beach in front of his cabin, and even the surrounding wilderness. He often canoed miles just to clean up trash left at campsites by hunters.

Matt, Robert, and I stepped onto the float of the plane and then onto the beach. A volunteer park ranger named Monroe was there to meet us. He knew we were coming because the park service tracks flights in the park on their two-way radios. Monroe and Kay (also a park service volunteer) spend their summers at Twin Lakes, living in a nearby cabin. They maintain Dick's cabin and give tours to park visitors.

Robert pronounced Monroe's name with the emphasis on the first syllable, which pleased Matt to no end. When Matt talks in his folksy accent, he stresses the first syllable of words like *De*troit and *po*lice. He worked Monroe's name into the conversation as many times as he could for the rest of the afternoon, just so he could say it – *Mon*roe.

Even though it was Matt's dream to visit Dick's cabin, I'd watched the documentary also and was looking forward to seeing this place. It was more impressive than I ever imagined. Dick was adamant that Twin Lakes and the wildlife should not suffer because of his presence. He reused almost everything, even carefully crafting buckets and storage boxes from used airplane gas cans. Everything that Dick had, most of which he made himself, was still in place in the cabin right where he left it: the furniture, his pots and pans, wooden spoons, clothing, books, shaving kit, the storage cache outside, etc. Some of Dick's belongings had deteriorated, and have been restored by Monroe using the same methods Dick originally used to make them.

Inside the cabin, it looked like Dick stepped out for a minute and would be right back; that's the feel the park service wants to maintain. Dick had many visitors when he lived at Twin Lakes. Babe Alsworth, park service employees, hunting guides (before it became a park), even the governor of Alaska – Jay Hammond – would fly in to visit Dick. Dick had a map of the Twin Lakes area that he kept on his desk in the cabin. On days he would venture away from the cabin, which were most days, he would stick a pin in the map at that location with a small tag attached that said, "Here Today." That way, if anyone came by the cabin and needed to find him or, if anything happened to him and he couldn't make it back, they would know where to look. The map and pin are still on his desk. I wish we could have hiked to that spot on the map, found Dick, and spent the day with him.

It's amazing he didn't have any life threatening – or life ending – mishaps considering the risk of living in the Alaskan wilderness in relative solitude. Dick didn't have a two-way radio like the park rangers do today. If anything bad happened to him – injury, sickness, or animal attack – he would have had to take care of himself until the next plane stopped by.

Soon after he finished his cabin, a grizzly bear tried to climb onto the roof while Dick was inside. Had he not shot his .357 magnum handgun into the air the bear surely would have made it to the top and quite possibly gotten into the cabin. When the shot rang out, the bear, rather than fleeing in fear, charged around the cabin, and threw its weight on the front door that Dick just closed and latched. He wrote in his diary that he could feel the weight of the bear against the door. Dick grabbed his rifle, and was about to kill the bear, when it walked off into the forest. After that day, Dick never saw that particular bear again. The claw marks the bear made on the log above the front door are still visible today. Imagine how frightening that would be, trapped in a small cabin with an angry bear, clearly not afraid of gunfire, trying to get in. It wasn't like our bear encounters in Katmai where there were always rangers nearby or a visitor center to duck into. Dick was on his own.

We wanted to hike into the high country above Dick's cabin, but after our Katmai bear encounters and seeing the claw marks on the cabin, we wondered if it was safe. I asked Robert if he had bear spray with him. He said, "No, but I have this." He unzipped the pocket of his windbreaker and slowly pulled out the biggest handgun I've ever seen; the bullets were the size of a roll of nickels. I realized at that moment that Robert was more than just our guide: he was our bodyguard. His job wasn't so much to guide us as to make sure nothing ate us. (I noticed later that Monroe had a large handgun in a holster just under his park service rain jacket.)

Robert and his gun made us feel more comfortable about hiking into the high country above the cabin. It was raining off and on and cool, so we only hiked a couple of miles up the hill on the south of the cabin, but it was far enough to get a panoramic view of the lakes and the surrounding mountains. Dick chose an incredible place to spend his retirement.

After our hour-long hike, we sat on the beach, leaning up against Dick's canoe, and ate the sack lunches the lodge had made for us. It was easy to picture the things happening on that very beach that Dick wrote about in his journal: Babe Alsworth parking his plane there while unloading mail and supplies, a wolverine on the frozen lake eating the moose meat Dick put out for it, Dick digging a three-foot deep hole in the lake ice to get fresh water to cook with.

With lunch finished, it was time to visit Monroe and Kay at their cabin. On the way, I had to make a side trip to the outhouse with Robert escorting me. The outhouse, about a quarter mile walk through the woods from Dick's cabin, was a shack pieced together from scraps of wood. It leaned to the left, and a big rock was propped against its sagging door. The huge gaps in the wood planks suddenly diminished the thrill of having a personal bodyguard by my side. I stepped inside and tried to close the door, but it was so warped that I had to reach through a gap and hold it closed with one hand while trying to do my business with the other. I could see poor Robert awkwardly standing about 20 feet away with his back to me, his hand in his gun pocket and his head moving back and forth as he watched for bears.

Monroe and Kay spend their summers living in Hope's Cabin. Hope was Spike's wife. Hope's cabin is the same size as Dick's, 11 feet by 15 feet, and just like Dick's, has a gravel floor. Although, Kay placed an area rug on the gravel inside their cabin. Space is at a premium inside these small cabins, and everything happens in the one and only room: eating, sleeping, cooking, bathing, reading and entertaining visitors – everything except outhouse business. While we were sitting in a circle inside their cabin, Kay told us how happy she is on sunny days because she can put their sun shower bag outside to warm. Once it's heated, they hang it from the rafters of their cabin, roll the area rug back, and shower in the middle of the room – one at a time I'm guessing. The water from the shower drains into the gravel floor, and in a short time, the floor is dry enough to roll out the rug again.

Monroe said that Dick may have been a packrat, but he was also fastidious about keeping his living space clean. Each year he would take everything out of his cabin, shovel out the gravel, wash it in the lake, let it dry in the sun, and then shovel the clean gravel back into his cabin. That sounds exactly like something Matt would do if he lived in a cabin, but Matt would have arranged the gravel according to size and color.

Monroe and Kay have organized their lives so they can spend three months every year at Twin Lakes volunteering for the park service. They live in California the rest of the year. Monroe is a talented wood worker, and from what we saw, he's on par with Dick Proenneke. When not giving tours, he's making reproduction furniture for the other park service cabins scattered throughout the park. Kay says that some days they're giving tours all day long, and don't have time to eat lunch, but other days, no one shows up.

We went back to Dick's cabin to take more pictures before we left. Monroe took our picture standing in the door of Dick's cabin. It's a Dutch door with the top and bottom halves on separate hinges. We had him take our picture with the bottom half of the door shut, and Matt and I leaning through the top half opening. We wanted this picture because there's an iconic picture from the 60's of Dick Proenneke in the same pose. Matt calls it the "Dick in the door" picture. It's a little cheesy, but it was a once-in-a-lifetime photo opportunity. This might be our Christmas card photo this year.

This week in Alaska has been amazing, and our Twin Lakes trip was an ideal ending. Lake Clark Air is flying us to Anchorage tomorrow where we'll catch a flight back to Seattle.

Your friend,
Karen

~.~.~.~.~.~.~

From: **Matt Smith**
Subject: **You won't believe this!**
Date: **July 10, 2011**

Dear Bob and Sue,

You won't believe what happened to us today. We still aren't sure it really happened. This afternoon, on our way to Anchorage from Lake Clark National Park, the plane we were in hit another plane in mid-air. We missed a total disaster by inches.

The other plane was coming straight at us and went right over the top of our plane, tearing off part of the tail and rudder. We never saw it coming. No one was hurt, thank God. We landed safely in Anchorage; the other plane was able to land safely on a lake.

It's a miracle we survived – an absolute miracle.

Your Very Lucky friends,
Matt and Karen

~.~.~.~.~.~.~.~

From: **Matt Smith**
Subject: **Happy to still be here**
Date: **July 12, 2011**

Dear Bob and Sue,

Wow. We're still shaken – and shaking – from our plane adventure. But, I've calmed down enough to give you the blow-by-blow description of what happened on Sunday.

Our nine-passenger plane was flying 165 miles per hour at 2,300 feet through Lake Clark Pass – not over the pass – through it. We had to look up to see the tops of the mountains. The peaks on either side of us were over 5,000 feet, and the valley below was narrow – a mile wide at most, even less in spots.

At the moment of impact, I was looking through the windshield of the plane. All I saw was a shadow flash across the cockpit. Instantly, I heard a loud bang and felt a metal-on-metal crunch. We hit something, something big. It felt as if we sideswiped another car, but there aren't cars at 2,300 feet.

Our pilot looked down at the yoke he was holding, unsure of what just happened. He checked his gauges, but they were reading normal. Everything seemed normal except for the loud bang. I thought it would be only a matter of seconds before we began an uncontrolled plunge into the wilderness below.

I looked out my window for places we could land, but our plane didn't have floats, and there was nowhere to put down on wheels. It was the second time in a week I had an "oh shit, I'm about to die" moment. I thought, "What just happened? Are we crashing or not? Is the plane damaged or is it okay?" It turned out to be something in between. And just that morning, Karen had said to me, "I think I'm over my fear of flying in small planes."

Our original plan was to fly from Port Alsworth to Anchorage at 6:00pm, and then catch a flight to Seattle, getting home about 3:00am. But, it was rainy in Port Alsworth, so we asked if there was an earlier flight to Anchorage. At 11:30am we boarded a Piper Navajo; Karen and I climbed to the front of the plane and sat in the row just behind the pilot.

From Port Alsworth, we flew to the village of Pedro Bay to drop off two passengers. One was a native Alaskan woman who had been in Port Alsworth attending Sunday church service. Before she got off our plane, she leaned forward and said to Karen and me, "This pilot is excellent." Then she handed us each a piece of green, round candy and said in a serious tone, "This is for your next flight." We didn't really want the candy, but it was a sweet gesture and we didn't want to hurt her feelings, so we took the candy and put them in our pockets.

In Pedro Bay, we picked up five more passengers. Judging from the boxes of fish they loaded onto the plane, they'd been on a fishing trip. From there, we flew to the small village of Kokhanok and picked up one more passenger. When we left Kokhanok, our plane had eight passengers and the pilot.

On our way from Kokhanok to Anchorage, we flew back over Port Alsworth and then northeast through Lake Clark Pass. The sky was overcast, but we were flying below the clouds. As we flew through the pass, we could see glaciers coming down from the peaks of the mountains. Even with an overcast sky, the crevasses in the glaciers were a deep blue color.

About half way through the pass, I was looking at the mountains on my side of the plane hoping to see sheep or mountain goats on the rocks. As I shifted my gaze toward the front of the plane, I saw the shadow and felt the crunch. We later learned that we hit the bottom of another plane that had been flying directly toward us. It was a Cessna 206 on floats with four people on board including the pilot. The stretcher bar across the floats of the Cessna took off the top two to three feet of our plane's tail and rudder.

The minutes ticked by, but the plane showed no signs of distress. It was obvious there was no place for the pilot to make an emergency landing, so he continued flying toward our scheduled destination, Merrill Field, close to downtown Anchorage. As he approached the airfield, he turned to me and shouted over the noise of the engines, "I don't know what's going to happen when I try to land because I think I lost part of the rudder when we hit that other plane. I've called for emergency services to meet us at the airport, so I don't want you to freak out when you see fire trucks and ambulances near the runway." He asked me to tell the other passengers behind me.

I didn't know until that moment that we hit another plane. I told the two guys behind me – a father and son – and asked them to pass it back. I looked at the other passengers, but it was too loud to speak to them. The woman a couple of rows behind us had a look of sheer terror on her face.

Despite his concerns about the rudder, the pilot made a smooth landing. He seemed to be in complete control, which was fortunate because the fire trucks and ambulances hadn't shown up yet. He taxied to his parking spot and shut off the engines. The propellers slowly came to a stop. No one, including the pilot moved or said anything for what seemed like a very long time. Then the pilot said, "Well, I got us here safely." There was nervous laughter followed by more silence. I asked him, "Have you ever hit another plane before?" He said, "No! That was my first time." He laughed and so did we. The pilot said he didn't see the other plane until its floats were going over the top of us. We later found out that he had over 10,000 hours of commercial flying experience in Alaska.

We didn't fully realize how close we were to being in a serious – if not fatal – plane crash until we exited the plane through the back doors. It was then we saw that the top of our plane's tail was broken off, and part of the rudder was missing. I hadn't noticed how tall the tail of our plane was when we boarded (I didn't know there would be a quiz after the flight), but it was clear a large chunk was missing.

Later I saw the other plane – the one we hit – on a news report. After comparing the damage of the two planes, I think we missed hitting the other plane's propeller by about a foot. Had either plane hit the other's propeller there would be no more emails from us – ever. (By the way, if something bad ever happens to us, we would like you to spread our ashes, 1/58th at a time, in each of the national parks. Good luck with the Alaska parks.)

I took several pictures of our plane's broken tail while all the passengers stood around looking at one another. We didn't know what to do. I thought to myself, "Is it okay for us to leave?" It was very strange. I don't remember anyone from the airline – except for the pilot – saying anything to the passengers. They didn't ask us how we were, or even what happened. It was as if they were afraid to speak with us. They just unloaded our luggage from the plane and wheeled it to the parking lot. It's not as if we were hoping for a certificate for a free flight, but how about a new pair of underwear, or something?

We took a taxi from Merrill Field to the main airport in Anchorage, which is named after Ted Stevens, the former US Senator from Alaska who *died a year ago in a small plane crash in Alaska!* We went to the Alaska Airlines customer service counter to change to an earlier flight. As the service agent looked for availability, I told her what happened and showed her pictures of our broken plane. She was very sympathetic, and assured us that we would not hit another plane on our next flight. Even though our earlier flight was not an Alaska Airlines flight, she felt so bad about us almost dying that she upgraded us to first class. (I don't recommend this method for getting an upgrade.)

It was exactly what we needed, to sit back and relax in a large plane, one flying in controlled airspace where someone with a radar screen is making sure the planes don't collide in mid-air. I had a couple of drinks; I think Karen had a few more than that - for medicinal reasons she said. We were somewhere over Vancouver, British Columbia before her facial spasm finally went away.

At home, I emptied my pockets and found the piece of candy the woman gave us in Pedro Bay. I threw it away with the other bits of trash left over from the trip. Later, Karen made me take it out of the trash can and put it in a safe place. She says they are our good luck charms, and we have to take them with us on every flight from now on. I don't know what it is with Karen and these elderly, native Alaskan women; she seems to think they have powers to protect us or curse us. I don't have to understand it. I'm just glad we were on their good side yesterday. Thank you Pedro Bay woman.

Your friend,
Matt

~.~.~.~.~.~.~

From: **Matt Smith**
Subject: **Lesson learned**
Date: **July 14, 2011**

Dear Bob and Sue,

The Seattle Times printed an article yesterday about our plane collision. They mentioned that we're visiting all the national parks. By dinnertime, reporters from three TV stations were standing on our front porch with their camera crews asking for interviews. I politely declined, in part because I didn't want to be on TV, but also because Karen was down the street at a friend's house, and when I called her to ask if she wanted to do the interviews she said she didn't like the clothes she was wearing or how her hair looked. By noon today they were back, so we let them in and did the interviews.

They all asked the same question. What have we learned from our experience? Other than *watch out for other planes when flying in Alaska,* the lesson that's stuck with us is, don't spend your life waiting for the *right time* to do the things you want to do. The right time may never come. If there's an experience you want to have, or a place you want to see, do it – soon.

We plan on taking our own advice. There are seven national parks left on our list, and in a few weeks, we will be continuing our parks trip when we visit Isle Royale National Park in Michigan. Ironically, two of the parks left on our list are north of the Arctic Circle in Alaska – Kobuk Valley National Park and Gates of the Arctic National Park – and we can't get to either without flying on a small plane.

Your friend,

Matt

~.~.~.~.~.~.~

From: **Matt Smith**
Subject: **#52 – Isle Royale National Park**
Date: **August 22, 2011**

Dear Bob and Sue,

Karen was excited for our ferry ride from Grand Portage, Minnesota to Rock Harbor on Isle Royale today. She only ate a granola bar for breakfast; she was saving her appetite for clam chowder and a beer on the boat ride. Unfortunately, our ferry today – the Voyageur II – was not like the ferries back home in Seattle. There was no clam chowder. There was no beer. The galley was a cardboard box with a few Snickers in it and the captain's Mr. Coffee machine. The captain graciously announced once we were underway that he would share his coffee with anyone on board who wanted some.

Sitting on the wooden bench at the back of the old fishing vessel –which was our home for the next eight hours – we laid out all our food, as if we were lost in the wilderness and needed to take stock of what we had to survive. We had three bottles of water, two peanut butter and jelly sandwiches, two plastic bags: one full of Cheez-Its and one with tiny pretzels, peanuts from the airplane yesterday, and four Dramamine. I took a Dramamine and told Karen to wake me up when we got there.

Isle Royale is an island in Lake Superior. Isle Royale National Park encompasses the entire island of Isle Royale, the nearby smaller islands, and the water within 4.5 miles of the islands. The park is in Michigan, but we got here by ferry from Minnesota. There are also ferries to the island from Houghton and Copper Harbor, Michigan. Visitors also can get to the island by floatplane. Flying on a small airplane was not something we were willing to consider so soon after our Alaska plane scare. We still duck when we hear small planes flying overhead.

We have no complaints about the Voyageur II; the boat was clean and safe, and the crew was professional, it just took longer than we expected to get to Rock Harbor. The schedule says eight hours, but we thought it couldn't possibly take that long. It did. It seemed longer for Karen than me; I was asleep for most of it. One Dramamine knocks me on my butt.

Two hours from Grand Portage we reached the west side of the island and landed at the dock in front of the Windigo Visitor Center. All the passengers had to disembark and listen to a ranger orientation talk. It was mostly common sense stuff: don't approach wildlife, stay on the marked trails, put out your fires, etc. The ranger also warned us about "inadvertently introducing aquatic invasive species" into the inland lakes. The park is particularly concerned about zebra mussels making their way into the lakes on the island. The park newsletter said about the zebra mussels, "Their potential to cause catastrophic change cannot be overstated." I promised the ranger I would check Karen thoroughly for zebra mussels before she attempted to swim in any of the inland lakes. He didn't appreciate my humor. This was serious business. The mussels hitchhike on small boats, such as kayaks and canoes that visitors bring with them to the park.

We took care of business at the visitor center and re-boarded our ferry. Isle Royale is about 45 miles in length, and, on average about five miles wide. From Windigo, our ferry sailed the length of the island on its north side and then looped back around to the south side for a few miles to get to Rock Harbor. That part of the trip took another five hours. We're spending the next three nights at the Rock Harbor Lodge.

From the ferry, the trees on the island looked impenetrable. It was easy to imagine teaming wildlife just inside the forest. At one time, there were caribou on the island, but they disappeared around 1925. Large mammals do that on Isle Royale; they appear and disappear. In 1905, there were no beavers on the island, now they are common. From the surrounding land –the closest being more than ten miles away –animals sometimes swim or walk across the occasional ice bridge to get to the island. But once they're on the island, they can struggle to maintain their population due to scarcity of food, predation by other animals, or by the ill effects of inbreeding. When only a single male and female make it to the island, their descendants have a pretty shallow genetic pool to swim in.

By mid-afternoon, we'd made it to Rock Harbor. There was enough time before dinner to check in to our room and hike a few miles along the rocky coast. We're staying in one of the Housekeeping Cabins tucked into the trees above the harbor. Each cabin is a duplex with large windows overlooking Tobin Harbor. The views from inside our cabin are excellent, but the big windows that looked out over Tobin Harbor don't open. We could only open a small, screened window at the base of the wall. There's no deck or porch outside to sit on. We feel a bit trapped when we're on the inside looking out. The cabins look like they haven't been updated in several decades. The rooms are fine, but expensive for 1960's vintage cabins.

Your friend,
Matt

~.~.~.~.~.~.~

From: **Matt Smith**
Subject: **Isle Royale continued**
Date: **August 23, 2011**

Dear Bob and Sue,

We read that the mosquitos are thick on Isle Royale in the summer, but they didn't bother us today. We brought our headnets, yet we never had to use them. Maybe we still have enough DEET in our bodies from our Alaska trip to keep the bugs away. Or, maybe the nights are getting cold enough to kill them off. Winter comes early here.

Isle Royale National Park is the only national park that completely closes to visitors in the winter. The only people who might be on the island then are researchers studying the wolves and the moose. The park's limited season – mid-April to the end of November – and isolation make it one of the least visited of the national parks. About 16,000 visitors make it to the park each year. That's fewer than the number of visitors to Great Smoky Mountain National Park on an average *day*.

It's also a very difficult park to visit for only one day. The ferries arrive at Rock Harbor late in the afternoon, dock for the night and then board passengers in the morning for the return trip. Unless you plan to spend only one night in the park (which wouldn't be worth the trip), you're there for at least two more days, when the ferry makes its return trip. That's if the ferry comes back. It's rare, but there are times the ferry can't sail due to bad weather. Yesterday our captain told us that the weather was so rough recently that there was a stretch of several days when they couldn't make it to the island. In those instances campers better hope they have extra food left over or that the lodge has enough provisions to last through the rough patch. Again, it's rare, but it happens.

The weather today was fine, and the forecast for the coming days looks good, so we're assuming our boat will show up on schedule. Today we went on a ten-mile hike from the lodge to Mt. Franklin and back. We started by taking a trail that followed the shore of Tobin Harbor, and then we climbed through the forest to the Greenstone Ridge Trail. A quarter mile later, we reached the top of Mt. Franklin where we ate lunch looking over Lake Superior to the north.

On our hike, we saw several areas that were permanently fenced off with signs warning of open pits. They were abandoned mine pits. None of them were very large, but a few were deep enough that you'd injure yourself, or worse, if you fell in. Before it became a park, the attraction to Isle Royale was copper. There's evidence that people mined for copper on the island as far back as 4,500 years ago. In the 19th century, many attempts were made to locate commercially viable mining sites on the island, but none were ever developed on a large scale. By the turn of the 20th century, all serious interest in mining on the island ceased.

After our hike, we hung around the lodge until it was late enough to eat dinner in the restaurant without feeling as if we were early birds. I'm happy eating dinner at 4:30pm, but Karen isn't; she thinks that's the first step down the slippery slope of turning old. I'm not so concerned.

At dinner, we saw a huge ferry docked at the pier in front of the lodge. It was the ferry from Houghton, Michigan. I'm guessing nine or ten of our ferries would fit inside of it. We looked at it with envy. I bet the passengers on that ferry had clam chowder and beer on their trip over.

The scheduled nightly ranger talk tonight was about the wolves in the park. We went to the community building where the rangers give their presentations and got a good seat. I was looking forward to learning about the wolves. When the time came for the talk a ranger walked to the front of the room, readied his slide projector, introduced himself and said, "I know you all came to hear about the wolves, but we have a slight change of plans. I'm going to talk about the history of mining on the island instead."

As if we rehearsed, all 75 people in the room shifted their gaze from the ranger at the front of the room to the exit doors and then back to the ranger. We'd been tricked. I hate being tricked. Everyone was silently asking the same question, "Would it be rude to walk out now?" No one did. We all stayed and learned about mining on the island, which the presenting ranger said was – I'm using his words so I can't be accused of being a jerk – "...the history of failure."

He went on to tell us about all the failed attempts at mining, and how they can tell the attempts were failures. It was an interesting study in forensic, historic research, but I had been looking forward to learning about the wolves. Instead, I had to settle for reading the free literature I'd picked up in the visitor center about the wildlife in the park.

I learned that the wolf-moose relationship on Isle Royale is the subject of the longest predator-prey ecosystem study in the world; it's been going on for over 50 years. Researchers are particularly interested in the wolves and moose on the island because of the unique conditions that have stayed constant for the entire time of the study: there's been almost no human interference (because the island has been a national park the entire time); there's been virtually no migration in or out of the wolf or moose populations, and the wolf and moose numbers are reasonably easy to track because the habitat area is finite and relatively small.

The wolves and moose have not always coexisted on the island. They believe the ancestors of the current moose population swam to the island around the year 1900. For five decades, they had no predators. The moose population grew nearly unchecked until the 1930s when, because of overpopulation, they destroyed their own food supply. Then they began to die off in large numbers.

In the late 1940's, a single pair of wolves came to the island by crossing an ice bridge that formed connecting the island with Canada. Wolves on the island today are the offspring from that original pair. (Some reports say that three wolves originally came across; others say it was only two.)

Researchers have learned much about how wolves and moose coexist by studying them on Isle Royale. They've learned that wolves rarely attack healthy moose that are in the prime of their lives. A healthy moose can outrun a wolf, and even if the moose can be caught, it's too dangerous for the wolves to take them on. The moose usually wins that fight. No, the wolves target the young, the old, and the sick. One article said, "The typical moose that a wolf kills... suffers from arthritis, osteoporosis, or periodontal disease, and in some case all of them." That sounds like us!

I went to bed after reading that pleasant fact. Tomorrow,

we're hiking again in the wilderness. Now that I know what the wolves are looking for I'll be sure to hike with good posture and try not to show any signs of joint pain. But, I do feel a toothache coming on.

Your friend,
Matt

~.~.~.~.~.~.~

From: **Matt Smith**
Subject: **#53 – Voyageurs National Park**
Date: **August 26, 2011**

Dear Bob and Sue,

Yesterday we took the eight-hour ferry from Isle Royale back to Grand Portage, and then drove 90 miles south to Silver Bay, Minnesota where we spent the night. This morning we drove to the Kabetogama Lake Visitor Center in Voyageurs National Park, making it just in time for our 11:00am boat tour. The park is in Northern Minnesota on the border with Canada. It's a lake park. Almost every activity in the park requires a boat; though, I could say that about the entire state of Minnesota.

Visitors come to the park to boat, fish, camp, and hike in the wilderness. There are wolves in the park, but the park's newsletter says visitors rarely seen them and that they are wary of humans. The wolves occasionally prey on moose but are more likely to hunt beaver.

The beavers are responsible for the park's existence. The European demand for beaver pelts in the 18th century brought fur trappers to the area, but the trappers needed a way to get the pelts to markets in Europe. Voyageurs – transporters of goods – filled the need and developed a trade route across what is now southern Canada. The lakes, especially Rainy

Lake, in Voyageurs National Park were part of that route. The mission of the park is to "preserve (among other things)... the route of the voyageurs who contributed significantly to the opening of the Northwestern United States."

At the dock in front of the visitor center we boarded a pontoon boat – named The Otter – with ten other visitors and two rangers, for a five and a half hour tour of the lake. Ranger Scotty was our captain and ranger Jessica was our tour guide. Jessica had a lot of energy and was intent on engaging us from the very beginning. Before we left the dock, she began talking. With a microphone in her hand, she looked at me and barked, "Where are we?" I needed more than that to formulate an answer. Even if I had an answer, she didn't give me enough time to respond. She barked again, "Come on, where are we?" Again, I had nothing. She answered her own question, "We're on Kabetogama Lake. Jeez!" She was annoying and endearing at the same time. I liked Jessica.

I'm glad Jessica said the name of the lake because I had no idea how to pronounce it. It still takes me a few tries to get it right. (It's pronounced KAB-beh-TOE-geh-muh, the emphasis is on the toe.)

Our tour took us on an indirect path to Kettle Falls, which is on the east end of the park. Scotty stopped at several eagle nests along the way. Eagles are one of the main wildlife attractions of the park. They were once endangered here but have made a recent comeback. In 1992, the park began a program of closing the areas around eagle nests to visitors for several months of the year in hopes of increasing their breeding success. The park's website says, "In early May, the park temporarily closes areas around the park's active bald eagle nesting sites to campers and other human activities. In mid-August the areas are reopened after the young eaglets fledge."

Both Scotty and Jessica were enthusiastic eagle spotters. Every time they found another, they acted as if it was the first eagle they'd ever seen. Jessica kept track of the number of eagles we saw and kept repeating the number to the group.

She said, "That was number ten. Or, was that eleven?" Ten or eleven?" She was quizzing us to keep our attention. I had flashbacks of being in third grade.

When Jessica was not pointing out eagles she was narrating the history of the park. As Scotty eased The Otter around Williams Island, she told us the story of Ingvald Walter Stevens, an immigrant from Norway. I.W. was a shoe salesman in the northern Minnesota town of Hibbing, when at the age 46, his doctor told him he needed to find a way to relax or else his chronic ulcers would be the end of him. He sought out the peace and quiet of Kabetogama Lake as his salvation. He bought the 400-acre Williams Island in 1932 and lived there for 47 years, until age 94. He makes Dick Proenneke of Lake Clark National Park fame look like a quitter by comparison.

The island was once the headquarters of the Virginia and Rainy Lake Company – a logging company – and already had a few tarpaper shacks when I.W. purchased it. He built a couple of additional cabins and turned the island into a small resort, which he operated until 1959. He once said he would rather not live if it meant leaving the island, but he also bitterly complained about how difficult life was there. He referred to his resort as the Slave Farm because of the effort it took him to accommodate his guests and to provide the necessities of survival in such a remote and harsh environment. In 1975, when the area was made a national park, the government gave him a life lease to the island. But Mr. Stevens left the island for good in 1979, and lived another ten years afterward; he died in 1989 at the age of 104.

Kettle Falls Hotel was our stop for lunch. Construction of the hotel began in 1910 and was completed in 1913. It's still a working hotel today, although the only way to get to the hotel is by boat. Kettle Falls is one of the many portages in the park – a portage is an impassible spot on a river where canoes and cargo must be carried around by land. It also marks the border between the United States and Canada. You can stand on the docks at Kettle Falls and look south into Canada. There are no longer falls at Kettle Falls; a dam was built at the site in the 1910's. One of the early uses of the hotel was to accommodate workers building the dam.

On the ride back to the visitor center the wind picked up unexpectedly, which made for a choppy voyage. There were times I wasn't sure our little pontoon otter was making headway against the wind. Waves kept splashing us, and it started to get chilly. Karen was sitting closest to the edge of the boat and squealed every time a wave soaked her. I took my raincoat from my backpack and covered her up until we made it to the protected cove in front of the visitor center. Once out of the wind we were warm again.

Tonight we're staying at a small resort on Kabetogama Lake a few miles from the visitor center, and tomorrow we'll drive back to Minneapolis and fly home to Seattle.

Your friend,
Matt

~.~.~.~.~.~.~

From: **Matt Smith**
Subject: **Travel day – to Kalispell**
Date: **August 31, 2011**

Dear Bob and Sue,

"I'm sorry. I can't sleep in a room that smells like body odor." That wasn't what Karen wanted to hear me say when we walked into our hotel room after a long drive from Issaquah to Kalispell, Montana – on the back roads no less.

"It's not a BO smell, it's a cleaning product smell. It'll be fine." Karen was trying to nip my odor concern in the bud. She was tired and wanted to go to dinner.

"Are you telling me that the hotel uses cleaning supplies that smell like body odor?"

"No, nothing in this room smells like body odor. Let's just open a window and go to dinner."

I was tired too; I'd been driving all day. Cannonball you know. I needed a few minutes to rest before getting back in the car. As I lay on the bed trying to relax there were moments when the BO smell went away, but then it came back in waves. "Sweetie, we have to switch rooms." I knew if we didn't move to another room the smell would drive me crazy all night.

We made the long trek back to the front desk. (It seems that whenever this happens to us, our smelly room is a mile away from the lobby.) I informed the front desk clerk that our room smelled like BO, but we were on our way out to dinner, so we'd like to switch rooms when we got back. She said, "We're sold out tonight, so if you want to switch we should do it now." Karen interrupted saying our room was perfectly fine and that we didn't need to change, but the woman insisted on making the switch.

She gave us keys to another room and said, "Check out this room and let me know if it's okay." The keys she handed me were to the room next to our original room. We hiked back to smell the new room. As soon as we opened the door I could smell it; the BO was there too. I silently went through the internal debate that every husband of 30 years has in a situation like this. Should I make my wife happy by acting like the new room is perfect, so we can get on with dinner and having fun, knowing the BO is going to drive me crazy for the next 14 hours? Or, do I have the woman at the front desk let me smell all their available rooms, so I can find one that doesn't stink, knowing my wife will be pissed off at me for the rest of the night?

I must have hesitated a bit too long because before I could say anything Karen said, "This one smells too, doesn't it?"

"No, it's fine. I can't smell a thing." She knew I was lying.

"I'm telling you, it's their cleaning supplies. Every room

in the hotel will smell like this," she said.

"Maybe a family who doesn't use deodorant stayed in both of these rooms." I replied. There was a door connecting the rooms.

Karen agreed that the previous guest – the BO family – was the source of the smell, but she would have agreed to anything just to get me out the door. It somehow made me feel better having solved the mystery, even though I had no evidence to support my theory. By that point, I was too tired to fight the BO. We kept our original room, opened a window and went to dinner.

Karen had researched our dinner options in Kalispell, and found the best pizza place in town, Moose's Saloon. She was excited to go there because "They serve peanuts and let you throw the shells on the floor." I don't understand why she thinks throwing peanut shells on the floor of a restaurant is an attraction.

The pizza was very good, so good I forgot about our BO room. When we got back to our hotel room, it was completely aired out from the window being open while we were gone. But, as soon as I shut the window the smell came back. I'm too tired to care anymore. It's time to get some sleep.

Your friend,
Matt

~.~.~.~.~.~.~

From: **Matt Smith**
Subject: **#54 – Glacier National Park**
Date: **September 1, 2011**

Dear Bob and Sue,

This morning started out clear and cool, but we could see clouds building to the south as we drove to the west entrance of the park. As close as Glacier National Park is to our home – about an eight-hour drive – we thought we would get here before now, park #54 of the trip.

The Apgar Visitor Center is just inside the west entrance of the park. The clouds were getting thicker by the minute, so we didn't linger at the visitor center after taking care of business. We had to get to our next hotel on the east side of the park. This meant driving the Going-to-the-Sun Road through the park and over the continental divide. The road is a spectacular drive from the west side of the park to the east side, but it's steep, narrow, and in the summer crowded. It's also the only way to get to the other side of the park short of driving outside and around the park on its south side.

Going-to-the-Sun Road begins at the Apgar Visitor Center. Before starting its ascent into the mountains, the road hugs the shore of Lake McDonald, at the end of which is Lake McDonald Lodge. Glacier National Park is home to several of the great lodges in the western United States; Lake McDonald Lodge is one of them. We're not staying there on this trip, but we're staying at two of the others: Glacier Park Lodge and Many Glacier Hotel.

Early promoters of the park built these grand lodges as destinations to attract visitors at a time when most people traveled to the park by train. All three opened for guests within a 25-month window from June 1913 to July 1915.

Past the lake, the road gradually makes its way into the heart of the mountains. The road was an engineering marvel when it was built, but lack of maintenance over the years has caused it to become a safety hazard. A multi-year rehabilitation project is underway, and for much of the climb, construction workers were close to the road. Traffic was slow, and I had to be vigilant about watching for workers. In the best of conditions, the road is nerve racking. With the added distraction of the construction work, it was a white-knuckle drive. Oh yeah, and the dark clouds we saw from the visitor center? We were now driving through them and the road was wet.

Traffic slowed and the visibility got worse the farther we went. By the time we reached Logan Pass Visitor Center, the high point on the road, the fog was so thick we could barely see the car 20 feet in front of us. I knew from driving this road before that there were sharp drop-offs along that stretch. Those drop-offs were on our side of the road, but I couldn't see them because I couldn't see where the edge of the road was. I knew there were at least a couple of feet of pavement on the passenger side, but I didn't know how much more than that.

At the Logan Pass Visitor Center, every car in front of us turned into the parking lot. We were the only ones who continued straight on the road. I no longer had the advantage of being able to follow a car's taillights in front of me. I didn't know if I was about to drive off the side on the mountain or not. I wanted to stop, but with such low visibility, if a car approached us from behind they wouldn't see us in time to stop. I thought the only thing worse than driving off the side of the mountain would be getting shoved off the side of the mountain from behind.

I crept along trying to watch the white line on the right side of the road that defined the outer edge. If I lost sight of that line there would be no telling what direction to go. That first mile past the visitor center was the longest mile I think I've ever driven. Slowly the visibility improved. Finally, I was able to see a couple of car lengths ahead of us. It was still not safe, but it was better than what we just came through. What a white-knuckle drive. We finally arrived at the Saint Mary Visitor Center on the east side of the park safely. I was glad to get out of the car and take a few deep breaths.

The drive across the park seemed to take forever, but it didn't. We still had half the day to fill. Two Medicine Lake was in the direction we were headed, so we stopped there and hiked for a couple of hours along the lake. There were many bear alert signs posted on trees along the trail. The huckleberries next to the trail were ripe and still on the bush. I've hiked enough in the mountains to know that if you're hiking through ripe huckleberries there's probably a bear close by. We kept scanning the forest as we hiked, but we didn't see any bears, just bear poop.

After the hike, we drove to East Glacier Park where we're staying at the Glacier Park Lodge. The rooms of the lodge were built around an open lobby framed by 60 enormous Douglas fir tree trunks. Each log is at least 40 feet long, has a diameter of 36 to 40 inches, and was 500 to 800-years old when cut down. In 1913, the builders couldn't find trees that large locally, so they shipped them in from Washington state. It's an amazing sight to stand inside the lobby and look up at these immense, arrow straight timbers, complete with their original bark. There are photographs in the lobby of the lodge during construction. One shows the solitary timbers, each standing in its final position before the rest of the lodge was built around them.

We had an early dinner in the lounge, and then sat around the huge fireplace with the other guests. It was starting to rain. In northern Montana it can feel like winter is just around the corner, even on the last day of August. It was very cozy though.

A woman was playing the piano in the lobby; she was very good, but we knew what was coming next, a group-sing. That's when we called it a night. We're lying in bed listening to the rain drum against our windows. From our room, we can hear the singing in the lobby. It's corny and oddly nostalgic, but it will be a nice sound to fall asleep to.

Your friend,
Matt

~.~.~.~.~.~.~

From: **Matt Smith**
Subject: **Glacier continued**
Date: **September 2, 2011**

Dear Bob and Sue,

The tops of the mountain peaks were dusted with snow when we woke up this morning. It can snow any day of the year in this part of Montana.

Our plan for today was to do a long hike starting from the Many Glacier Hotel in the northern section of the park, so we checked out of the Glacier Park Lodge early and got on the road. As we drove past Two Medicine Lake, we saw a black bear on the road close to where we hiked yesterday. I pulled over and got out to try to take his picture. He saw me and began climbing up the hill away from the road eating berries as he went. This time of year, when the berries are ripe, bears spend every waking moment eating as much as they can.

Driving on the road into the park toward Many Glacier Hotel, the scene in front of us was spectacular. The sun broke through the clouds and was in the east behind us as we drove west toward the hotel. I stopped several times to try to capture the scene with my camera. My photos never seem to capture how amazing the real scene was. We made it to the hotel by mid-morning.

Many Glacier Hotel sits on the shore of Swiftcurrent Lake in the northeastern quadrant of the park. It was the largest lodge built by the Great Northern Railway; it's five stories tall with 214 guest rooms

The lobby is essentially a half-sized version of the Glacier Park Lodge lobby. And, a section of the lobby has been walled off to create a gift shop, which makes it look even smaller still. Similar to Glacier Park Lodge, builders used huge, 40-foot long timbers from Washington state to frame the lobby.

Since it was too early to check in to our room, we made sandwiches in the car and prepared for our hike to Grinnell

Glacier, an 11-mile round trip from the hotel parking lot.

The hike was amazing, one of the best hikes we've done on our parks trip. The weather couldn't make up its mind if it wanted to be summer or winter. We went from hot to cold and back again several times; it rained on us briefly. None of that mattered though; we were enjoying the hike just the same.

The Continental Divide splits the park in half from north to south. Grinnell Glacier sits just below the divide to the east. The glacier is high on a plateau; the runoff spills over the edge of the cliffs and feeds Grinnell Lake below. The lake was a deep green-blue color, and was in front of us to the left for most of our climb to the glacier. It's worth the trip just to come halfway up this trail to sit and look at the falls and the lake below.

From the trail, the mountain sloped steeply down to the lake. We could see bighorn sheep grazing below us. They were about a half a mile away, and I needed my binoculars to get a good look. On our way back from the glacier, we saw the sheep again; they had climbed higher on the mountain from where we first saw them. I kept my eye on them hoping we would get a better look this time. I was glad but a little surprised when I saw two bighorn sheep about a quarter mile away standing on our trail.

The brush was thick around the area where they were standing, so they chose to use the trail rather than push their way through the bushes. They were moving slowly toward us, and we were moving slowly toward them. When we were about 100 yards away, I realized they weren't going to move off the trail. At that point, there was nowhere for us to go; the bushes were several feet tall and very thick on either side of the trail. They kept coming at us, and the one in front was big – and getting bigger.

When they got to about 30 feet from us, I finally realized we needed to get the hell out of their way. The big one in front stopped briefly, looked straight at us, and then lowered his head – his horns wrapped 360 degrees around. He had a "full curl." Then he raised his head and continued to stare straight at us. It was a very clear message. He was saying, "This is how big I am. How big are you?"

I said to Karen, "We have to get off this trail now."

"Where?"

"Into the bushes," I said. Pushing into the bushes reminded me of when we were in Alaska and had to hike through the wet alder bushes. We got thoroughly soaked in the process. Karen pushed a couple of feet into the thick vegetation. I said, "You're gonna have to go farther than that. We need to give these guys plenty of space." With a deep exhale, Karen moved deeper into the soaking wet bushes. The sheep by this time had started moving toward us again.

We pushed about 15 feet off the trail, which didn't seem like a safe distance, but it was as far as we could go. When the big one reached the point on the trail where we had moved off, he stopped and looked at us. I thought for a moment he was going to turn and follow us. I pulled my bear spray out of the side pocket of my backpack and took the plastic safety cap off the trigger – we always carry bear spray now after our close encounters in Alaska.

The lead sheep stood and looked at us for a moment. We talked to him in a soft, calm voice hoping he would move along. Finally, he did. The one behind him followed. I never thought of big horn sheep as potentially dangerous animals, and maybe they aren't, but standing a few feet away from this one I was impressed by his size. He was huge. One pop from his horns would crush a person's chest.

We were also spooked because about a year ago a mountain goat in Olympic National Park gored a man. (I know, different animal, but still...) The goat severed an artery in the man's leg, and he bled to death as the mountain goat stood over him, not letting other hikers come to his rescue.

It was frightening to be so close to a wild animal that large, but it was also a thrill. I got a couple of good pictures; I had my camera in one hand and my bear spray in the other.

Back at the hotel, we still had some time to kill before we could get into our room, so we went to the bar and ordered fondue. We were expecting it to be like the fondue we ate in Switzerland: a big pot of cheese and a huge basket of bread. It was similar only in name. They brought us a small bowl of cheese that was heated by a votive candle, a couple of pieces of bread, four cherry tomatoes and six carrot sticks. Karen called it "measly" and waved our waiter over twice, asking for more bread. She's a big eater. I like this about her.

We spent the rest of the day hanging out in the hotel and driving around the area. We drove to the other hotel down the road, the Swiftcurrent Motor Inn. There wasn't much to see inside the Inn, but a crowd gathered in the parking lot. They had cameras and telescopes set up on tripods pointed toward the mountain behind the Inn. They were spotting grizzly bears. We tried to find the bears with our binoculars, but they were too far away.

Tomorrow we're driving back to Issaquah. We've decided we need to visit Glacier National Park more often; we say this about nearly every park we visit. But this one is so close to home we have no excuse not to.

Your friend,
Matt

~.~.~.~.~.~.~

From: **Matt Smith**
Subject: **Kings Canyon National Park revisited**
Date: **September 26, 2011**

Dear Bob and Sue,

Karen gives Kings Canyon National Park one of her highest accolades; she says it's a *hidden gem*. If you're keeping track, *hidden gem* is just below *magical place* and just above *Who-ville* and *darling* on the Karen Smith rating scale. *Ramshackle* is now the lowest rating a place can get; *shithole* was recently removed from the scale. Karen says she prefers to act like a place doesn't exist rather than call it a shithole.

This week we're on a road trip from Issaquah to Southern California. We're visiting Channel Islands National Park. Because of the forest fire in Kings Canyon National Park last September, we didn't drive into the canyon, so we decided to go back and see it as part of this trip. Last night, we stayed in Clovis, California and this morning we drove into the park.

From the Kings Canyon Visitor Center in Grant Grove Village, we drove north on highway 180. The highway goes out of the park and through the Sequoia National Forest. It then drops into Kings Canyon, and follows the South Fork of Kings River to the east back into the park. The drive was beautiful: steep canyon walls, a rushing mountain river, big trees close to the road. If it wasn't so hard to get to, this park would be crowded with people. We saw very few other cars. The highway dead ends in a valley that looks very similar to Yosemite Valley. Except, Kings Canyon does not have the masses of people, cars, shuttle busses, gift stores, etc. that Yosemite Valley has.

John Muir, the original champion of Yosemite, had this to say about Kings Canyon. "In the vast Sierra wilderness, far to the southward of the famous Yosemite Valley, there is yet a grander valley of the same kind. It is situated on the south fork of the Kings River, above the most extensive groves and forests of the giant sequoia, and beneath the shadows of the highest mountains in the range, where canyons are the deepest and the snow-laden peaks are crowded most closely together."

It was pristine, and in September it was deserted.

In the valley, we parked our car close to the Cedar Grove Visitor Center – it closed for the year just yesterday – and hiked the Hotel Creek Trail. We hiked to the Cedar Grove Overlook, which was a five-mile round trip. It was perfect weather for a hike.

After we ate PB&J sandwiches for lunch in our car, we drove back to Grant Grove Village. On our way out of the park, we noticed an overhang of smoke. On the visitor center bulletin board, a sign was posted saying the park service was starting prescribed fires in the park. We drove a short distance to the General Grant Grove (home of the General Grant Tree), and were shocked to see fire fighters setting fires at the bases of the big trees. Clearly, they knew what they were doing; they even had a tent set up to explain to visitors how and why they set these fires. The purpose of the fires is to remove combustible material that might ignite if an uncontrolled fire were to come near the big trees.

From there, we drove to Bakersfield where we picked up dinner, and then to Oxnard where we're spending the night. Tomorrow we're visiting Channel Islands National Park.

Your friend,
Matt

~.~.~.~.~.~.~

From: **Matt Smith**
Subject: **#55 – Channel Islands National Park**
Date: **September 27, 2011**

Dear Bob and Sue,

Being from Kansas, I've never seen squid before, unless you count those deep-fried rubber rings that Karen sometimes orders in restaurants. Today on our boat ride to Channel Islands National Park there were more jumbo squid than we could count; it looked like there were at least 100 of them feeding close to the surface of the water. One of the deck hands said, "I've been doing this for 38 years and have never seen this before." Large squid were feeding on smaller squid. The captain said the big ones were Humboldt squid, and he called the smaller ones bait squid. As the big ones darted through the water, they would grab the smaller ones with their tentacles. They were *flashing* –changing colors from black to red –as they chased their breakfast. Sometimes they would come to the surface and squirt streams of water into the air. It was the main attraction this morning on our boat ride to the park, a jumbo squid feeding frenzy.

Channel Islands is our 55th national park. At 8:00am our boat left from Ventura, California for Santa Cruz Island, the largest of the five islands that make up the park. The boat ride normally takes an hour, but today we made several stops to look at wildlife – the squid put us behind schedule but it was worth it.

As the boat was pulling into the dock at Scorpion Harbor, the captain reminded us that he would pick us up for the return trip at 3:45pm; the boat would leave the island at 4:00pm sharp. He then repeated the message no fewer than ten times and made us all answer him when he asked over the public address, "What time does the boat leave?" We shouted back, "four o'clock!" We got the feeling that he wasn't joking when he said that if we miss the four o'clock departure we would be "unintentional" campers on the island until the boat comes back tomorrow.

After a short but mandatory orientation on the beach, we were free to roam the island for six hours. We stored our cooler in one of the food caches by the visitor center. The volunteer rangers were adamant that all food brought on the island be stored in the metal food caches. Their main concern is to keep food away from the foxes that live on the island. They don't want them to see humans as a source of food and lose their ability to survive in the wild – it's for their own good.

The east quarter of Santa Cruz Island is open to general park visitors; the western three fourths is a nature conservatory, and requires a special permit to explore. We stayed on the national park side of the island, hiking over a 1,400-foot ridge to Smuggler's Cove on the other side. We were the only hikers on the trail. The park literature says the way the island looks today is what most of Southern California looked like before the cities, suburbs, and industrial complexes were built: rolling hills, tall grass, and not many trees. Being the end of summer, the entire island was the color of dry grass with the exception of the few trees in the valleys close to the shore.

Smuggler's Cove was empty except for a handful of very large crows and a couple of sailboats anchored offshore. At Smugglers Cove, there's an abandoned orchard with hundreds of olive trees, which early settlers planted for subsistence. We felt as if we were the only ones on the island. Had the sailboats not been there, we could have imagined that we were thousands of miles from civilization on a deserted island; odd considering we were only a few miles across the water from one of the most populated cities in the U.S. (Los Angeles).

The hike back to Scorpion Beach was a trudge, although there were decent views of the ocean and nearby islands. The temperature was bearable today, but it can get dangerously hot on Santa Cruz Island, especially for hikers. A couple of years ago a 49-year-old man hiked 14 miles from Prisoners Harbor to the Scorpion Campgrounds in 94-degree heat. He set out at 11:00am, and according to his hiking partners, struggled mightily to reach the campgrounds; by 7:30pm he had died of heat stroke.

Once we were back at the beach, we pulled our cooler out of the food cache. Having heard the captain's warning we made sure we were at the dock early – two hours early. We sat at the picnic tables close to the dock and ate lunch.

On the boat ride back to Ventura, there was more excitement in the channel where we saw the jumbo squid; dozens of dolphins were swimming near the surface. The captain said they were probably feeding on the squid we'd seen earlier. We had a front-row view of the circle of life. The extraordinary thing about this group of dolphins was that many had babies with them. Our captain called it a nursery. The mothers would come up out of the water with their babies right by their side. The little ones mimicked their mothers. It was really quite amazing; there were dozens of baby dolphins with their mothers. It was way better than a visit to Sea World.

Tonight we're staying at the Hampton Inn in Oxnard. Tomorrow we're going to cannonball it to Chico, California, to tour the Sierra Nevada Brewery. By the way, since we're almost finished visiting the national parks, Karen and I have decided our next thing will be to tour every brewery on the planet. Maybe you could join us.

Your friend,
Matt

~.~.~.~.~.~.~.~

From: **Matt Smith**
Subject: **#56 – Hot Springs National Park**
Date: **October 24, 2011**

Dear Bob and Sue,

Truth be told, of all the parks we've been to, Hot Springs National Park has been the one we had the lowest expectations of prior to visiting. But, it's a national park, and we pledged to see them all, so here we are. Last weekend we were in Kansas to visit Matthew at KU. Yesterday morning we drove seven hours from Overland Park, Kansas to Hot Springs, Arkansas, the home of the park.

The park has about 5,500 acres of land, some of which is heavily treed with hiking trails, but the main attraction is the bathhouses. There's nothing wrong with the trails but it wouldn't make sense to travel a long distance to get here just for the hiking. The attraction is the mineral water, both hot and cold. The hot water was piped into bathhouses where people would bathe, believing the hot mineral waters had medicinal benefits. They also drank the cold mineral water coming out of the springs. They still do – we saw many people filling up plastic water jugs from the public spring water faucets.

The area that is now the park became a government

reservation in 1832. The park brochure says, "It was the first U.S. reservation created to protect a natural resource." In 1921 Stephen Mather (the first Director of the National Park Service), convinced Congress to make it a national park. The park literature also says that during the Golden Age of Bathing, over a million visitors a year came to bathe in the mineral waters. Visitors also, "strolled the Bathhouse Row with cups to quaff the elixir." They walked around smelling the water. They say that by the 1950s "changes in medicine led to a rapid decline in the use of water therapies." I should hope so.

We first stopped at the visitor center inside the Fordyce Bathhouse and took care of business. The Fordyce building, in addition to being the visitor center, is a preserved bathhouse from the golden age. Karen and I walked through the rooms in back ("golden age" is an exaggeration). It was very weird; there were stalls that looked like they came straight out of a horror movie. I told Karen it looked like they filmed the *Alien Autopsy* movie in there.

People still come to Hot Springs National Park to bathe in the mineral waters. A couple of the buildings, Quapaw and Buckstaff, still operate as active bathhouses. One of the old bathhouse buildings, the Ozark, has been converted into an art museum.

I can see that it made sense at one time for Hot Springs to be a national park – when people believed bathing in the mineral waters improved their health. But now that's an obsolete idea, a novelty. Hot Springs National Park is more about historic preservation than an activity destination.

After visiting the park, Karen and I walked to a Mexican restaurant by our hotel. We ordered Margaritas in memory of 2011, the Summer of the Margarita.

This morning we woke up to a cold and foggy day. Instead of hiking we drove the Hot Springs Mountain Drive through the park, and then on to Little Rock. Right now we're sitting in the Little Rock airport waiting for our plane. We should get back to Seattle tonight about 10:00pm.

Your friend,
Matt

~.~.~.~.~.~.~.~

From: **Matt Smith**
Subject: **Death Valley National Park revisited**
Date: **January 13, 2012**

Dear Bob and Sue,

"A *borax* museum? I can't believe there's enough interest in borax for it to have its own museum." Don't say that in front of the lady running the Borax Museum in Death Valley National Park. I made this mistake and had to listen to a lecture about why borax is the most important mineral known to man.

It's a key ingredient in household cleaners; it's a fire retardant; it's used as a flux in making glass and ceramics – Pyrex couldn't be made without borax. It's even used to control radioactivity in nuclear power plants. But, my favorite use for borax is—it's used to make Slime, the silly putty stuff we used to make with our kids. No, do *not* make fun of borax, at least not in the Borax Museum.

Borax was mined in the area that is now the park until as recently as 2005. Mining is the only conceivable reason why humans would inhabit such an inhospitable place as Death Valley.

Karen and I visited Death Valley National Park in

September 2010, but then we were pressed for time, and the temperature in the park was well over 100 degrees. We came back now, in January, because it's an ideal time to see the park without the oppressive heat. The average daily high temperatures from May through September are over 100 degrees, but in January, the average daily high is in the upper 60's.

The easiest way for us to get to the park from Seattle is to fly to Las Vegas, rent a car at the airport and drive. That's how we got here yesterday. It was about a two-hour drive. We're staying at Furnace Creek Ranch, close to the Furnace Creek Visitor Center smack in the middle of the park. (Death Valley National Park is the largest national park in the lower 48 states. It's roughly 120 miles long and 40 miles wide.) We looked online at The Inn at Furnace Creek across the highway from the ranch, but their rooms were much more expensive. Our room at the ranch is just fine; we didn't feel the need to spend extra to stay at the Inn. The Inn has a nice bar and restaurant, but we can drive over there for dinner then come back to the ranch to sleep. Besides, the ranch has a general store, several restaurants, a saloon and the Borax Museum.

The paved roads in the park are well maintained and suitable for everyday vehicles, but there are many rough, gravel side roads that lead to some of the best parts of the park, the backcountry areas. The valley runs through the center of the park; mountains flank it to the east and west. In the mountains, there are countless slot canyons that are spectacular to hike and drive through – if you have the right type of vehicle.

Our rental car doesn't have high clearance, nor does it have the kind of tires needed to drive over the sharp rocks and rough roads in the backcountry. That's why I reserved a Jeep for two days from Farabee's Jeep Rentals. Richard Farabee rents Jeeps that are equipped to handle the unpaved roads in the park. His shop is just across the highway from The Inn at Furnace Creek. We were there at 8:00am this morning to pick up our Jeep.

Renting a Jeep isn't cheap, but it's less expensive than breaking down in the middle of nowhere and having Richard tow you out; Richard also runs a tow service. I asked him, "How much do you charge for a tow?"

"Well," he hesitated, "I charge $200 an hour."

I said, "Some of the places where people could get stuck are a couple of hours or more from here. That could get expensive."

"Yeah, we pull people out of the Racetrack all the time. From here, that's a five-hour round trip. It costs them $1,000 just to get their car back here to my shop, and I don't fix 'em, I just tow 'em. If they've rented a car in Las Vegas, they have to make arrangements with their rental car company to get it fixed or towed back to Las Vegas. It can be a pretty expensive outing."

"Just the other day I pulled two cars out of Echo Canyon. Both belonged to the same group of guys. They were on a bachelor party. This seems to be a popular bachelor party spot. Anyhow, both cars lost their oil pans trying to get up into the canyon. That kind of put a damper on their party."

Inside Richard's office, he pulled out a map of the park and highlighted several popular roads and sites we could explore. We decided on our itinerary for the next couple of days, and Richard wrote it down, not just for us, but also for him to keep. He said he likes to keep track of where people are in the park, just in case they run into trouble.

Our first destination was Titus Canyon. From Richard's shop, we drove north through the park toward the ghost town of Rhyolite. We had to drive a couple of miles outside the park to pick up the one-way road that would take us over Red Pass and then through Titus Canyon. It didn't take long after we turned onto the Titus Canyon road to realize we'd made the right decision to rent a Jeep. The road was so rough that we would've never made it in our rental car.

About eight miles from where we entered the road, just past Red Pass, we came to the ghost town of Leadfield. Richard told us that every road in the park exists because it once led to a mine. The 15-mile Titus Canyon road was built to provide access to Leadfield. No one lives there now, but in 1926, the town had 300 residents and a brand new post office. Leadfield is a good example of the boom and bust nature of mining in the early 20th century. Very little ore was ever mined at the site, and by early 1927 the residents deserted the town.

West of Leadfield, the road drops in elevation and the walls of the canyon squeeze in on both sides. For several miles, the road follows the twisting path of the slot canyon; at times, the road was barely a single car's width – the reason why it's a one-way road. Once the road exits the canyon, the gravel continues for another mile or so before it reaches the paved main park road. If we had more time, I would have driven that road again. It was that beautiful of a drive.

On our way back to Furnace Creek, we stopped at Stovepipe Wells Village to fill the Jeep with gas. You always need to keep an eye on the fuel gauge when you're driving in Death Valley. Distances can be deceiving, and there are only a couple places to get gas. Just outside the village, we stopped at the Mesquite Flat Sand Dunes and hiked out onto the dunes.

Many people who haven't been to Death Valley think the park is mostly sand dunes, but less than one percent of it is covered with dunes. Sand from the eroding canyon walls is carried by the wind and trapped between the mountain ranges. In a few places, it piles up into sand dunes. The Mesquite Flat Sand Dunes are about 100 feet tall, and once you walk into them and are surrounded by sand you feel like you're in the Sahara. We climbed to one of the highest dunes and plopped down in the warm, soft sand. We sat there looking at the mountains change colors as the sun set.

Your friend,
Matt

~.~.~.~.~.~.~

From: **Matt Smith**
Subject: **Death Valley National Park continued**
Date: **January 14, 2012**

Dear Bob and Sue,

The place I wanted to see the most in Death Valley National Park was the Racetrack. It's not an actual racetrack; it's a dry lakebed, or playa, tucked between the Cottonwood Mountains and the Panamint Range on the west side of the park. It's named the Racetrack because on the dry lakebed are rocks – that move. They appear to be racing one another across the desert. No one has ever seen the rocks move, but when they do, they leave tracks of their path. I can't think of a stranger sight we've seen on our entire parks trip.

To get to the Racetrack, we had to drive on a washboard-rutted gravel road for 28 miles; that's 28 miles one way. We rarely went faster than 15 miles per hour. Just getting there took over two hours from when we left the paved road. And, that was with half the length of the road having been recently graded smooth. I now understand why Richard gets calls to tow cars out of this area of the park; we passed several crowded minivans that should not have been driving this road.

A few miles short of the playa is Tea Kettle Junction, a fork in the road that leads to an abandoned mine. It's become popular for people to hang teakettles on the Tea Kettle Junction sign. There were dates and messages written on the kettles; some looked brand new, others were rusted antiques. At first glance, it looked trashy, but at the same time it was an interesting sight; the sun reflecting off the kettles made them look like jewels in the desert. I liked it. We took our picture by the sign.

We were lucky to be able to get an early start this morning. By renting the Jeep for two days, we skipped having to wait in line this morning to pick it up. When we got to the playa, there were only a couple of other visitors there.

The playa looked like the kind of dry lakebed you would see on TV commercials for sports cars, where the cars are speeding across an endless flat surface with mountains in the background. At first, that's why I thought this particular dry lakebed was called the Racetrack.

The distance across the playa was deceptive. From where we parked we could easily see to the other side, which looked to be a short distance away, maybe a couple of city blocks in length. But, once we got onto the playa and started walking toward the rocks in the distance, it seemed as if we were walking in place. It was at least a mile and a half across the playa.

After a few minutes, we reached several small rocks but didn't see any sign of movement or tracks. I thought for a moment that maybe this was a big goof and there weren't any moving rocks. Then, we found one. It was square and about a foot and a half wide on each side. It was just sitting there in the early morning sun like it probably has every morning for dozens if not hundreds of years. But trailing away behind it was a slightly curved, indented path in the dry, hard playa surface. It looked like someone got down on their hands and knees and pushed it across the lakebed when the mud was wet, and then the trail hardened when the lakebed dried. But there were no sign of footprints, or handprints, or any prints except the path the rock made as it "raced" across the playa.

As we walked farther we saw many other rocks that had moved, each with a trail coming from a different direction. Some of the trails even crossed each other. Whatever was causing these rocks to move, it wasn't a force that moved in the same direction. If it had, all the trails would also be moving in the same direction.

Still early in the morning, the sun was at a low angle. It was a perfect time to photograph the rocks because the light caused a slight shadow on the ridges of the rocks' trails. Had the sun been directly overhead, the trails would have been difficult or impossible to see in our pictures.

There are several theories about how the rocks move.

The most plausible is that strong winds come through the valley, and when the lakebed is wet, the surface is slippery enough for the wind to push the rocks along their path. If that were true, though, why would the paths be moving in different directions? And, some of the rocks are too big for the wind to move them. A few that we saw looked to be at least a couple of hundred pounds. Then there are people who believe that aliens moved the rocks – of course they believe that. Whatever the correct explanation is, I'm glad no one has ever seen it happen. It keeps the mystery alive.

While we were walking amongst the mysterious rocks, we met another couple. They were older; I'm guessing they were in their seventies. They told us that they had been to this playa years ago, and back then there were many more rocks. People, it seems, have been coming to the Racetrack and taking the rocks. How stupid – and selfish – is that? It's not the rocks that are special; it's the fact that they move mysteriously, and no one can figure out how it happens.

On the way back to the car, I began noticing trails in the playa that would stop abruptly with no rock at the end. Rock poachers!

We were fortunate to pass only a few cars on the way to the Racetrack; the road was rarely wide enough for two cars to pass safely while both were moving at the same time. One of the two cars would have to pull over and let the other pass. As we were leaving, we could see several rooster tails of dust in the distance approaching us. The Jeeps were coming.

With our high-clearance vehicle, we were always able to find a spot to pull over and let an approaching car pass. Except once. It was a particularly narrow stretch of the road, and the graded gravel made a high bank on either side that was too high to climb over with our Jeep. The other car, also a Jeep, approached us and stopped. We were facing each other and neither of us could pass.

Looking behind me, the nearest place I could see to pull over was a long way off, at least a quarter mile. I wasn't going to back up into a cloud of dust, with zero visibility, for a quarter mile. I could see a spot about 50 feet ahead where the other Jeep could back into. I got out and told the other driver if he just backed up a short distance we could pass each other. He didn't speak a word of English and he looked terrified from having driven on the rough road. I kept motioning for him to back up, but he shook his head no. He must have thought I was telling him that he had to back up for the entire length of the road – several miles. Finally he understood me, backed up and we made it through. That guy was in for a long day.

We explored other areas of the park with our Jeep: the Ubehebe Crater, Mosaic Canyon, and Echo Canyon. Toward the end of the day we went back to the Stovepipe Wells Village gas station, filled up with gas and bought refreshments. Karen and I drove to the sand dunes and hiked back to our favorite dune with my backpack filled with beer and snacks.

We took off our shoes and socks and rested our heads on our backpacks. Lying there, watching the sun set on the stunning vista, we were deeply satisfied. Our parks trip has been more than we expected when we started out. More incredible, more expensive, more exhilarating, more time-consuming, more eye-opening. I can see us doing it all again.

We've now visited 56 of the 58 parks. We've gone as far as we can without going back to Alaska and getting in a small plane. We're still not ready for that. The two parks we have left, Kobuk Valley and Gates of the Arctic, are both north of the Arctic Circle in Alaska. They're wilderness parks, with no roads or visitor services. We'll have to hire a guide to take us in. We plan on visiting them this August once the bugs are gone, but before it starts snowing. It's not too late for you to join us.

Your friend,
Matt

~.~.~.~.~.~.~

From: **Matt Smith**
Subject: **Unfinished business**
Date: **May 26, 2012**

Dear Bob and Sue,

It's time to take care of some unfinished business. With my new job about to start, Karen and I are off to Grand Teton and Grand Canyon National Parks. We don't feel we properly visited these parks on our first pass through. It's going to be a 4,000-mile, old-fashioned road-trip.

Last night we drove from Issaquah to Coeur D'Alene, Idaho, where we stayed at the Days Inn. Before going to bed, Karen suggested we shouldn't be in a hurry in the morning – that we should feel good if we were on the road by 8:00am. This morning at 5:45 she said to me, "Why are we just laying around?" We were on the road by 6:30.

It was sunny when we started out, but that only lasted about 20 minutes. By the time we got to Butte and stopped for lunch, it was snowing. We're celebrating the beginning of summer by driving back into winter.

Just east of Bozeman, I noticed a car next to us in the left lane. Whenever I sped up or slowed down, it would too. This was very annoying, and a little dangerous given that we were driving through a snow shower. After several minutes I looked over to see the driver, a young woman, with a Dairy Queen sundae in one hand and texting on her phone with the other hand. She must have been steering with her knees. Apparently the curvy mountain roads, the snow and the traffic were not enough to hold her attention. Eventually she sped away and disappeared into the distance.

By mid-afternoon we arrived in Gardiner, Montana where we're staying tonight. Gardiner is a small town that sits just north of the Yellowstone National Park border along the Yellowstone River. Several years ago when we were here with the kids, we spent a couple hours poking through the stores.

One had an impressive offering of animal pelts, from grizzlies to weasels. It was on that trip I got the idea to start a pelt collection. I didn't buy any pelts at the time because I thought they would be plentiful on our travels through the west. They're not.

Since then, I've regretted not buying a pelt and I've mentioned it to Karen so often that she's tired of hearing about it. She doesn't like the idea of me accumulating a closetful of dead animals, but she prefers that to listening to my laments. Karen's been looking forward to our trip back here so I can finally buy a pelt, although she's said there's one condition, "We're only buying pelts of animals that died of old age or were road killed."

When we pulled into Gardiner this afternoon, the light rain that had been falling was turning to a mix of rain and snow. Standing under the eaves of the old west storefronts, we could barely see the Roosevelt Arch just a few hundred yards away.

We walked the entire length of the row of shops but couldn't find the pelt store. I was in a mild state of panic. "What if they went out of business? Where would I get my pelts? What if there are no more pelts? What if...?" Karen could sense my growing anxiety so she distracted me with an offer of food and drink.

We stopped in a bar to have a beer. There were only two other people in the place besides the bartender and us. Karen did her best to calm me down. There had been one closed shop along the strip with a "We just stepped away" sign on the door. She assured me that was the pelt store and we would go back later this afternoon. I wasn't so sure. I had looked through the windows of the closed store and hadn't seen any pelts.

In an attempt to end my worries, she waved the bartender over to ask him about the pelt store. I thought to myself, "Here we go."

He walked over and leaned toward us across the bar. The crucifix tattoo on his arm brushed against my beer; Jesus was staring right at me.

Karen said, "Excuse me. Where's the pelt store?"

"What kinda pelt you looking for?"

Karen just stared back at him, suddenly mute.

"I got a bear pelt outside in my trunk I'd sell you. The bear charged me during bow season, so I shot it in the head with my .45 pistol."

Karen squeezed my thigh under the bar. She was silently asking me if we should run for our lives.

Doing her best to act like she shops for bear pelts regularly, she asked, "What type of bear was it?"

"A black bear." There was a pause. After a confident sniff he continued, "Yeah, it's the 15th largest black bear shot in Montana."

We weren't sure if he meant that it was 15th largest black bear shot *in the head* in Montana or if it was the 15th largest black bear shot anywhere in Montana.

Karen replied, "I'm looking for something a little smaller than a bear."

The bartender could tell she didn't have a clue what she was looking for.

When he left to serve one of the other customers Karen turned to me and said, "Everything about that exchange was offensive."

I replied, "Where's the pelt store? What was that? We might as well be wearing t-shirts with 'STUPID TOURIST' printed on them."

She said, "I should have asked him if he has the 15th smallest penis in Montana."

I was glad their conversation ended so quickly. For a moment I thought we would end up in the parking lot, digging through this guy's trunk full of animal remnants. I could imagine a stray antler accidentally setting off one of his loaded weapons. After we left the bar, Karen agreed not to start anymore conversations with strangers in Montana, or anywhere, about pelts.

I'm still peltless though, except for the two rabbits Karen

has packed away with her Christmas ornaments, and those have glitter on them.

Your friend,
Matt

~.~.~.~.~.~.~

From: **Karen Smith**
Subject: **If I had a hammer**
Date: **May 28, 2012**

Dear Bob and Sue,

Memorial Day weekend is supposed to be the kick-off to summer. In Yellowstone it was still winter; many of the roads in the park were closed yesterday morning when we drove through on our way to Grand Teton National Park. The snow from the recent storm was still being plowed. Fortunately, there was one route open so we were able to drive through the park and exit to the south rather than taking the six-hour detour around the park entirely. When we stopped at the Old Faithful Visitor Center, Matt was disappointed because their pelt collection was not on display. He likes to look for the bullet holes, but you already know that.

When we pulled up to our cabin in Colter Bay Village, we were surprised that it was on a lake. Not Jackson Lake, which is down the street, but a huge puddle right outside our front door. Matt quickly named it Smith Lake. He estimated that the parking lot hadn't been draining properly for at least a couple of years, leaving a puddle about ten yards long and a half foot deep in some places. We had to park in front of another cabin and drag our luggage around the lake and through some long wet grass to get to the front door.

Matt said weeds were blocking the water's path to the drainage ditch, and if he had the proper tools he could easily fix it. We looked in and around the cabin, but couldn't find anything he could use to clear a channel for the water to escape.

We also looked in the car. I asked Matt if there was a small shovel in our emergency roadside tool kit. He said no, there wasn't a shovel, but he did pack a hammer. We had a lengthy debate about why he would choose to bring a hammer over a small shovel. It seemed to me that in an emergency, like getting stuck in the snow or coming across a forest fire, a shovel would be useful. I pointed out that a hammer isn't a tool usually called upon for any kind of rescue attempt, unless you need to bludgeon someone. Matt dismissed my opinion and assured me that a hammer is an essential emergency tool. Whatever.

A little while later, we left our cabin to drive to the visitor center to take care of business. I asked Matt to stop by the rental office so I could inform them we had a lake where our car should be.

"Tell them your husband needs a hoe," he called out to me as I jumped out of the car.

At the front desk, I waited for a few minutes while other guests checked in. When it was my turn, the front desk clerk looked at me expectantly, "May I help you?"

"My husband needs a hoe." The woman stared at me blankly. She didn't get Matt's humor. I explained the problem to her and she said, "Our maintenance workers are over at the lodge until 5:00, and when they get back here they won't have time to deal with anything unless it's an emergency."

I tried again: this time changing my request to a shovel. "My husband can take care of the problem."

"I'm sorry, we can't give our guests tools. They might hurt themselves."

OK, then how about a life jacket? I thought to myself.

The next morning, after Matt went on a coffee run, we got dressed in layers for our hike in the snow. Matt said he had to get something out of the car, and when he didn't return I glanced out the front window of the cabin. I saw him at the edge of the lake, hacking away at the weeds with the claw end of his hammer. And that is why I love this man.

I found the camera and took some pictures of him in action. The man staying in the cabin next door, who was also inconvenienced by the lake, came out and wandered over to watch him. I'm pretty sure he thought Matt was a maintenance worker, although he must have wondered why Matt was using a hammer. His only comment to Matt was a sarcastic, "Thanks for doing this *now*, just as I'm ready to check out." I couldn't decide if this guy was the dumbest man on the planet or the bravest. Who takes that tone with someone straddling a weed patch, splattered with mud, crazily wielding a hammer?

It took Matt only about ten minutes of hacking for the water to flow freely into the drainage ditch. Afterward, he wiped off his hammer, put it back in the emergency roadside kit and came into the cabin. We stood at the window and watched the water drain. Matt pointed to the stream of water flowing into the drainage ditch, "See there?" he said. "That's Smith Creek." Matt stayed there in the window, watching with pride as Smith Lake drained into Smith Creek. And then, the lake and the creek were gone: just wet pavement remained.

Matt turned to me with a sigh. "I needed a win."

Now, and for the rest of our road trip, I'll have to listen to Matt talk about what a great idea it was for him to pack a hammer. So much better than a shovel.

Your friend,
Karen

~.~.~.~.~.~.~

From: **Matt Smith**
Subject: **Hiking in the Tetons**
Date: **May 28, 2012**

Dear Bob and Sue,

While I would be happy to believe that "Grand Teton" means "Big Breast," no one knows for sure if that's the correct origin of the name. The French owned the land that's now Grand Teton National Park prior to the 19th century, and since téton means breast in French – nipple actually – some think the mountains were named Tetons because they look like big breasts. After some quick research, I'm not convinced this is the correct etymology of the name, but it works for me.

With Smith Lake drained, I was ready for a hike in the Tetons. From Colter Bay we drove to Jenny Lake. On the way, we saw several cars parked alongside the road. People were standing on the shoulder looking toward a meadow. A brown bear, a grizzly, was pawing the ground in search of food about 100 yards from the road. It never stops being a thrill to see a bear in the wild. There are very few places in the lower 48 states that are home to grizzlies, but the federal government has protected Yellowstone for so long (since 1872) that it and Grand Teton to its south still have brown bear habitats. Grand Tetons also has a diverse population of other large mammals: moose, elk, and black bears.

At Jenny Lake, we wanted to hike into Cascade Canyon, but when we spoke with the ranger he told us it would be a treacherous hike today because of the newly fallen snow. Instead, we hiked the trail that circles the lake.

We asked the ranger at the visitor center if there had been any bear sightings close to the lake. He showed us a map with a couple of shaded areas with dates indicating recent brown bear sightings. When we started out on our hike, we saw a park service sign warning visitors not to run or jog along the trails because of the brown bears that frequent the area close to the lake. If a bear sees someone running, they're likely to give chase; the bear doesn't know the difference between someone training for a triathlon and someone running away out of fear. Their predatory instinct isn't well tuned enough to tell them apart – that, and they don't care why you're running, they're going to chase you regardless.

It was a gray day and when we started our hike, the trail had a dusting of snow. We hiked single-file with me in front; Karen insists I lead. Every time I looked back, Karen would smile and hold the bear spray up for me to see. She was ready for a bear encounter. At least I think her gesture was indicating her readiness. Either that or it was a gentle threat. I had recently shown her how to remove the safety from the bear spray trigger; we even practiced so she would know how to do it in an emergency. I have to say, I'm more hesitant to be a smart-ass when she's got the bear spray in her hand.

Halfway around the lake, the trail climbed a couple of hundred feet. The snow was six inches deep and there were no footprints other than ours on the trail. Even though I was ready for summer, it was pretty special hiking through virgin snow, just the two of us.

Occasionally we saw animal tracks, mostly small tracks that looked like rabbits. But then we came across a set of prints we'd never seen before. Each print looked like a pair of teardrop-shaped hooves. They were too large for deer to have made them. Later we learned that they were elk prints. We stopped often to look for wildlife hoping to see an elk or a moose. On the backside of the lake the Tetons rise up dramatically from lake level. On one of our stops Karen spotted a moose on the rise above us. It's a wonder that you can drive to these incredible national parks, hike a few miles into the wilderness and be surrounded by magnificent wildlife.

As the day wore on, the snow began to melt and Karen's "winter wonderland" faded away. Eventually, we followed the trail around the far side of the lake. Heading back toward the visitor center, the final couple of miles were free of snow. Usually we're the ones passing other hikers, so we were startled by the sound of heavy breathing and footsteps from behind. We moved aside to let a man and woman run past us. I thought of yelling to them the warning about not running on the trail, but they were out of earshot in an instant. The spot on the trail where they passed us was smack in the middle of one of the shaded areas the ranger showed us on his bear sightings map. I wonder if bears prefer Nikes or Adidas?

The parking lot was crowded with visitors when we finished our hike. The summer crowd was just beginning to arrive. Karen and I made a loop through the gift store then stood outside under the half-mast flag looking at each other. After three rounds of "I don't know, what do *you* want to do," we decided we'd had enough winter for one year. We drove back to Colter Bay, checked out a day early and headed toward Utah. It's time for summer and warmer temperatures.

Your friend,
Matt

~.~.~.~.~.~.~

From: **Matt Smith**
Subject: **Ready to hike the Grand Canyon**
Date: **June 6, 2012**

Dear Bob and Sue,

This week was the bonus round of our parks trip. We re-visited many of our favorite parks and added a couple of new destinations to our "must see again" list. Since leaving Wyoming last week, we've been to Arches, Canyonlands, Mesa Verde, Canyon De Chelly (national monument), and Zion National Parks. We also found a spectacular slot canyon hike in southern Utah: Buckskin Gulch.

Right now we're at the Thunderbird Lodge on the south rim of the Grand Canyon, packing for our hike tomorrow to Phantom Ranch at the bottom of the canyon. We're staying there tomorrow night and hiking back here the next day. Our original plan was to hike from the north rim to the south rim, spending one night at Phantom Ranch, but a water main running beneath the trail on the north side of the canyon broke a couple of days ago and washed out the trail.

An agent from Xanterra called me while we were in Zion, and told me about the washed-out trail and said the park service didn't know when they would re-open it. So, we changed our plans and will instead hike down and back from the south rim. I'm disappointed, but maybe it's just as well for our first attempt. Since the trailhead on the north rim is 1,400 feet higher in elevation than the south rim, the trail down from the north is steeper; it's also five miles longer.

We've wanted to hike to the bottom of the Grand Canyon for years. My research assistant has read all the information she could find on how to do this hike safely, what to bring, and how to prepare, but her "training regimen" has been mostly limited to reading about it.

A couple of weeks ago she hiked Tiger Mountain – once. The day after her one and only training hike she took two naps. I found her taking the first one at 9:30 in the morning after breakfast. When she woke up I told her that on the day after hiking down the Grand Canyon, instead of napping she would have to hike back up the canyon, which is the equivalent of two Tiger Mountains. She said she wasn't worried because the training hike activated her muscle memory and served as a "wake up call" to her muscles. "They've reported for duty," was the way she put it. (I don't think Karen knows what muscle memory is, but I didn't point this out to her.)

Still, she thought there should be another option available to hikers who might need some assistance. "They should rent mules to hikers," she suggested.

"What do you mean *rent* mules?" I asked.

"The parks service should rent mules that you guide with a rope on the way down the trail. You could put your backpack on its back instead of carrying it yourself."

"Really?"

"Yeah, and at Phantom Ranch you could tie it up and feed and water it. The mule would be like your pet for a couple of days."

"Really?"

"Yeah, *really*. When you're ready to go back up the canyon, you could ride on its back."

"They can't *rent* mules. Most people wouldn't know how to care for them. And besides, what if it bolted and ran away?

(Big sigh from Karen) "You have it on a rope! It's not going to run away."

"*OK*—we'll set aside the fact that mules weigh 1,500 pounds and can go wherever they want. What if it was a biter?"

"A biter?"

"Yeah, what if you got a mean one and it tried to bite you?"

"They could put muzzles on them."

"Do you even know what a mule is?"

"It's a brilliant idea," she insisted.

When Karen was getting dressed for the Tiger Mountain training hike, I suggested she wear the Asolo hiking boots I bought her last summer, but she insisted on wearing her old tennis shoes because they were "broken in and comfortable." They were so broken in that the treads on the bottom had worn slick and she pretty much slid all the way down the mountain. Halfway down, she fell. Her leg bent in an awkward position and her knee took the brunt of the impact. Gravel embedded into her knee. Since it was not a long hike, I didn't have my first-aid kit in my backpack. All I could do was wash her knee with my drinking water. She limped the rest of the way with blood running down her leg.

Karen knows she's stubborn – belligerent actually – but she rarely admits it. When she finally comes around to seeing things my way she defends herself by saying, "I just wasn't ready to hear that message." Gravel sticking out of her knee got her ready in a hurry. Her hiking boots are sitting by the hotel room door.

Your friend,
Matt

~.~.~.~.~.~.~.~

From: **Matt Smith**
Subject: **Down and Back**
Date: **June 8, 2012**

Dear Bob and Sue,

At 5:00am yesterday, I pulled the curtains back from the window of our room at the Thunderbird Lodge to see three enormous elk standing ten feet away. They were stunning. I've never seen wild animals that big before, including the moose in Alaska. Karen said it was a good omen for our Grand Canyon hike.

The weather was perfect when we started down the Bright Angel Trail at 5:45am. We'd hiked this trail before but we'd never gone more than a few miles down before turning back. The trick to hiking in the Grand Canyon during the summer is to avoid the warmest hours of the day. The park service recommends not hiking between 10:00am and 4:00pm in the summer. By getting a start before 6:00am, we expected to make it to the bottom by 10:00am. As it turned out, the hike down took a little over four hours. We shuffled into Phantom Ranch at 10:15am.

The first couple of miles down the trail were uneventful.

The scenery was spectacular and the weather perfect, but we'd experienced this before. Many visitors to the park get a mile or two down the canyon, but few go farther than that. I was looking forward to getting past the point where most people turn back.

Four and a half miles into our hike, we reached Indian Gardens. With shady Cottonwood trees, a campground, restrooms, and potable water, it's an oasis. It was also our first stop on our way down. Very few campers seemed to be awake as we sat on a bench along the trail and got out our granola bars for breakfast. We didn't sit for long; squirrels made herky-jerky movements toward us, looking for any crumbs we may have dropped. There's a high concentration of squirrels around the campsites in the park, so we put our backpacks back on, filled our water bottles and kept moving down the trail eating our granola bars as we hiked.

The elevation change from the south rim to the river is 4,400 feet. It takes less energy to hike down than up, but the constant pounding took its toll on our knees. Anyone with knee or hip joint problems should not try to hike down without trekking poles to take some of the weight off the down steps. Also, Karen swears that taking an anti-inflammatory like Ibuprofen at the start of the hike helps prevent aches and pains in her knees.

The Colorado River is a seven-mile hike from the south rim. From the river, it's another couple of miles to Phantom Ranch, a collection of cabins and a canteen catering to overnight visitors at the bottom of the canyon.

We reached the river about three hours from the start of our hike. It was a spectacular sight. The water was deep green and moving swiftly. The Spanish named it the Colorado River (red river) because the silt in the river gave it a deep red color. Since the Glen Canyon Dam was completed in 1963 upstream, the silt has been trapped behind the dam and the water now has a green color. With the dam controlling the river's rate of flow, it's no longer a wild river, but its currents looked menacing to us as we hiked along the ridge a couple of hundred feet above. It may not be wild but it's extremely dangerous. The parks service warns visitors not to swim in the river.

About a mile before Phantom Ranch, the Bright Angel trail led us to a footbridge across the river. The Silver Bridge is a modern era suspension bridge and is only used for foot traffic. Mules that take visitors and supplies up and down the canyon must cross the river on Black Bridge, a short distance to the east of Silver Bridge.

The bridge swayed in the wind as we walked across it. We stopped at the middle and looked down at the currents braiding back and forth underneath us. Small eddies formed along the banks where large boulders jutted out into the river. The deck of the bridge was an open grate and through it we could see a large pipe attached to the underside. It's a high-pressure pipe running from the north rim to the south rim that provides all the water to the south side of the canyon. This is the same pipe that ruptured on the north side of the canyon earlier in the week and washed out the trail. They've repaired the pipe, but for a couple of days, the campgrounds in the canyon were without water. Hikers and campers in the canyon had to filter or treat creek water. I'm guessing the south rim has a water storage system that holds a reserve supply because they were never without water during the pipe repairs.

Just past the bridge, we stopped again to have a snack. The park service suggests eating often when doing a strenuous hike like this one. The Grand Canyon National Park website says, "This is not a time to diet," (that's reason enough to do the hike) and hunger is not a good indicator of when you should eat; you need fuel to keep your energy up. They also recommend salty snacks. In the desert heat, you sweat more than you realize because much of it evaporates quickly. Staying hydrated and getting plenty of salt is a must.

I was expecting Phantom Ranch to be just on the other side of the river, but it wasn't. The trail followed Bright Angel Creek a mile upstream before it reached the ranch. Even though it was only 10:00am, the temperature was in the 90's and we were ready for a rest in the shade. A ranger we spoke with at the south rim visitor center the day before described to us the symptoms of heat exhaustion: low energy, disorientation, dizziness, and nausea. She warned us to watch for these signs and gave us tips for staying cool: wear light colored clothing, wear a wet bandana around the neck, stay hydrated, and if those don't cool us down she suggested we sit in the creek – Bright Angel Creek *not* the Colorado River.

We made it to the ranch in better shape than we anticipated, but we were still whooped and needed a long rest. The next time we do this hike, I'll pack lighter. I'd brought more water than necessary, which made my pack heavier than it needed to be. While it's important to drink a lot of water, there are several places along Bright Angel Trail to fill a water bottle, so you don't have to carry all the water you need for the entire hike.

We had reserved a cabin at the ranch, but check-in time wasn't until 3:00pm. There's not much to do at the ranch besides laze in the shade or hike. Since the ranch sits in a small side canyon, the only hiking options are to go up the North Kaibab Trail, or cross back over the river and hike up the South Kaibab or Bright Angel Trail. We didn't have the energy for more hiking so we sat our tired butts on a couple of park benches in the center courtyard under a large tree. It was warm even in the shade but we were very relaxed. I don't think we spoke for about a half an hour. Karen and I just stared silently into the distance. Eventually we dug our smashed peanut butter and jelly sandwiches out of our backpacks and ate them quietly as a few other hikers filtered in and joined us in a half-trance lunch.

Karen took off her hiking boots, tied them to her pack and slipped on a pair of flip-flops. I did the same. Flip-flops have never felt so good. It wasn't long after we'd eaten the PB&Js that Karen laid back on her park bench and dozed. Her feet hung off the end of the bench and her flip-flops fell onto the dusty ground. She looked very peaceful.

As I sat there half-dozing myself, I watched a green-tinted squirrel pop his head up over the stone wall that encircled the courtyard. Each time his head appeared he was a little closer. I didn't move a muscle, hoping he would be brave enough to check us out at close range. Pretty soon he did. He (or it could have been a she) sniffed my backpack and searched around my feet for a fallen nut or Cheez-It. I amused myself with the thought of how startled Karen would be if she opened her eyes at that very moment to see a squirrel poking around two feet away from her. There must have been a smear of peanut butter or jelly on one of her flip-flops because the squirrel sniffed it, grabbed it in his mouth and tried to run off with it. I hollered loud enough that the squirrel dropped the flip-flop and shot off for the safety of the bushes. Karen sat up and said, "What was that?" I replied calmly, "Oh nothing. You should try to go back to sleep."

We killed the afternoon by walking up and down the trail close to the ranch and checking with the staff every half hour as to when our cabin would be ready. The answer each time was the same, "About 3:00pm." There was an un-manned ranger station a couple of hundred yards away from the ranch's main building that had a few interpretive signs and a small library of books about the canyon. We kicked ourselves when we saw there was a passport stamp sitting on the table in the middle of the ranger station: we hadn't brought our passports with us on the hike.

At 3:02pm, we got the key to our cabin from the extremely patient, young woman in the canteen whose job it is to keep the restless hikers at bay until 3:00pm. Our cabin was number four, directly across from the canteen. It had a small metal silhouette of a chicken on the front door. Karen loved the little chicken. Every cabin had a different animal. I presume that's to help guests remember which cabin is theirs. When you're in a post-hike stupor, it's easier to mutter, "chicken" than "number four" to the staff when they find you wandering around the grounds disoriented.

The cabin was tiny. It had two sets of bunk beds, a sink in one corner and a rustic table and chair in another. A toilet was tucked into a space the size of a broom closet. Showers are in another building. It was small but we didn't care. Most of the cabin lodging at the ranch is dormitory style. We cranked the AC and climbed in bed to take a nap. Each of us took a lower bunk where the temperature was comfortably in the 70's. It was easily 20 degrees warmer just a few feet higher at the upper beds. As comfortable as it was, neither of us slept for more than a few minutes. We found a couple of sheets of Phantom Ranch stationary on the table and decided to go back to the ranger station to stamp them with the passport stamp as souvenirs.

Upon our return from the ranger station, Karen insisted I take pictures of our chicken cabin from several angles. While I took the pictures, Karen stood at a distance with her arms folded looking at the cabin with a smile. This had the markings of the beginning of a fantasy that ends with me building an exact replica of the cabin in some remote mountain setting. I think the heat and the direct sun was making her light-headed. My combination whistle / thermometer / compass / magnifying glass read 106 degrees. I snapped her out of her dream world by mentioning that the ranger talk in the courtyard was about to begin.

Normally we don't attend a lot of ranger talks because I can't sit still for more than five minutes unless I'm getting paid to do so or there's food being served. But, we were truly out of things to do so we joined the group for the talk. When we got there the only place left to sit was right next to the ranger. Ranger Jenny had prepared a game of National Park trivia in Jeopardy format. She gave a brief introduction of herself and launched into the game.

She chose the first category – wildlife – pulled the first card from her duct taped game board, and read it to us. "This pink snake is the most common rattlesnake found in the canyon." I raised my hand immediately and said loudly, "The Grand Canyon Rattlesnake."

Karen tilted her head at me and said, "*What* is the Grand Canyon Rattlesnake?"

"*It's* the answer. Jeez!"

"No. You're supposed to say it in the form of a question. Haven't you ever seen Jeopardy? Jeez!"

"Oh. What is the Grand Canyon Rattlesnake?"

Jenny looked concerned. It could have been my unexpected enthusiasm, or the banter between us, but whatever her concern she casually moved a few feet farther away from us before she explained the prizes.

For every correct answer you would get a sticker that read, "DOWN IS OPTIONAL. UP IS MANDATORY." They were courtesy of Grand Canyon National Park Search and Rescue. It's their way of getting the message out that they are not there for the sole purpose of dragging your sorry ass out of the canyon when you hike to the bottom and can't make it back up. Jenny explained how some hikers think they can "call the helicopter" when they can't or don't want to hike back to the top. Jenny was adamant that the rescuers should not have to put their lives at risk to assist people too out-of-shape or unprepared (or both) to handle the round-trip hike. I found her attitude refreshing. As I was nodding my head in firm agreement, Karen leaned over and whispered to me, "Now what do you think of my rent-a-mule idea? It's gold, I'm telling you, pure gold."

Jenny turned to me and said, "You answered correctly so you get to choose the next card."

"Jenny, I'll take History for 100," I said.

"This female architect was hired by Fred Harvey to design the permanent structures at Phantom Ranch."

"Mary Colter," I shouted.

(No, Colter Bay in Grand Teton National Park was not named after her. It was named after John Colter, one of the members of the Lewis and Clark expedition. I had hoped that might be the Daily Double question, but it wasn't.)

Now I had two stickers and no one else had any. I started to imagine what it would be like to answer every question and end up with all the stickers for myself. Karen could sense this might be going through my head and squeezed my thigh as

Jenny read the third card. I knew the answer right away but I used every ounce of self-control to keep from shouting it out. A young girl behind the picnic table beamed as Jenny handed her a sticker for the correct answer. I looked down at the two stickers in my hand and placed one on Karen's lap. I was making a kind gesture but she took it as a show of pity, meaning that I thought she couldn't possibly answer a question correctly. She looked at me with an incredulous, opened-mouth expression, threw the sticker at me and said, "Oh, it's on now."

I don't remember the final sticker tally but let's just say Karen had no interest in counting when the game was over. After the ranger talk, we messed around in our cabin until 6:30pm – time for hiker's stew.

There are two dinner options at Phantom Ranch: steak at 5:00pm or hiker's stew at 6:30pm. Both have limited seating and must be reserved ahead of time. That's something to keep in mind if you ever plan to do this trip. It would suck to get all the way down to the ranch and think you could mosey on in to the canteen at suppertime and order dinner only to have the dinner host say, "Sorry, we don't see your name on the list."

Inside the canteen were five or six tables each seating about 14 people. The staff had assigned all of the guests to a specific table and they served the food family style. In addition to stew they served us salad, cornbread, and chocolate cake for dessert. There was enough for everyone to have seconds. The stew was fantastic; it was one of the best meals we've ever had. Of course after our hike down the canyon, had they served us boiled shoelaces they would have tasted pretty good.

Close to the end of dinner, the canteen manager gave us the details about breakfast the next day. He said the first breakfast seating is at 5:00am, but the cook will have sack breakfasts ready for pickup by 3:00am for hikers who want to get an early start up the trail. We hadn't reserved breakfast; instead we brought extra granola bars to eat on the way up the canyon. Our plan was to be on the trail by 5:00am the next morning. Ranger Jenny had to cancel her evening ranger program to help a hiker in distress, so we called it a night early. We were asleep by 9:00pm.

At 4:45 this morning, we left Phantom Ranch and our chicken cabin to begin our hike back to the south rim. It was light enough for us to see without flashlights. There were several other hikers hanging out in front of the canteen waiting for breakfast. It would have been nice to eat a hot meal before our hike, but every minute spent eating would have put us a minute later in the day at the end of the hike.

The first couple of miles were fairly easy with almost no elevation gain. When we reached the first steep upward section of the trail, Karen decided it was time to sit and eat a granola bar for breakfast. I tried to get her to eat quickly, but my attempts only caused her to slow down. I was anxious to get to the top before the hottest part of the day, but regardless of my intention, Karen took offense and stuffed her half-eaten breakfast in the side pocket of her backpack and huffed along the trail.

It didn't take long after that for us to begin to overtake hikers that had left Phantom Ranch earlier than us. From behind me I could hear Karen say between gasps, "The parks service website says..."

"What?"

"The park service website says... it says we're supposed to hike slow enough... slow enough that we aren't out of breath."

"What?"

"We're supposed to be able... to be able to carry on a normal conversation."

"What?"

"We're supposed to be able to carry on a normal... a normal conversation!"

I could hear her fine; I just wanted to see how many times I could get her to repeat herself. There was no way I was going to slow down and she knew it. I had a foursome of slow hikers in my sights ahead of us and I wasn't going to let up until we were well past them.

By the time we reached Indian Gardens, I was feeling bad about rushing Karen through her breakfast. I asked her if she wanted to take a break. At first she said no; when we were there yesterday we saw so many squirrels hovering around that today she wanted to hike through the area as quickly as possible. So, when we reached the restrooms I was surprised that she took off her pack and sat on one of the benches by the side of the trail.

"I thought you didn't want to stop here because of the squirrels," I said.

"Yeah, but I've been on the lookout and there doesn't seem to be any here right now. Maybe they're still asleep."

"O -kay, " I replied. Karen was sitting on the bench facing me. Looking at her I could see a squirrel perched on a rock wall right over her left shoulder staring intently at her granola bar. I sat my backpack next to her on the bench and went off to use the restroom.

After a five-minute break we filled our water bottles, put on our backpacks and continued up the trail. The trail is fairly flat at Indians Gardens, but soon after it got steep again. That was the point my headache began. I'd been eating plenty of salty snacks, drinking enough water and I wasn't dieting, so "What's with the headache," I thought. It started as a mild nuisance, but grew to the point of being a real concern. I took some Ibuprofen, but other than that I would just have to tough it out.

Having been preoccupied with my head, I'd stopped checking on Karen behind me. A little more than three miles from the rim I looked back at her. She had a look of concern that I've rarely seen on her face when we hike. She was beginning to crash. It took me by surprise that we both were struggling as much as we were. We were in good shape. We've done strenuous hikes before without much difficulty. What was going on? Was this heat related? It couldn't be; it wasn't *that* hot.

A tip we read while planning for this hike suggested

wearing a wet bandana around the neck while hiking in the heat. The moisture evaporates and keeps the bandana and your neck cool. Karen was wearing the bandana I bought her for this trip. We stopped in a small patch of shade at one of the switchbacks so I could pour water on her bandana. Then she asked me to pour water over her head as well. That seemed to help a little but I knew the best thing we could do was get to the top before the day grew much hotter.

At the three-mile marker, we stopped at the resting hut for more water and to sit in the shade for a few minutes. The crowd of day hikers coming down the trail was starting to get thick. As we sat there, a mule train came past us. None of the mules had riders or saddlebags except for the one in front that had a single rider leading the train. It was tight quarters as they passed us on the trail; they were less than a foot away from us as they walked by. After they were gone we sat without expressions as the dust settled around us.

The break didn't make either of us feel much better. What did make us feel better was the fact that we'd hiked this far down before, a couple of times, and had a pretty good idea of how much work was left to get to the top. Also, there was another rest area at the one-and-a-half-mile marker. If we could get there in fair shape, it would be a huge mental boost.

My head was pounding and every step for Karen was a struggle. Even so, we passed several sets of hikers on those next two miles. Nearly everyone hiking up from the bottom of the canyon was flagging by that point in the hike. A ranger on her way down the trail stopped us and asked us how we were doing. "Fine," I said unconvincingly. She asked us a few more questions: where we started from, when we started, did we have water with us. She wasn't just being friendly; she was assessing us. We must have looked worse than we felt. I completely expected her to ask me next what day or year it was, but she didn't. She must have been satisfied with our responses because she wished us a good rest of our hike and continued down the trail.

At the one-and-a-half-mile marker we rested again.

Karen was wearing her white hiking shorts that were by then soaked from the water I'd poured on her. She parked her butt in the red dirt, knowing but not caring that they would be bright red for the rest of the hike. A young man and woman who looked to be about twenty-five years old sat beside us. We had seen them at dinner the night before at the ranch. They told us they left the ranch about the same time as we had this morning. Before we got to our feet, they got up and continued hiking up the trail in front of us. They were the first hikers to pass us today. Karen likes to remind me that our hikes are not races, but I could see a little disappointment in her face as she realized they were going to beat us to the top.

We sat there for a few more minutes before gathering the strength to continue. We had just put our backpacks on when an energetic older gentleman with very white teeth approached us.

"Good morning!" he said. Then he stood there with a wide grin waiting for our reply. Neither of us could remember what the correct response was to "Good morning." We looked at him with blank stares.

"You guys coming up from the river?" he barked.

We nodded slowly.

"Great hike was it?" He asked each question with more enthusiasm than the one before.

Again, we nodded slowly.

"Well, let me ask you this," he said as he came a little too close. "Was it worth it?"

Karen leaned away from him and said quietly with a weak smile, "Now's not a good time to ask that question. Ask us again if we make it to the top."

The last mile was hell, but we kept passing other hikers. As slow as we were going, I don't know how we could pass anyone, but we did. It reminded me of semi trucks on steep mountain highways: when one truck going 12 miles an hour passes another truck going 11 1/2 miles an hour. We were the 12 mile an hour truck coming up the trail. Every time I would move into the passing lane, Karen followed. I've never been so proud.

A half-mile from the top, a woman with trekking poles, a large fanny pack and too much make-up to be hiking the Grand Canyon approached us. In a mildly panicked tone she asked, "How much farther is the next water station?" She'd come only a half-mile down and was already in desperate need of water. Karen replied, "There's water at the one-and-a-half-mile marker."

"Well, how far down are we now?" she asked.

We both just shrugged our shoulders. "Half a mile maybe?" I said.

Nervously she glanced up the trail from where she'd come, and then proceeded on down the trail toward the water. She clearly was unprepared to be hiking such a difficult trail during the heat of a summer day. But, we didn't have the energy or attention span to convince her to turn around. She just slipped past our unfocused stares.

When we finally reached the top we took off our packs and high-fived. We don't high-five very often. It took us a couple of tries to hit each other's hand. My watch read 10:15am: five and a half hours. We were pretty happy with our time. We'd reserved a room at the El Tovar Hotel but it was too early to check in so we were essentially homeless. We also looked homeless. The layer of red dust that covered almost every inch of our bodies was streaked with sweat, so we hobbled to our car, discarded our hiking boots and grabbed some clean clothes.

After a stop at the El Tovar bathrooms, where we wiped off the dust the best we could and changed clothes, we sat on the porch of the bar and ate lunch. There wasn't much talking at lunch; Karen was recovering quickly but my head still pounded. Then it dawned on me: I hadn't had coffee yet. I never skip coffee in the morning. I ordered coffee from our waiter and once I drank it my headache began to ease up. By the time we finished our lunch my headache was nearly gone. That must have been it. Note to self: don't attempt a hike up the Grand Canyon without having your coffee first. I'm convinced this is the reason Karen crashed as well, although she's not so sure.

By 12:30pm our room was ready. It was the first room down the hallway across from the front desk. We shared a wall with the gift shop, and the front door to our room couldn't have been thirty feet from the entrance to the bar. Karen was hesitant about having a room so close to the lobby and bar area but we didn't have the energy to ask for another. As it turned out we loved being so close to the lobby and all the action.

In our room, we pulled the curtains closed, cranked up the air-conditioner and took turns showering. I don't remember a shower feeling so good. It was as if my headache was washing off me and running down the drain. It gave me shivers it felt so good. Outside it was sunny and hot, but our room was dark and cool. We climbed in bed, sore but clean; and took a two-hour, body-twitching, open-mouth snoring, semi-comatose nap.

Right now we're back in the bar, this time having a celebration drink – beers and shots of tequila. The round-trip hike, including our overnight stay in the chicken cabin, took fewer than 30 hours. Looking back though, it feels like we were gone for days. It's amazing how quickly the pain goes away and you're left with the satisfaction of accomplishment. We still want to hike from rim to rim, but now we have a reason to come back and do it again. Next time though, you're coming with us.

Your friend,
Matt

~.~.~.~.~.~.~

From: **Matt Smith**
Subject: **Travel day – to Fairbanks**
Date: **August 25, 2012**

Dear Bob and Sue,

When I started my new job in June, I told them I already had this trip to Alaska planned, but we still had to make this final trip a quick one. Kobuk Valley and Gates of the Arctic national parks are both wilderness parks north of the Arctic Circle, and the ideal window of time to visit them is tight. The part of the arctic we're visiting has permafrost just below the surface that prevents water from draining quickly, which makes it damp and mushy in the summer. Mosquitos and flies are relentless from spring until late summer when the nights are cool enough to kill them off. That's why we waited until now to visit these last two parks. We were hoping we wouldn't have to break out the headnets again.

This was one of the hardest trips to plan. There are no roads into the parks and no services, so one of our concerns was where to get the passport stamps and where to get our picture taken in front of the parks' signs. The three national parks visitor centers that serve these parks are in Kotzebue, Coldfoot, and Bettles. All three of them are difficult to get to, but we chose Bettles because it is centrally located and Bettles Lodge offers a flight-seeing tour into both parks. Ironically, Bettles is easier to get to in the winter because you can drive there on an ice road. In the summer you must fly in.

Planning a trip to Alaska, anywhere other than to Anchorage or Fairbanks, requires a shift in expectations. The time of day your plane, train, boat, bus, or tour will depart or arrive is merely an estimate; even dates are approximations. Most of the delays and changes are weather related, which is why it's suggested to build in an extra day or two into your itinerary, but the lack of communication is aggravating. Even getting the mom and pops to return your phone calls and emails takes persistence. This was the case with going to

Bettles. I could go on and on about how difficult it was to nail down specific dates and times for this trip, but I won't. Karen finally said to me one day when I was bitching about it, "Move on." That's her short way of saying, "These people aren't trying to be difficult, they're juggling the million details of running a small lodge in the middle of nowhere, so cut them some slack." I've moved on.

Today we flew from Seattle to Fairbanks and tomorrow we're taking a small plane to Bettles, thirty-five miles north of the Arctic Circle. The next day we'll take a floatplane into both parks; landing in each of them to make our visits official. There aren't many options to visit the two northernmost national parks in Alaska. You can take a half-day flightseeing tour, or you can get dropped into the park for days or weeks. We no longer have the luxury of time, which is why we opted for a flight-seeing trip into both parks.

Sitting in the Seattle airport this morning, I asked Karen, "Are you going to cry?" She said, "No," shaking her head as if my question was too childish to consider. A few minutes later I looked up from my phone and she had tears in her eyes. It's sad to think about this being our last parks trip.

We flew to Anchorage and changed planes for a quick flight to Fairbanks. I had a window seat on the plane and the views of the coastline, mountains, and glaciers were magnificent. Seeing them made me wish we had more time to spend in Alaska on this trip. Maybe next time.

The weather in Fairbanks when we arrived was cool and rainy. We took a cab to the Hampton Inn – we've lost count of how many Hampton Inns we've stayed at over the past two years – and walked across the street to buy last-minute supplies at a grocery store. After a quick dinner down the street, we went back to our room and called it an early night, although it's hard for me to sleep when it's perfectly light outside.

Karen is sleeping as I'm writing this email. Recently she was fitted for a mouth guard to protect her teeth while she sleeps. It's difficult for her to talk with it in her mouth, so she usually won't say anything after she puts it in. Tonight was an exception though. A few minutes after closing her eyes she opened them again and with a startled look on her face said to me, "Tomorrow don't forget, we need to find the vithitor thenter and get our nathional parkth thtamps."

I said, "Don't worry. There's no way I would forget that. Good night, Thweetie."

Your friend,
Matt

~.~.~.~.~.~.~

From: **Matt Smith**
Subject: **Bettles, Alaska**
Date: **August 26, 2012**

Dear Bob and Sue,

Karen and I looked out of place sitting next to our fellow passengers in the one-room office of the small airline that was taking us from Fairbanks to Bettles: we'd bathed in the last week, and weren't wearing a stitch of camouflage clothing. Two hunters were there when we arrived. Both had Australian accents; we later found out they were father and son. They looked as if they'd already been in the bush for days, but according to them they were just beginning a trip into the wilderness. They were flying north to hunt caribou in the Arctic.

Everything gets weighed before it goes onto the plane. Two more hunters joined them, and their packs and supplies were stacked near the scale where a baggage handler was recording the weight of each piece. He shook his head as he placed the third, large box of ammunition on the scale. "Why do these guys need so many bullets?" he muttered to himself. They were so far over the allotted fifty pounds per person that half of their stuff was sent on another plane.

The pilot helped Karen, me, and the four hunters board the plane, and then he shut and locked the back door of the Piper Navajo. A faint flashback went through my head. We were taking the same make of plane to Bettles that we'd flown from Lake Clark to Anchorage just over a year ago. I quickly reached into the outside pocket of my backpack to make sure I had my green candy with me.

After our plane collision, we tried to find a way to visit these parks that didn't involve flying in small planes. Gates of the Arctic can be reached by driving north of Fairbanks on the mostly-gravel Dalton Highway, parking along the road and bushwhacking your way into the park (there's no trail). When a ranger told us we would have to cross a couple of mountains and swollen streams to get to the park, Karen said, "There's no way we're doing that. Besides, it's a long ass way on a bad highway." After considering the risks and insect annoyance factor of that method, we decided to suck it up and take the plane.

Kobuk Valley National Park is a different story. I'm not sure there is a way to get there without flying in. Six months ago our original plan was to fly into Kotzebue, and from there take a small plane into the park. We wanted to float the Kobuk River through the park for a week or so in late August or early September, hoping to see the caribou migration, but as it turned out, we didn't have that much time, and we wouldn't have seen the Gates of the Arctic. We'll put that trip on the list for our next swing through all of the parks.

A smooth hour and ten minutes after taking off, our plane touched down on the gray patch of airstrip in front of Bettles Lodge. We were thirty-five miles above the Arctic Circle and one step closer to visiting the final two parks on the list. Bettles – population twelve – is one of the few places above the Arctic Circle that has an airstrip and fuel for planes, so they get a lot of air traffic from pilots needing to gas up. The lodge was built in the 1950's and the current owners have been managing it for the past thirty years. It has a main building with a kitchen, dining area, front desk lobby, and six rooms that share community bathrooms. A separate building has additional rooms for guests. The entire complex looked as if it had capacity for about thirty guests.

For being so remote there was a lot of activity at the lodge when we arrived. A seriously equipped outdoor film crew filled the dining area/lobby, and they'd spread out their cameras and camping gear in the common areas of the adjacent building as if they were planning a major trek into the wild. Later we made friends with a few members of the group. They swore us to secrecy about the nature of their adventure, which was easy for me to promise since my short-term memory is about four minutes anyway. All I can tell you is they are filming in the parks over the next couple of months and taking a lot of electronic gear with them. But, until the weather clears, they aren't going anywhere.

To our relief, a very short distance from the lodge was the national park visitor center with a Gates of the Arctic National Park sign in front. After checking in to the lodge and putting our packs in our room, we walked over to the visitor center to take care of business for the last time. The Gates sign hung on the building about fifteen feet off the ground. I pushed a picnic table underneath it and set my tripod at a distance so we could get a photo of us with the sign in the background.

Inside the visitor center we found passport stamps for both parks. We weren't sentimental as we stamped our passports, completing the collection of 58 national park stamps. It was all business. I'm hoping, though, this will not be the last time we handle these stamps. At each park, I felt like we'd be back someday; I even felt that way in American Samoa.

The ranger figured we must be national park collectors because she'd seen us take our picture in front of the sign outside. When we told her these were our last two parks she pulled a thin plywood sign from behind a bookshelf and handed it to us. It had the words, "Kobuk Valley National

Park" burnt onto its surface. She told us, "There's no official Kobuk sign, so when people fly there from here they take this sign and get their picture taken with it while they're in the park." An earlier visitor had it made and left it at the visitor center so others like us could use it.

We poked around the visitor center for a while then went for a walk on the road leading out of town. We weren't sure where the road led; we just wanted to stretch our legs. I kept looking off into the meadows along the road hoping to see a moose, but we didn't. I always hope to see big animals on our walks in the wilderness, but on those rare occasions when we do, like in Glacier Bay National Park when a moose ran in front of us while we were biking, I think "Oh shit! What do we do now?"

Back at the lodge, we were early for dinner so we killed time talking with the camera crews who were busily planning their trip into the park once the weather breaks. We also met Tom, who works at the lodge during the summers. He said his job was to make the coffee, but every time we saw him he was busy doing other odd jobs or talking with guests. He asked a lot of questions of us: where were we from, what did we come to see, had we been to Alaska before, how long had we been married? He was curious with a sharp mind, especially for someone 89 years old. Karen liked Tom instantly. She said, "We'll be lucky if we're like him when we're 89 – working every day, living in an interesting place, and still having a curiosity about life."

Dinner tonight was what Karen calls "Mexican Fiesta," which to her is anything that looks like it might be served south of the border. It was a large enchilada and very good. A small dog named Chloe worked the dining room looking for handouts while the guests ate. She spent most of her time parked at the foot of our table. We must look soft. Dogs can sense that. We'd seen her hanging around the lodge since we arrived, and each time we saw her she was wearing a different outfit. By dinnertime it was getting cold outside so she was dressed in layers: a thin base layer with a sweater over that and a camouflage outer shell. Even the dogs wear camo in Alaska. She stared at me while I ate. My enchilada was about her size. Karen was finished eating when Chloe's owner, one of the lodge's staff members, came by and asked, "Is she bothering you?" Karen said, "No. She's being a good girl," then picked Chloe up and let her sit on her lap while I finished my dinner.

We were too tired to stay up to see the northern lights. Even though the days are getting shorter, dusk still lingers until about midnight. It needs to be completely dark to get a good view of the northern lights, which means staying up past 1:30am this time of year. For sure we will stay up tomorrow night; we've come too far to miss out on the chance to see them.

Your friend,
Matt

~.~.~.~.~.~.~

From: **Matt Smith**
Subject: **#57 – Kobuk Valley and #58 – Gates of the Arctic National Parks**
Date: **August 27, 2012**

Dear Bob and Sue,

Chloe, the enchilada dog, stared at me again while I ate breakfast this morning. She was wearing a new sweater; one I hadn't seen yesterday. Karen didn't invite Chloe on to her lap this time though. Breakfast was huge. I ate all of mine and then ate Karen's bacon. Just once in my life I'd like to see how much bacon I could eat in one sitting. Never have I thought, "No, I can't eat that last piece of bacon. I'm full." Karen said we have to finish our parks trip before I eat enough bacon to kill me. Her concern for my health is touching.

Tom sat and visited with us while we drank our third cup of coffee. The more we talked with him, the more interesting his life seemed. Tom, like many Alaskans, is a pilot. He became familiar with Bettles Lodge during his many stopovers to refuel his plane. I was surprised when he told us that he stopped flying just a few years ago. He also told us about the large game he'd hunted over the years and then with a distant stare out the window said, "I don't have guns anymore." Tom's hunting days are over.

Before he retired, Tom taught college courses on interpersonal relationships. He told us that he knows just by looking at a couple if they enjoy being together. He said he watched us when we first arrived at the lodge, and could tell by our body language and the way we looked at each other that we are a couple who has fun together. Karen smiled at me when he said that. It was one of those times when I got extra points for doing absolutely nothing, but I'll take them because it doesn't happen very often.

Clouds were still hanging around at mid-morning, but the lodge manager was fairly certain the weather would clear enough by the afternoon for us to fly into the parks. The manager didn't seem to like me very much, even though I used all my charm on her, so I made Karen ask her when we should be ready to go. I heard her say, "Probably not until 3:00 or 4:00pm, but late afternoon is a great time to go because the lighting is perfect for pictures. We can pack a picnic dinner to take with you. Check back with me at 11:00am for an update." At 11:00am I took the bait and made the mistake of asking her for an update. She snapped back, "Didn't someone already tell you when you're going?" I didn't have an answer for her that wouldn't get me thrown out of the lodge or put on the next plane back to Fairbanks, so I just smiled and went back to writing my emails to you guys.

There's not much to do in Bettles, so we didn't stray too far from the lodge all day. We went back to the visitor center and watched an hour-long documentary about Gates of the Arctic. In the middle of the film, the door to the screening room opened and in walked a guy, dressed entirely in buckskin, carrying a large bow with several arrows attached to it. He walked through the room and exited through a side door. It was surreal for us – I'm sure for him as well – like he had somehow taken a wrong turn in the wilderness and ended up in front of a large flatscreen TV. "It's Alaska," Karen said to me, and went on watching the film.

The rest of the time we hung out at the lodge because I was pretty sure had we left to go for a hike for a couple of hours, we would have returned to learn we missed our window of good weather, with a curt message of, "Sorry you missed your chance. We'll have to try again later this week, or maybe next. Now, just sit in the corner until we call your name."

During lunch I commiserated with a man and woman who'd been sitting in the lodge all morning. The woman said to me, "Don't feel bad. We've been here since 8:00am this morning and no one has told us yet when we'll be leaving." They were waiting to be flown into Gates of the Arctic National Park for a weeklong float trip, just the two of them, father and daughter.

We drank beer with our lunch, a couple of beers. Karen felt that would calm me down a bit. It worked. After lunch we looked through the lodge's guest books, reading where the guests were from and the comments they left. Apparently a lot of people had been stranded here, waiting for the weather to clear enough to fly out. Around 3:00pm one of the pilots, Bill, came in the lodge and told us he thought we would be going shortly. He said, "Yeah, I'll be taking you up in the 206 pretty soon." After he walked away I asked Karen, "What is a 206; is that a plane? Why do they do that?" Pilots always refer to their planes by names that would not make sense to anyone except another pilot: Beaver, Otter, Skywagon, 206.

Bill had been flying all morning and was taking a break before our flight. After a quick lunch in the dining room, Bill went outside to the front porch and lit a cigarette. Karen was already apprehensive about taking the 206 into the parks, but finding out that Bill was a smoker gave her one more reason to worry.

She whispered to me, "What if something happens to him on the flight?"

I said, "What are you worried about? Do you think he'll develop lung cancer and die all during the course of our four-hour flight?"

"No, what if he has a heart attack? Who will fly the plane?"

I wasn't going to let this turn into a serious conversation. I said, "Don't worry. If he keels over, I think I could bring the plane down."

She replied, "*I* could bring the plane down. We need someone to bring it down without killing us."

While we watched Bill finish his cigarette a young man bounced through the front door of the lodge. He looked at us and said, "Hi, I'm Patrick. You ready to go?" We'd never seen Patrick before that moment. We're pretty sure he didn't know we were the couple that was scheduled to take the flight into the parks. I'm guessing he would have whisked away any couple standing in the lobby at that moment.

Outside he led us to an old pickup truck where Bill joined us. Karen and I slid into the back of the cab; Patrick and Bill climbed in front. Patrick drove us out of town on the gravel road we'd walked last night. We were headed to the small lake where the float planes take off and land.

A mile out of town, Patrick looked at us in the rearview mirror and said, "I'm gonna be taking you into the parks today. Is that okay?" I knew he was joking but Karen wasn't so sure. He continued, "Yeah, I'm still learning to fly so Bill thought this would be a good chance for me to get some experience flying through the storms between here and the Kobuk." Bill didn't react: he just stared out the front of the truck and kept quiet. Karen started looking a little green. For a moment, I thought our parks journey was going to end right there. Patrick had no way of knowing we were *not* the people he should be joking with about plane safety. I shook my head at Karen trying to assure her that Patrick wouldn't be our pilot.

At "the pond" Patrick and Bill readied the plane. Bill was putting gas in the left wing when he looked over at us and said, "You okay with a little turbulence?" Without hesitating I answered, "Yeah, no problem." I thought about it for a minute then asked, "How much turbulence are we talking about?"

"It shouldn't be too bad."

Then why did you mention it? I thought to myself. Now *I* was the one worried. I dug through my backpack and found my tube of ten-year-old Dramamine. Karen had a full water bottle so I swallowed a pill with a couple of long gulps.

Bill asked which one of us wanted to sit up front with him. I looked at Karen and she said, "God no!" Karen climbed in the single back seat and Bill placed our backpacks next to her. Karen kept the plywood Kobuk sign at her feet. With the co-pilot seat pushed back into Karen's knees, I wriggled my way across the pilot's seat and settled in the front right seat of the plane. It was hard getting in without bumping against the controls and switches on the dashboard. I could imagine the windshield wipers flapping and the radio blaring like a high school practical joke when Bill started the engine. Or worse, that in flight he wouldn't find that one critical setting that I'd changed until it was too late and the plane was plunging to the ground. I decided to not say anything and assume he would check them before the flight like pilots are supposed to do. Besides, I'm sure he's had more clumsy passengers with bigger butts than me shoehorn themselves into the co-pilot's seat before.

Bill taxied the plane slowly to one end of the pond giving us room to takeoff and allowing the engine to warm up. When Bill turned the plane toward the direction of our takeoff and gunned the engine, I was surprised at how close we were to the trees on the approaching shore. But my concern was unnecessary; by the time we reached the trees we were well above them.

In an instant, we were high enough in the sky to see for dozens of miles in every direction. The dark grey, treeless mountains to the north had a dusting of snow from earlier today. We'd made it here with no time to spare; winter was coming soon. Bill said their last flight to pick people up in the backcountry would be September 16th. After that, all the planes are flown to Fairbanks, where they spend the winter.

Twenty minutes into the flight, I felt a slight urge to pee. I thought nothing of it at first; I can hold it with the best of them. The first leg of our flight to Kobuk Valley National Park was 175 miles. In another hour we would be there and I could go then – no problem.

We flew in and out of rain showers but could see the sun most of the time. Multiple rainbows in the distance rose out of the unspoiled landscape. I was trying to concentrate on the scenery and take pictures but the "urge" was growing at an unusually fast pace. Maybe it was the two beers I had at lunch or the huge amount of water I drank with the Dramamine, but soon there was only one thing on my mind: where's the bathroom? There wasn't, of course, a bathroom. We were quite literally in the middle of nowhere. Bill wasn't going to land the 206 on some random lake so I could relieve myself. I needed to start thinking about plans B and C, and possibly D.

I could see the controls; we were flying at about 110 knots and the park was 175 miles away. I didn't like the way the math worked out: I wasn't going to make it. I thought to myself, "This is ridiculous: man up and hold it." My silent pep talk made me feel better, for about thirty seconds. Then, the urge came back even stronger than before.

The three of us were wearing headphones with microphones attached to them that rested right in front of our mouths. The microphones were voice activated, but there was about a one-second delay from when I started talking to when I could hear the microphone activate. But, if I stopped talking and waited for the microphone to activate, it would shut off again and I would have to start over. I finally realized that I needed to start every sentence with "Uh—" then continue talking. It was important that I figured this out because it was the only way to communicate with Bill. Once I knew he could hear me I said, "Uh, Bill, I'm going to have to pee before we get there. I'm going to go in a dry bag that I brought with me."

Without expression, Bill said back to me, "Yeah, no problem."

I looked back at Karen and her face was stricken. With wide eyes she mouthed, "What!" to me. She had long given up on trying to talk into her microphone. She thought because of the odd delay of the voice activation that her microphone wasn't working. I could see her slink down in her seat in disbelief.

Once I had notified everyone I still needed to come up with a plan on exactly how to do it. It wasn't like I could unbuckle my seatbelt and climb in back to have some privacy. We were in close quarters: Bill and I were sitting so close we were nearly touching shoulders. Whatever my plan, it was going to happen right there in the co-pilot's seat. I reached my left arm around Bill to feel for my backpack. I couldn't reach it and had to ask Karen to kick it toward my hand so I could dig through it for my dry bag. Karen reluctantly helped me out; she was trying to act like she didn't know me and we weren't together. Nice.

I was able to feel through my pack and locate the dry bag. It was full of snacks. I pulled it into the front of the plane, took my snacks out and put them in the pockets of my rain jacket. This took way longer than I thought it possibly could. I had enough in there to survive for a week. It made me think about whether I really needed to carry around so many year-past-their-expiration date Cliff bars in my backpack.

Once the bag was empty and ready for duty I still had some things to work out. To add to my dilemma, I was buckled in tight. A shoulder harness was over my chest and connected at a very inconvenient spot with my seatbelt. I'll fast-forward past the other problems I had and skip to the part where I'm holding a warm bag of pee on my lap. Whew! I'm glad I had that dry bag with me.

I'm glad I had it with me, but this particular dry bag wasn't as "dry" as I had expected it would be. I think it was designed to keep moisture out, not so much to keep moisture in. I began to think about how that could be; shouldn't it work both ways? Soon my contemplation about directional moisture flow was quickly interrupted by a more immediate problem: I needed a dry bag for my dry bag!

Luckily I came prepared. I reached around Bill again to dig through my backpack to find the 13-gallon, tall kitchen trash bag I always carry with me. I double bagged my pee, placed it on the floor at my feet and relaxed. Just then the Great Kobuk Sand Dunes came into sight in front of us; it was perfect timing.

There are three active sand dune areas in the park totaling over 20,000 acres, the largest being the Great Kobuk Sand Dunes. Even though they're in the Arctic, temperatures on the dunes in the summer can reach 100 degrees Fahrenheit. Bill told us he would land the plane on a lake close to the sand dunes so we could take our picture before leaving again for Gates of the Arctic. We would have liked to have gone ashore and hiked the dunes, but there wasn't time. Bill took our picture as we sat in the plane holding the Kobuk sign. It was the shortest visit we'd made to any of the parks but certainly the hardest to get to. Within twenty minutes we were back in the air and heading toward the next park.

It was roughly another hour of flying before we reached Walker Lake on the southern edge of Gates of the Arctic National Park. Bill first circled the area of the lake where he planned to land, looking at the water to determine the strength and direction of the wind. He put the plane down and taxied to a small point of land that had a shallow approach and a narrow sandy beach.

Bill cut the engine as we neared the shore and got out onto the float. A few feet from dry ground, he stepped into the water and guided the plane into its final resting position, tail-first toward the beach. I don't remember one specific moment when I felt a sense of accomplishment that we'd made it to the final park, but once we were on land and climbed to the top of the small bump-out, Karen turned to me with a raised hand for a high-five. This time I connected with her on the first try.

We'd made it.

The mosquitoes were thick as they hovered around our faces. I could imagine they would drive someone crazy who was camping here. We only stayed long enough for Bill to put another few gallons of gas in the plane and take our picture. He wanted to fly us over the Arrigetch Peaks on the way back to Bettles, and that was going to use up our remaining time. Arrigetch is an Inupiat word meaning "fingers of the outstretched hand." The peaks are part of the Brooks Range of mountains that cut through the park.

As we taxied away from shore I looked at the peaks rising in front of us. Their highest point was over 7,000 feet in elevation; on the lake, we couldn't have been higher than 1,000 feet. I wondered to myself if our little 206 could climb that high that fast, but with calm determination, Bill got us up and over them with ease. He'd done this countless times before.

The peaks are spectacular, charcoal grey spires reaching up to the sky. Clouds from earlier in the day had mostly cleared and the sun was in perfect position to give high relief to every rock on the surface of the peaks. Despite my bitching about waiting around all day for our flight, this was the perfect time of day to fly over the peaks. We were close enough to the mountains to see every detail. I scanned each one, looking for wildlife, hoping to spot a mountain sheep or goats. At one point I looked back at Karen to find her slumped down in her seat; I think mentally she was done with our journey and just wanted the plane to get back on the ground safely. The scene outside the plane looked a little too much like Lake Clark Pass for her comfort.

Once past the peaks, Bill angled the plane toward home and followed the Alatna River out of the mountains. With the sun at a low angle, the river looked like a silver thread lying on a green carpet. Where the valley leaves the park to the south the elevation drop is so slight that the river meanders back and forth nearly connecting with itself on each switchback. I can only imagine how this landscape will change in the next couple months as the temperature drops and the snow falls.

A few miles from the pond, we heard over our headphones one of the other Bettles pilots calling for Bill. He had just taken off from the pond with another couple from the lodge for a flight-seeing trip into Gates. He announced his position and altitude, as pilots are supposed to do, so Bill could keep a safe distance.

"Bill this is Brad, I'm at 2,000 and just over the bend in the John," the other pilot said. He was referring to the John River, which connects with the Koyukuk River a few miles west of Bettles. "Where are you?" he asked.

Bill replied, "I'm at 2,600 just west of the bend. I should be able to see you, but I don't."

Brad said, "I don't see you either. You must be right on top of me."

Karen and I were frantically looking in every direction trying to spot Brad's plane.

Bill calmly replied, "You stay at 2,000 and I'll keep it at 2,600 for a little bit longer and we should be fine."

Compared to our fender bender – tail bender actually – in Lake Clark Pass, 600 feet of separation seemed more than safe to me. Karen wasn't so sure and kept looking for the other plane until we were almost on the pond.

At the dock, Karen and I climbed out through the door on the pilot's side of the plane. We unloaded our backpacks – mine a little heavier than when we started – and the Kobuk sign and waited by the pickup while Bill tied up the plane and did a few post-flight chores. Regardless of how outrageously expensive the flight is, it's customary to tip the pilot for his or her services; that is if they've done a good job. I got out my wallet and Karen and I agreed on a reasonable amount for Bill's tip. I added an extra $40 to the tip: $20 for not killing us and $20 for letting me pee in his plane. Bill seemed genuinely appreciative.

Back at the lodge, the other guests were finishing dessert. I grabbed two beers from the cooler by the front desk and Karen claimed the corner booth in the dining area. Since there was no picnic dinner on our flight into the parks, we were hoping they had saved us some dinner, but eating was merely an afterthought. It was beginning to sink in that our two-plus-year journey to visit all the national parks was complete. We were deeply relaxed and satisfied.

One of the lodge workers brought us dinner and just as we were about to eat, Tom came by and asked if he could join us. He asked, "Are you sure it's okay for me to sit with you while you eat?" We welcomed his company. Tom was beaming; we had told him earlier that these were the last two parks on our journey. He was happy for us. We ate slowly and talked about our flight into the parks and how good it felt to reach this milestone.

The conversation turned to a variety of subjects, but eventually Karen began asking Tom about his future. "Are you going to stay here this winter?" she asked.

"No, I'm going to go back to Washington state next month. My kids keep asking me to stay with them. They want to take care of me," he said.

Karen asked, "So, when will you come back here? Next May?"

Tom paused before answering, "I don't know if I'll be coming back. This might be my last summer up here. I say this without feeling morose, but I feel the end coming."

Karen's eyes watered.

I replied matter-of-factly, "It comes for all of us, doesn't it?"

Tom nodded in agreement. "And, I'm fine with it. It's natural. I've had a good life."

He left us to make more coffee and we sat there quietly for a few more minutes. We avoided a sad goodbye with Tom knowing that we'd see him in the morning before our flight to Fairbanks. The only thing left on our list was to see the northern lights.

We still had several hours before the sky would be dark enough to see the aurora. That's what they call the northern lights here in Bettles. One of the lodge staff said, "For us, the lights aren't in the north, they're right overhead. We just call it the aurora." Some of the camera crew and another couple staying at the lodge had the same plan to stay up to see the lights. We visited with them and wandered around the grounds waiting for the sky to darken. Some of them were drinking beer and playing horseshoes on the side yard of the lodge. Every now and then we'd hear the clank of metal on metal. They were still playing well past the point where it was light enough to see what they were aiming at. I was waiting for the inevitable yelp when one of them scored a ringer around someone's shin, but it never came.

At 1:00am, Karen and I were pacing the gravel runway trying to keep warm. We were wearing all of the clothes we'd brought with us. The moon was nearly full and on the rise, making it harder to see the lights. At 1:30am, we heard someone say they could see them. We walked over to where they were standing and looked into the sky in the direction they were pointing. At first I couldn't see them and was ready to give up, but a few minutes later they came into faint focus. I'd thought they would be stationary but they weren't; the lights were wispy and moved quickly as if being blown by the wind. We stood on the cold gravel for another half an hour watching, as the lights got brighter and the shades of green intensified. I'm glad we stayed awake long enough to see them. On the last day of our two-year journey to some of the most spectacular places on earth, this incredible lightshow was a fitting finale.

Your friend,
Matt

~.~.~.~.~.~.~

From: **Matt Smith**
Subject: **Going home**
Date: **August 28, 2012**

Dear Bob and Sue,

The lodge was bustling when we arrived for breakfast. Like yesterday, clouds hung low in the sky, but the forecast was for clearing. The camera crews had their gear stacked in piles outside; everyone was ready to fly into the park.

Karen and I slid into a booth with our coffee. Tom came over and sat across from us. Pointing to the group standing outside he said, "These guys told me last night they would be up at 4:30 getting ready for their trip, so I got up at 4:00 to make the coffee."

"What time did they show up?" I asked.

Tom chuckled and said, "6:30."

A staff member brought us breakfast of bacon, eggs, and French toast. (All of our meals at the lodge were fantastic.) We ate and shared small talk with Tom. He looked tired. Tom asked us if we'd enjoyed our trip. Karen said, "The two great things about this trip were seeing the parks and meeting you, Tom." That was very sweet. Karen always knows the right thing to say.

Our plane was scheduled to leave at 9:00am, but we were packed and ready to go well before then, so we killed time visiting with the other guests. I stood outside in the cold morning air and talked with one of the cameramen. He told me about all of the adventures he'd had filming amazing places around the world. He looked to be about my age. He shuddered and said, "I only have a couple years of this left in me. I need to go somewhere warm like southern California and just sit on a beach."

The plane taking us back to Fairbanks landed at Bettles about 8:45am. There was a rush of activity getting the bags onto the plane and making sure everyone who was supposed to go was there and ready. Karen ran back inside to say goodbye to Tom, and then we climbed into the Piper Navajo through a door in the back.

Our pilot buckled himself in and gave us the speed-talking version of the safety briefing. I could tell Karen wanted to say, "Slow down; this shit's important." Instead she looked at me and slowly shook her head. Within a few minutes we were accelerating down the gravel runway and into the air. It was an uneventful flight to Fairbanks, but Karen was on the lookout for other planes the entire time.

At the Fairbanks airport we were hours early for our flight to Seattle, but we went through security anyway. There couldn't have been 10 other people in the airport as we sat in the snack bar staring out the window at the planes. Karen started to tear up. I knew it wasn't because our parks trip was over.

She said, "When I said goodbye to Tom, he told me that he would think about us often." She choked up and had to stop for a moment. "He said we're rich, and he wasn't referring to money. He said we're rich because we have each other and we have time. And, that's all we need."

Neither of us spoke for a long while.

Karen and I don't know what our next adventure will be. There's a part of me that wants to do it all over again – exactly the same – and another part that doesn't want to ever see another list. Whatever we do, I'm sure we'll have fun. Anyway, we have time to figure it out. Next go-around, you should come with us.

Your friend,
Matt

~.~.~.~.~.~.~

The End
(almost)

From: **Matt Smith**
Subject: **#59 - Pinnacles (don't call me a Monument) National Park**
Date: **April 1, 2013**

Dear Bob and Sue,

Three months after we published *Dear Bob and Sue,* our book was obsolete. Out of nowhere came a new national park, #59. In January 2013 Pinnacles National Monument in central California became Pinnacles National Park.

As soon as we found out, Karen and I started making plans to visit the new park. We already had a short vacation scheduled to Palm Springs for late March as a break from the Seattle rain, but this news gave me an excuse to extend the trip. And, a chance to combine visits to two of my favorite places: a national park and a brewery. My new plan was to rent a car in Palm Springs, drive from there to Pinnacles, and then drive back to Seattle visiting Russian River Brewery along the way. Karen was totally on board; she has visions of loading up the rental car with as much Pliny the Elder as they will let us buy. (Pliny the Elder is a double IPA that is extremely difficult to get anywhere outside the Russian River Brewery tap house.)

One thing we had to consider when planning our drive was which side of the park to visit. The road into the park, Highway 146, enters from both the east and the west but doesn't continue all of the way through. You can't drive from one side of the park to the other; a ridge of mountains - the pinnacles - divides the park north to south. We decided to visit the east side because that's where the visitor center is located. Yesterday afternoon we left Palm Springs and drove to Paso Robles where we spent the night. This morning, after turning into the park off a mostly deserted Highway 25, we drove straight to the visitor center to get a stamp for our park passports and some advice for a hike.

The ranger at the visitor center asked us a few questions, and then recommended High Peaks Loop Trail, about a seven-mile hike. He gave us a park map and explained in detail how to find the trailhead. With map in hand we left the visitor center and took our picture by the new park sign on the side of the building. It's the only sign in the park that reads "Pinnacles National Park." After one more check of the map before leaving the parking lot, we realized that neither of us could remember which trail the ranger recommended.

"Wow, we *are* getting old. I thought it was just you losing your memory." I don't remember which of us said this to the other - doesn't matter. We looked up from the map and without hesitation went back into the visitor center for round two of our information session with the ranger.

This time he used a green highlighter to outline the trail. I had to keep myself from diving in front of the map when he pulled out the marker. But, knowing where we're going when we are in the middle of the wilderness is more important than having a pristine map for the files back home. I was pretty sure this wouldn't be the last time today we'd forget what he told us. As we headed back to the car I slipped a second park map into my backpack.

The ranger had originally suggested a hike that led to a bat cave. He said it was "easy and family-friendly." "What else you got," I thought to myself. The hike he suggested had two strikes against it: 1) it leads to a cave, and 2) we don't do family- friendly. It's not that we don't like hiking amongst families; really, I enjoy tiptoeing through a young family's picnic when they've decided to have a mid-morning snack - right in the middle of the trail. (That's how those goldfish crackers got stuck to the bottom of my hiking boot.) Or, listening to parents speak every thought that comes into their head while learning to parent. "Alexandra, this is a leaf. Can you say leaf? Oh, here is another leaf. It's green. Can you say green? Here is another... don't eat the leaf, Alexandra. Do not! Honey, I could use a little help here! Don't let Alexandra eat the leaf. Where's Zebulon? He was right here... Zebulon! Zebulon, don't eat the dirt. Honey! Zebulon!" Nope, we're past that point in our lives. We're at the stage where we're looking for family-hostile hikes. As it turned out, the High Peaks Loop Trail was just the right amount of family-hostile for us. (Who names their kid Zebulon?)

Pinnacles hasn't gotten the same attention as many of the other national parks, but it has a long history of being part of the national park system. In the span of seven days in 1908, Teddy Roosevelt made it a national monument along with John Muir and the Grand Canyon. The main entrance sign, which still reads Pinnacles National Monument, has an old stone foundation that looks like it's from the CCC (Civilian Conservation Corps) days of the 1930's and 1940's. I'm sure the visitation numbers will be up this year now that it has "national park" in its name.

Since it was still early in the day, we were able to find a place to park in a pullout alongside the main park road just before it forks toward the Bear Gulch Day Use Area. It took a little while to figure out exactly which direction we were supposed to go and to find the trail, but after a couple of false starts we were going in the right direction.

The first mile or so of the hike was flat and followed the park road to a dead end parking lot. From there the trail became steep, switchbacking up a canyon. Up to then we had no idea what a pinnacle was. What I mean is, we knew what pinnacles are - tall pointy rocks - but it's not clear when driving through the park where they are or what they look like. It's not like Mt. Rainier where you can see the peak from fifty miles away.

Karen started pointing to every rock larger than a Volkswagen asking, "Is that a pinnacle?" As the terrain became rockier, with large rocks grouped together, she'd ask, "Do you think those are the pinnacles?" It got annoying by about the twenty-fifth time she asked. (It actually got annoying sooner than that but I'm being kind.) How would I know a rock from a pinnacle? Does she think that sometime during our last thirty-two years together I secretly became a geologist and never told her? I had no idea what a pinnacle was.

Finally I distracted her with a rare offer to stop for a rest and have a snack so I could take some pictures of the view. She said, "I hope you're taking pictures of the rocks. These could be the pinnacles, you know. We don't want to get all the way to the top and find out that..." she changed her voice to what sounded like Yogi Bear, "Oh sorry, those were the pinnacles you passed earlier. There aren't any more along this hike. Hope you got some good pictures."

Before I could figure out who would be telling us this at the top of the mountain, a pair of hikers interrupted us as they walked through our mid-morning picnic. As they tiptoed around our backpacks and water bottles, I apologized, "Sorry, we didn't realize we'd spread out in the middle of the trail."

The elevation gain on this hike is about 1,500 feet. Before we got to the top, we came to where the trail met the shorter Condor Gulch Trail. We stopped and thought about turning off and going back down toward our car. It was tempting: we were tired and we couldn't see anything interesting ahead, but we kept hiking up the trail. By the end of the hike we were glad we hadn't wimped out.

Over the next half of a mile or so the trail continued to gain elevation, but more gradually than before. Pretty soon we were hiking amongst massive boulders. Not quite pinnacles but impressive still. An older hiker - older than us - was on our tail the entire time. My instinct in these situations is to hike faster to put some space between us, but no matter how fast we went he hung right behind us. He must have been in his mid-seventies - at least. We couldn't shake him. Finally, reluctantly, with simultaneous shame and awe, we let him pass us. (My desk job is making me soft; I need to spend more time on the trail.) As he sprinted past us we decided it would be a good time to stop for lunch.

Karen and I ate while sitting on boulders next to a quiet stretch of the trail. This morning on our way to the park we picked up sandwiches in King City. Besides the camping supply store in the visitor center, there's no place to buy food in the park.

Being early spring, the weather changed by the minute. When the sun came out it was instantly a beautiful warm day. A moment later it would be cloudy and cool enough to remind us that winter was just two weeks ago. Like so many of the wilderness areas in the national parks, the space around us looked like it had been professionally landscaped; every plant put in just the right spot to make a perfect scene. Many plants were blooming with bees buzzing about.

The park's website says there are nearly 400 species of bees in the park; 260 species of bees have been spotted along the 2.3-mile Old Pinnacles Trail alone. How do they know that? I've hiked hundreds, if not thousands of miles in the national parks, and seen countless types of bees. But, there's no way I could describe a bee to a ranger in such detail that they could tell it was a different species than one of the other 259 species already described by passers-by: "about this long, bug-eyes, yellow body with black stripes, two wings and furry legs."

I said to Karen, "How could they know that 260 species of bees have been seen along a single trail in the park? It would take teams of etymologists forever to categorize that many bees."

Karen laughed so hard water came out her nose.

"What's so funny?"

"An etymologist studies the history of words."

"I thought they studied bugs."

She laughed again. "They might, in their spare time, but their job is to study words."

"Who studies bugs?"

"Entomologists study *insects*."

"I thought that was the guy who did my root canal."

"I think that's an endodontist."

"I think you're making up words."

Regardless, I'm calling bullshit on this one. Even if

endocrinologists spent years hovering along the trail looking for bees, it's hard to believe they would have found 260 distinct species.

Far above the bees, circling the pinnacles, were large black birds. We thought they were California condors, like the ones we saw along Bright Angel Trail in the Grand Canyon. Farther up the trail we came across two researchers who told us the birds we saw were turkey vultures, not condors, which are a different type of vulture. (The researchers had a radio antenna and were trying to pick up signals from tagged condors.) Karen was disappointed; she had been hoping to see a condor. I'm not sure why. I've seen a California condor close up. They're just as butt-ugly as a turkey vulture, and they share some of the same charming features. They both have bald heads so they can clean them after sticking them into rotting animal carcasses, they pee on themselves to regulate their body temperature and they throw up in self-defense. And, we saved these birds from extinction why?

I made the mistake of saying this out loud in front of Karen. What followed was an impassioned and near encyclopedic explanation of why saving the condors was important. Apparently she had been reading about the plight of the California condor as part of her research on the park. Finally I said, "Ok! Ok! I get it. The world is a better place because we saved the condors. But they are *condors* not *conders*."

"No, they're condors." She was pronouncing it *conders*.

"Con - doors." Not, conders."

"No one calls them con-*doooors*, they're called conders."

"No, they're con-*doors*."

"No, they're con-*ders*."

This dialogue continued for a quite awhile without much variation - you get the gist. Suffice it to say I stopped making fun of the condors and Karen made a point of emphasizing the *door* part of the word condor for the rest of the day. (Maybe conders is the correct pronunciation now that I think about it, but I'm not going to take it back now.)

I have to admit though, the story of their survival is impressive. In 1987 the 22 remaining wild condors (Karen stressed that they were the last 22 wild condors *in the entire world*) were captured and the species was bred in captivity until there were enough to begin reintroducing them into the wild. Pinnacles has been a part of the California Condor Recovery Program since 2003. The park now manages over 30 free-flying condors. We didn't see any condors today; at least we don't think we did.

After lunch we packed up and continued hiking along the high ridge. There's no sign along the trail that announces that you are officially "in the pinnacles," but by the time we had reached our lunch spot we were clearly amongst them. We'd thought we were already at the highest point of the trail when suddenly we were standing at the base of a series of footholds carved into a pinnacle. Running alongside the shallow steps was a metal railing. "There's no way Alexandra and Zebulon would make it up these," I thought to myself as I started climbing.

That wasn't the last set of carved footholds and metal railings we encountered. There were several steep pitches and sudden drop-offs along the trail that required our undivided attention. The stairs were so narrow they could only be climbed single-file. Hikers coming from the opposite direction had to wait. When we came to a section that looked out over the west side of the park it was easy to see from our vantage point why there isn't a road that crosses the park east to west: there's no way through the pinnacles.

The views from the top were beautiful, but hard to capture with my point-and-shoot camera. At one spot along the top I stopped, no longer hearing Karen's footsteps behind me. She was fifty yards back taking a picture. I thought for a moment she was trying to capture the landscape but instead she was focusing on a squirrel, which seemed to be posing for her on its hind legs. She was breaking her own trail etiquette rule: it was clearly below the two-pound limit to qualify for a wildlife sighting.

She kept taking picture after picture on her phone. As I made my way back to where she was standing, she glanced at me and put her finger to her lips.

"Finally making friends?" I asked.

"Never," she whispered. "Oh, how the tables have turned."

"What does that mean?"

"It means I have this little guy right where I want him. He's completely exposed on this big rock, nowhere to hide, no friends around to call for backup. I think he's frozen with fear. Look how he's holding his paws. It looks like he's praying."

"And what's preventing him from taking a flying leap and landing on your head like the last time you cornered a squirrel?"

She took a step back and put the camera in her pocket. "I'm done," she said.

Soon after that we came to the point where the trail started back down in elevation, looping back to where we'd parked. There's always a feeling of relief when you start back down after a steep climb. The hikers we met coming up looked exhausted and could barely breathe. We were joking with one another and greeting each person we passed with a cheerful, "How's it going?" I think Karen may have been skipping behind me. Needless to say we were glad to be on our way down.

Toward the end of our hike we came to a turnoff that led to the Bear Gulch Cave. While I doubt I'll ever be a fan of caves, I like bats; they're amazing creatures, and Karen regrets calling them blood-sucking, rabid rats with wings. Maybe we'll put up a bat house when we get back to Seattle. (By the way, many species of bats have excellent eyesight despite the fact that many people think they are nearly blind; bats get a bad rap.) The ranger here had told us that they close part of the Bear Gulch cave ten months a year in order to protect the Townsend's big-eared bats, a "sensitive species". From mid-May to mid-July the entire cave is closed because it's pupping season. A baby bat is called a pup. Fourteen species of bats live in the park; in addition to Bear Gulch Cave, bats also live in the Balconies Cave area.

While Pinnacles protects their condors and bats, they've removed pigs from the park because they're not native to the area. Exotic, invasive, feral pigs were once a big problem in the park. They competed for food with deer and other wildlife and had the potential to spread disease to other animals in the park, including humans. Their rooting behavior was destroying plants and insect habitat and caused soil erosion problems. They were being pigs, so the park service had to get rid of them. In 2003, the park constructed a 24-mile fence around the perimeter to keep them out. After the fence went up, it took another few years to rid the park of the pigs that were on the park side of the fence. Since 2006 the park has been mostly pig free - of the four-legged kind anyway.

The last couple of hundred yards of the hike ran through a dry, sandy creek bed. Pinecones were scattered about: big, perfect pinecones. They were just big and perfect enough that I wanted to take one home for my pinecone collection. I have two pinecones in my collection so far. But, it's against the rules to take anything out of a national park, so I left them where they were.

We drove out of the park and headed north toward San Jose. Again, there was very little traffic on the road just outside the park. I drove about two miles an hour close to the shoulder, looking for just the right pinecone take home. At first Karen was encouraging, but her attitude quickly soured. The first one I stopped for looked perfect from my vantage point in the car. Karen got out and held it by its tip like she was holding a fine piece of artwork so I could inspect it.

"How's this?" she asked.

"Spin it around," I said. "Nope, it's wet on one side."

With a deep breath Karen flung the rejected cone into the ditch alongside the road and got back in the car. We repeated this scene several times. Each new candidate looked good from the car, but had some flaw that required me to reject it: too dirty, crooked, color faded on one side, too sappy.

By the fifth stop Karen didn't ask my opinion. She grabbed the closest one to the car, tossed it in the back seat without even looking at it and said, "It's perfect. Let's go." I'd flown too close to the sun and knew better than to push my luck any further.

As I drove away I could see in the rearview mirror my brand new, crooked, dirty, two-toned pinecone in the back seat, with its sap side stuck to my backpack. It was time for a beer.

We are official again; we can now say we've visited all of the national parks. Although, I'm getting tired of explaining that we've only been to the fifty-nine parks that are "national park" national parks. I suggested to Karen that on our drive back to Seattle we take a side trip to visit the John Day Fossil Beds National Monument east of Bend, Oregon. She looked at me with raised eyebrows and asked, "Why?"

"Well, you know, since we are going right by we should stop and see the park."

"We are not going right by; it's at least a three-hour detour. Seriously, why do you want to go?"

"You know why."

"No. We are not going to visit all 342 remaining national park sites."

"Why not?"

"My park passport is nearly full. I don't have room for 342 more stamps."

"I'll buy you another passport."

"What about all the park sites we've already visited? Are we going back to Bent's Old Fort?"

"Well, next time we're in the area, we could stop by. Besides, you liked it. Remember how all the park employees were dressed like trappers and traders from the 1840's, and had to stay in character even when I asked them where we could find a gas station in the area?"

"So, we're going to spend every free moment we have for the next twenty years driving to places like that in the middle of nowhere?"

"Exactly! It'll be fun."

I didn't mention to her that at the rate they're adding new park units it might take more than twenty years to visit them all. Karen didn't put up as much of a fight as I had expected. I'm taking that as a yes. Bob and Sue, how about you?

Your friend,
Matt

The End

~.~.~.~.~.~.~

About the Authors

Matt and Karen have been married for over 34 years and live in the Seattle, Washington area. Having both grown up in the Midwest, they met at the University of Kansas and have been together ever since. *Dear Bob and Sue* is their first book project together.

~.~.~.~.~.~.~

We welcome your feedback.

Email: mattandkarensmith@gmail.com